D0312343

TROUBLE MAKER

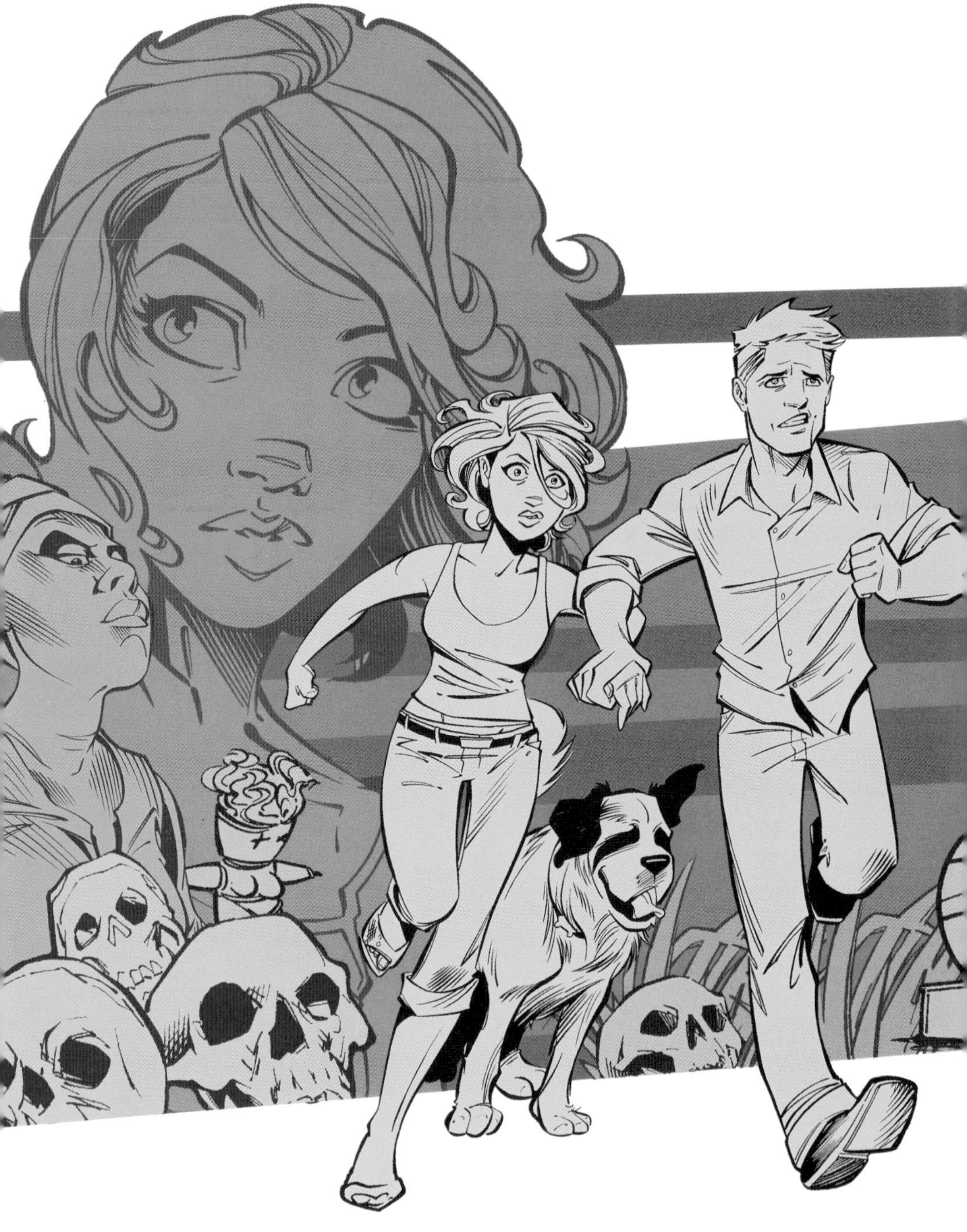

TROUBLE MAKER

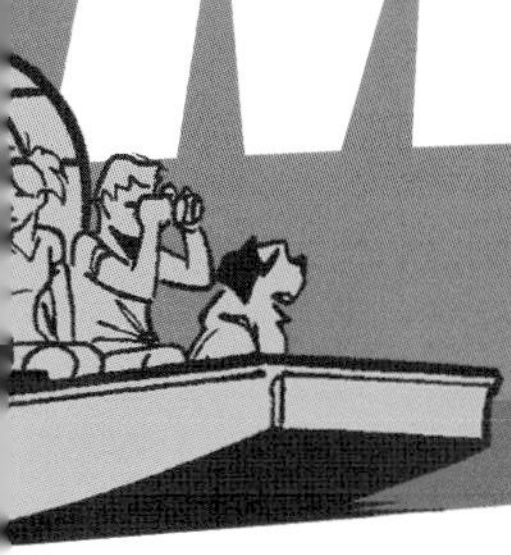

BOOK ONE
A BARNABY AND HOOKER GRAPHIC NOVEL

WRITTEN BY
JANET AND **ALEX EVANOVICH**
DRAWN BY **JOËLLE JONES**

BACKGROUND PENCILS – BEN DEWEY | INKS – ANDY OWENS
COLORS – DAN JACKSON | LETTERS – NATE PIEKOS of BLAMBOT®

DARK HORSE BOOKS®

FOR BARNABY, THE GREATEST ST. BERNARD A GIRL COULD HAVE.

President & Publisher
MIKE RICHARDSON

Editor
SIERRA HAHN

Assistant Editor
FREDDYE LINS

Collection Designer
DAVE NESTELLE

Special thanks to Anita Nelson and Dark Horse Comics for giving us the opportunity to make a lifelong dream come true.

Thanks also to Matt Dryer and Lia Ribacchi.

executive vice president Neil Hankerson • chief financial officer Tom Weddle • vice president of publishing Randy Stradley • vice president of business development Michael Martens • vice president of business affairs Anita Nelson • vice president of marketing Micha Hershman • vice president of product development David Scroggy • vice president of information technology Dale LaFountain • director of purchasing Darlene Vogel • general counsel Ken Lizzi • editorial director Davey Estrada • senior managing editor Scott Allie • senior books editor Chris Warner • executive editor Diana Schutz • director of design and production Cary Grazzini • art director Lia Ribacchi • director of scheduling Cara Niece

Published by Dark Horse Books
A division of Dark Horse Comics, Inc.
10956 SE Main Street
Milwaukie, OR 97222

www.darkhorse.com
www.evanovich.com
www.joellejones.com

To find a comics shop in your area, call the Comic Shop Locator Service toll-free at (888) 266-4226.

First edition: July 2010
ISBN 978-1-59582-488-2

10 9 8 7 6 5 4 3 2 1
Printed by Solisco Printers, Ltd., Scott, QC, Canada.

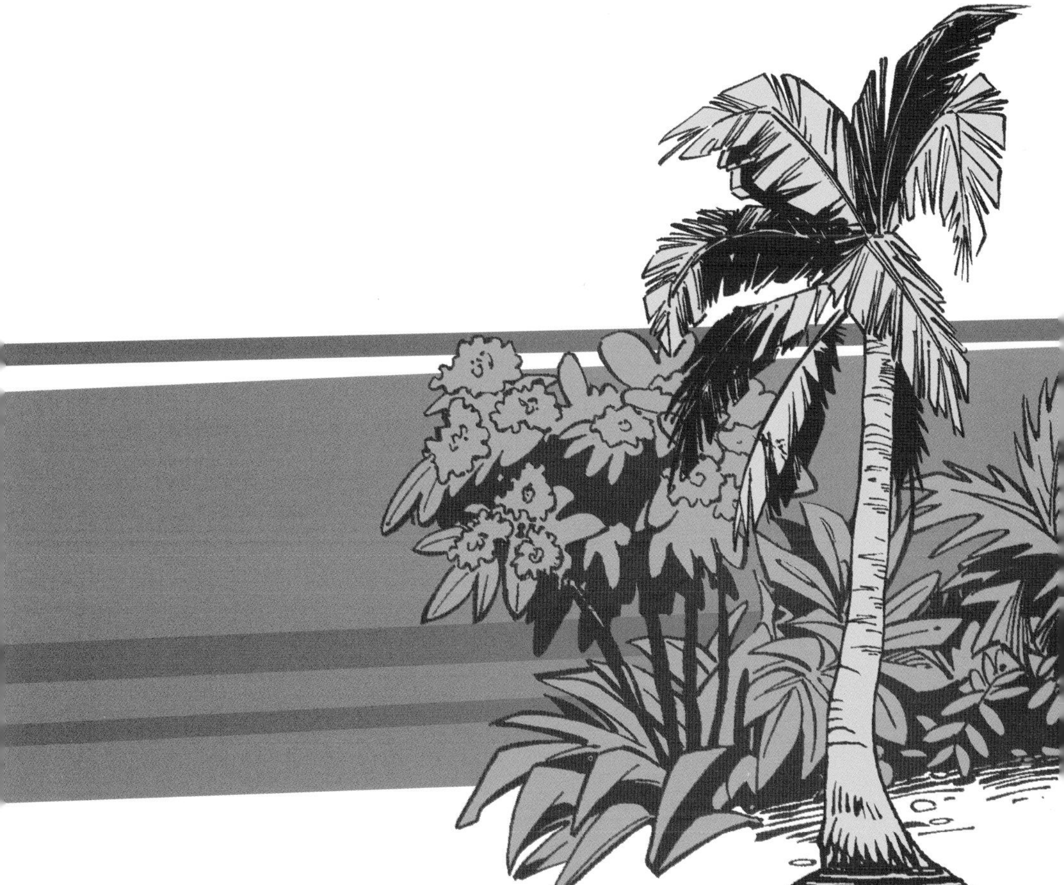

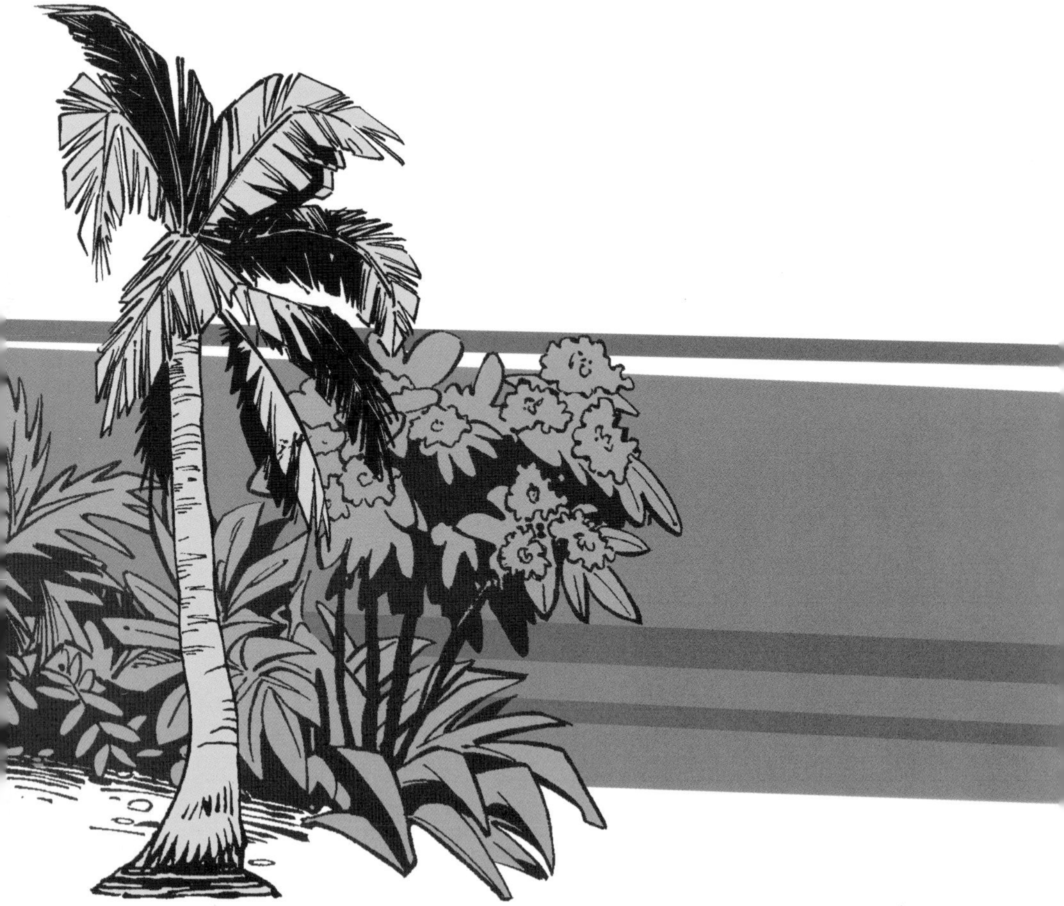

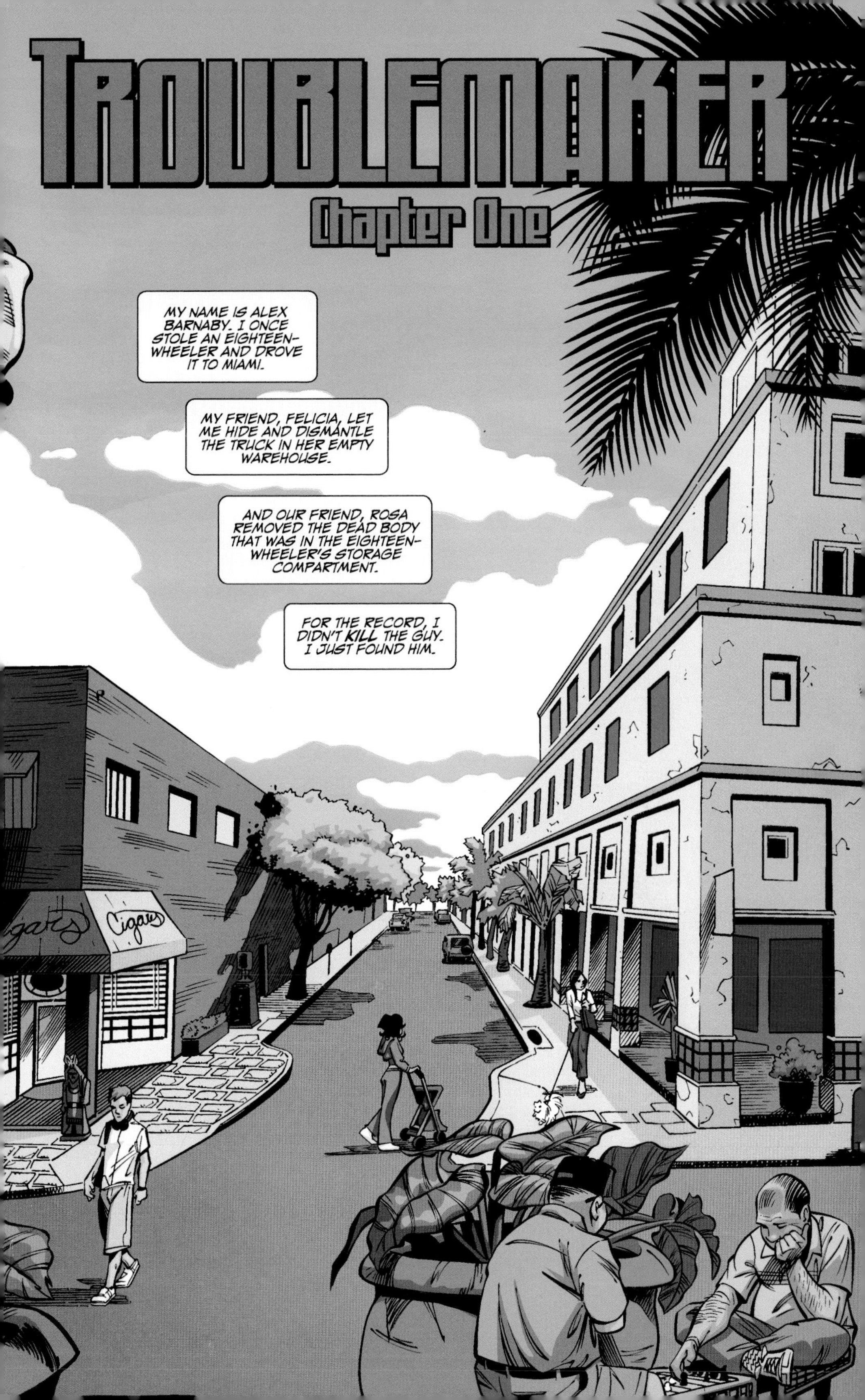

TROUBLEMAKER
Chapter One
MY NAME IS ALEX BARNABY. I ONCE STOLE AN EIGHTEEN-WHEELER AND DROVE IT TO MIAMI.
MY FRIEND, FELICIA, LET ME HIDE AND DISMANTLE THE TRUCK IN HER EMPTY WAREHOUSE.
AND OUR FRIEND, ROSA REMOVED THE DEAD BODY THAT WAS IN THE EIGHTEEN-WHEELER'S STORAGE COMPARTMENT.
FOR THE RECORD, I DIDN'T KILL THE GUY. I JUST FOUND HIM.
Cigars

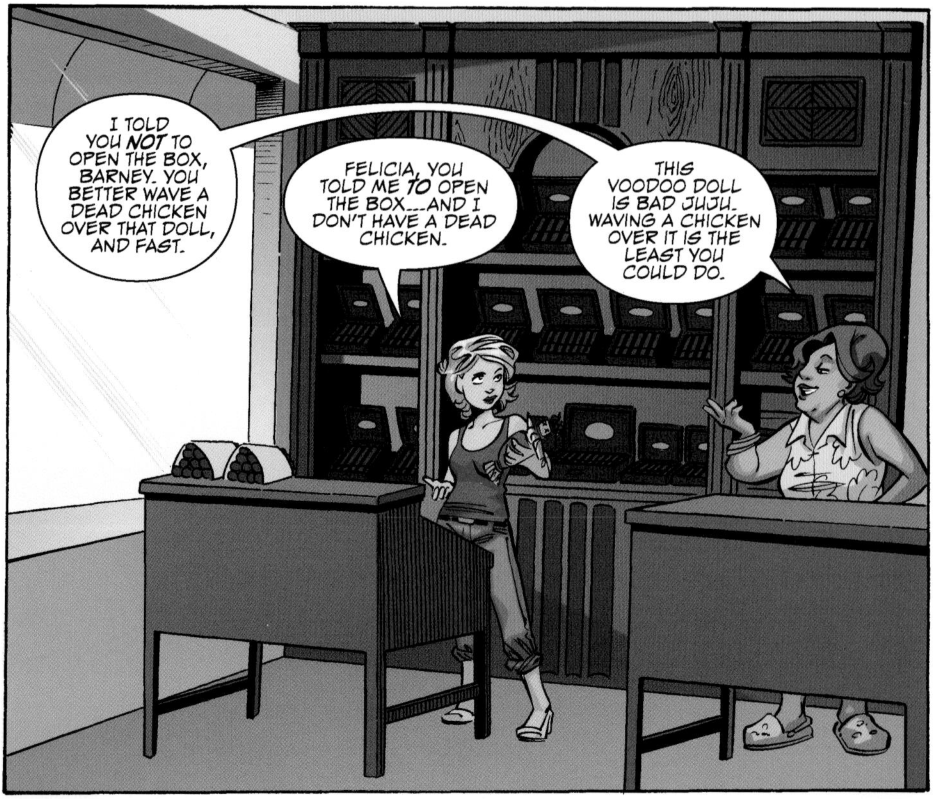
I TOLD YOU *NOT* TO OPEN THE BOX, BARNEY. YOU BETTER WAVE A DEAD CHICKEN OVER THAT DOLL, AND FAST.
FELICIA, YOU TOLD ME *TO* OPEN THE BOX... AND I DON'T HAVE A DEAD CHICKEN.
THIS VOODOO DOLL IS BAD JUJU. WAVING A CHICKEN OVER IT IS THE LEAST YOU COULD DO.

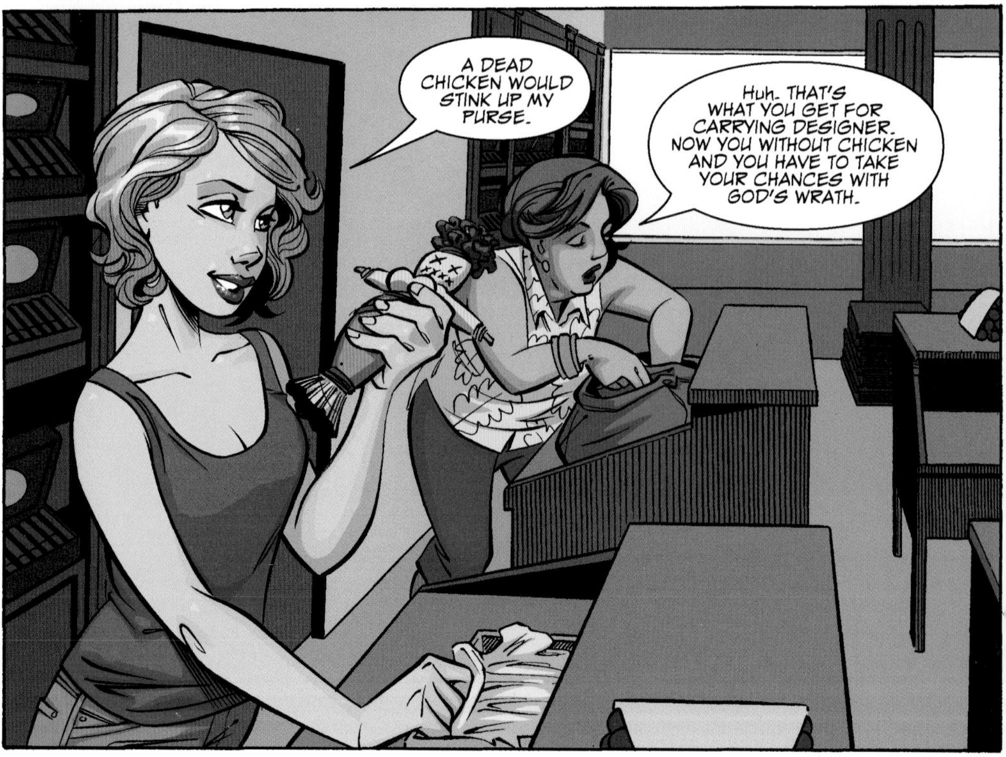
A DEAD CHICKEN WOULD STINK UP MY PURSE.
Huh. THAT'S WHAT YOU GET FOR CARRYING DESIGNER. NOW YOU WITHOUT CHICKEN AND YOU HAVE TO TAKE YOUR CHANCES WITH GOD'S WRATH.

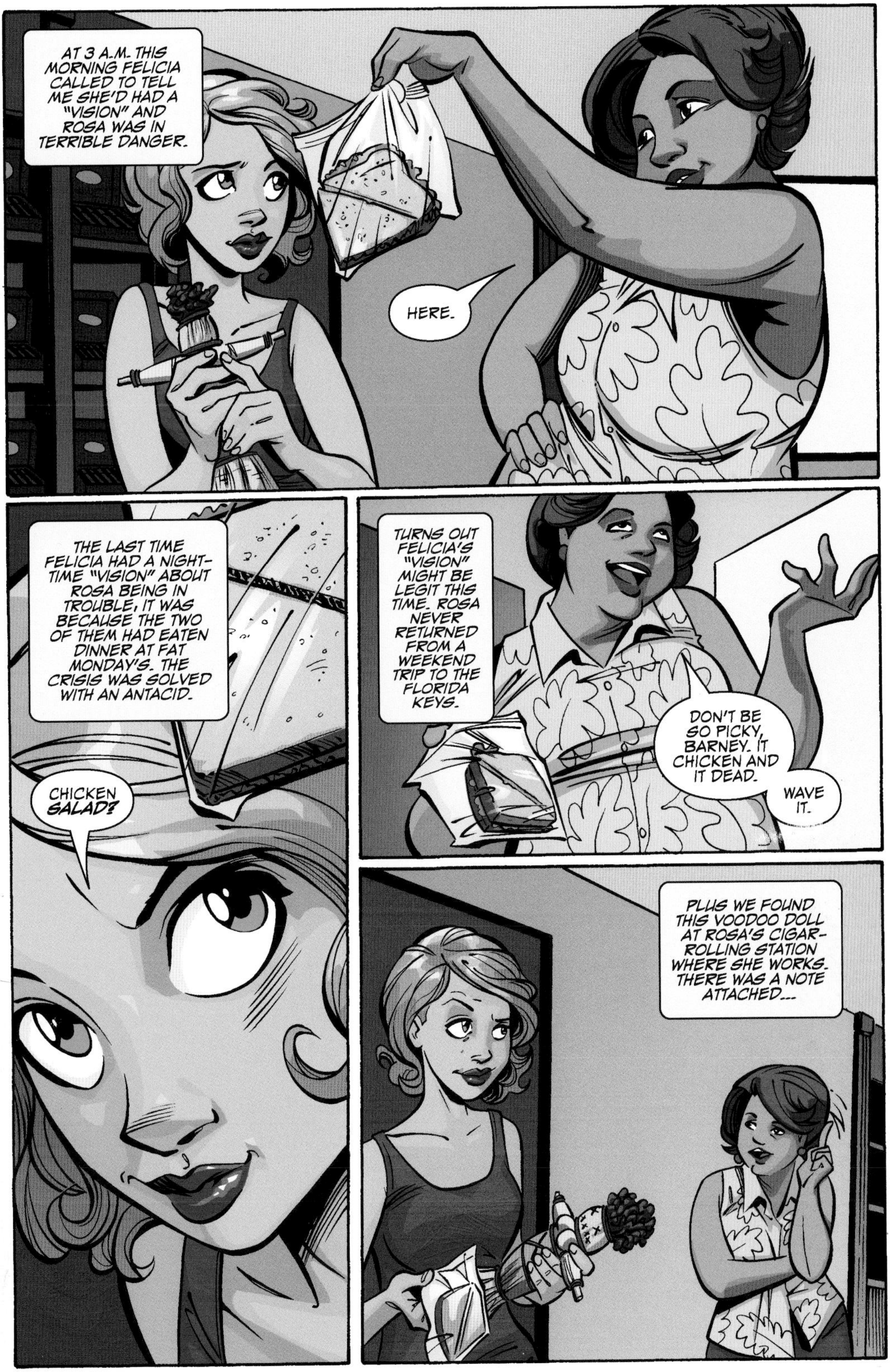

AT 3 A.M. THIS MORNING FELICIA CALLED TO TELL ME SHE'D HAD A "VISION" AND ROSA WAS IN TERRIBLE DANGER.
HERE.
THE LAST TIME FELICIA HAD A NIGHT-TIME "VISION" ABOUT ROSA BEING IN TROUBLE, IT WAS BECAUSE THE TWO OF THEM HAD EATEN DINNER AT FAT MONDAY'S. THE CRISIS WAS SOLVED WITH AN ANTACID.
CHICKEN SALAD?
TURNS OUT FELICIA'S "VISION" MIGHT BE LEGIT THIS TIME. ROSA NEVER RETURNED FROM A WEEKEND TRIP TO THE FLORIDA KEYS.
DON'T BE SO PICKY, BARNEY. IT CHICKEN AND IT DEAD.
WAVE IT.
PLUS WE FOUND THIS VOODOO DOLL AT ROSA'S CIGAR-ROLLING STATION WHERE SHE WORKS. THERE WAS A NOTE ATTACHED...

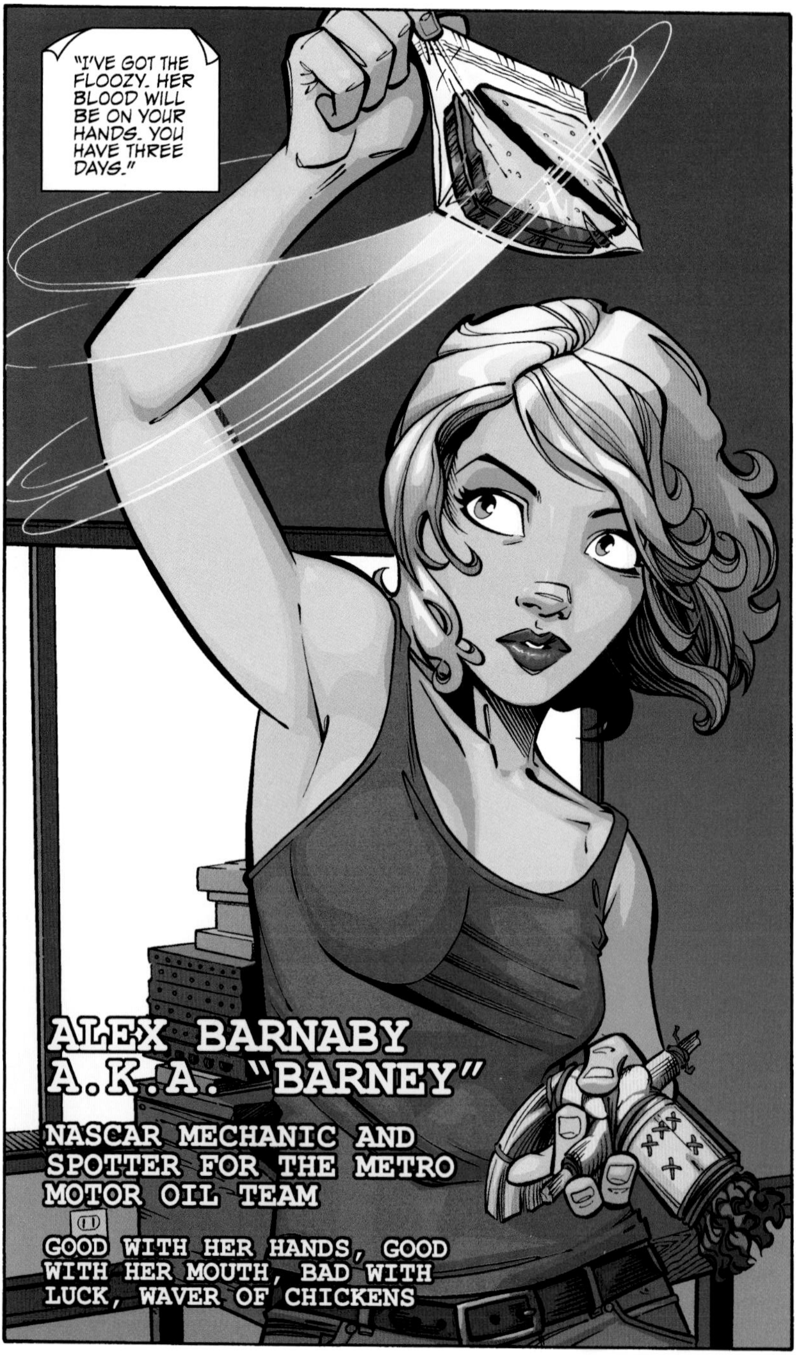
"I'VE GOT THE FLOOZY. HER BLOOD WILL BE ON YOUR HANDS. YOU HAVE THREE DAYS."
ALEX BARNABY A.K.A. "BARNEY"
NASCAR MECHANIC AND SPOTTER FOR THE METRO MOTOR OIL TEAM
GOOD WITH HER HANDS, GOOD WITH HER MOUTH, BAD WITH LUCK, WAVER OF CHICKENS

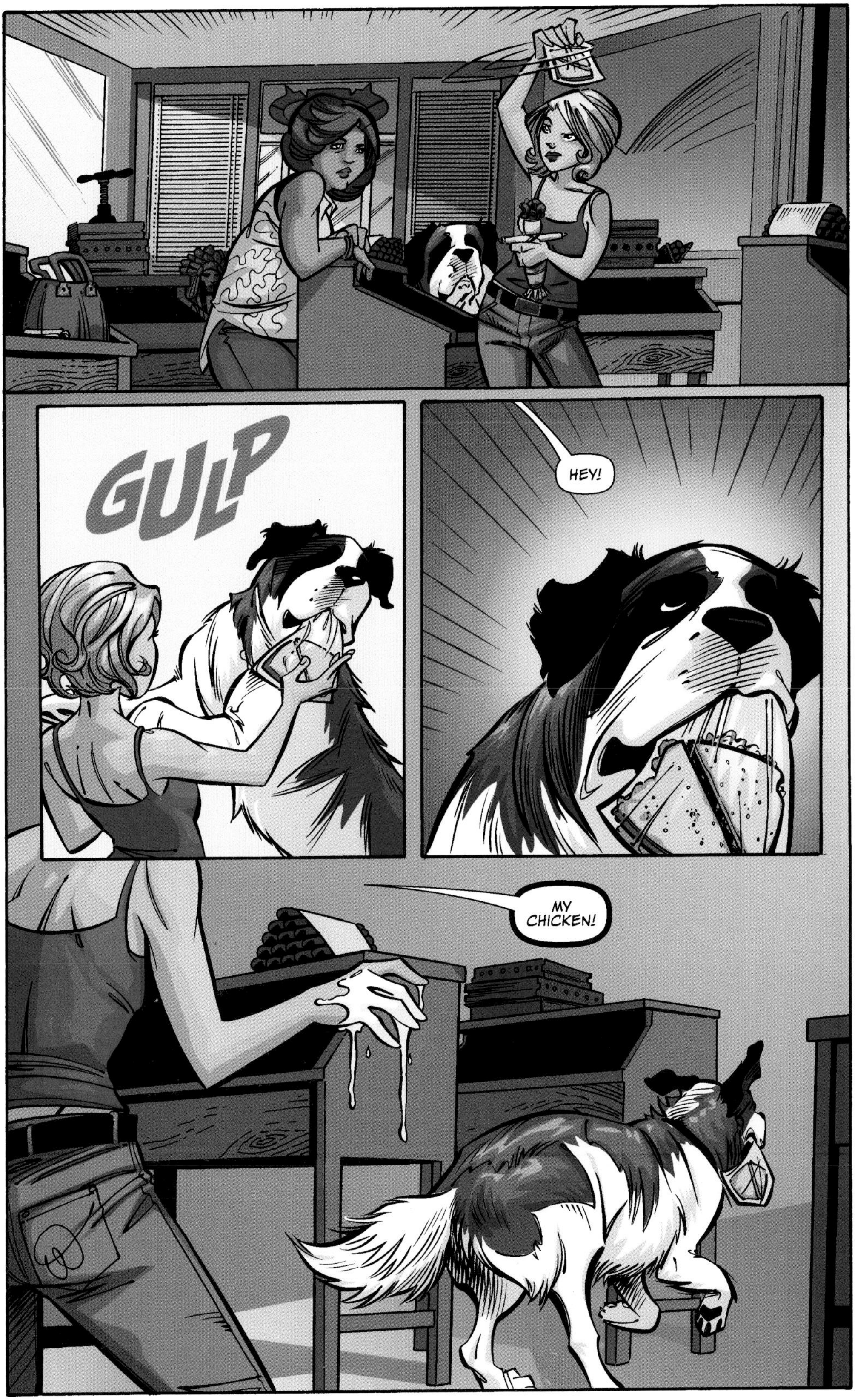
GULP
HEY!
MY CHICKEN!

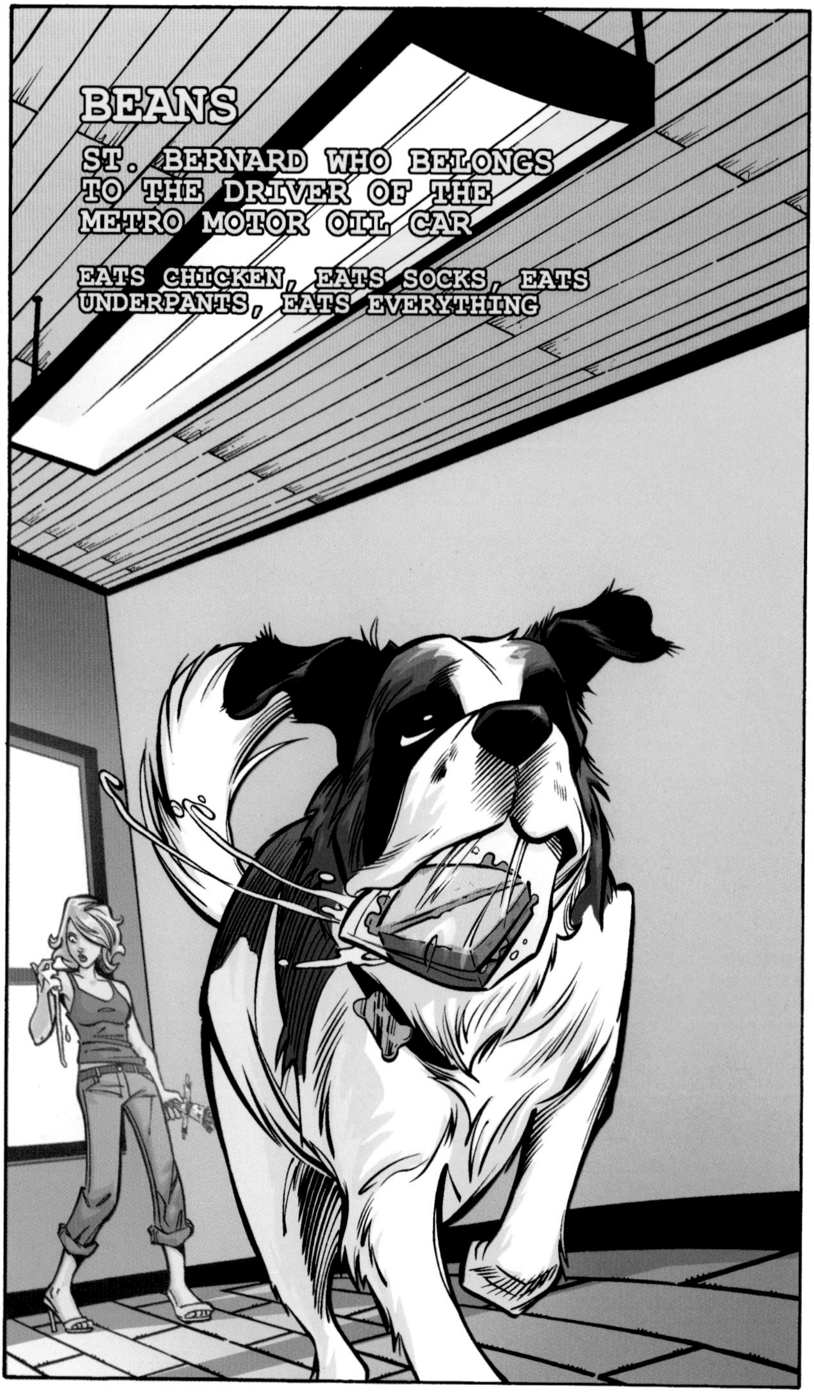
BEANS
ST. BERNARD WHO BELONGS TO THE DRIVER OF THE METRO MOTOR OIL CAR
EATS CHICKEN, EATS SOCKS, EATS UNDERPANTS, EATS EVERYTHING

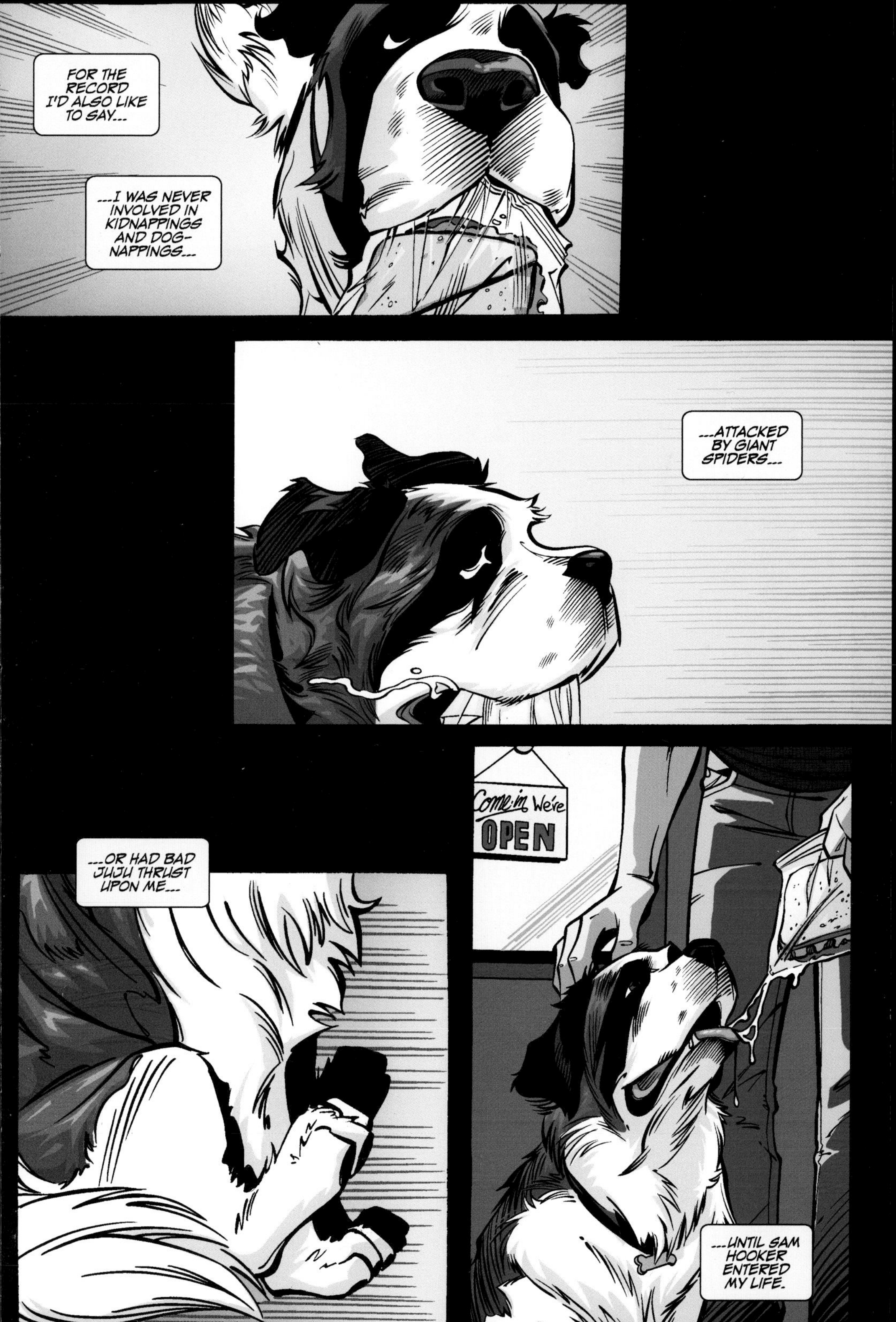
FOR THE RECORD I'D ALSO LIKE TO SAY...
...I WAS NEVER INVOLVED IN KIDNAPPINGS AND DOG-NAPPINGS...
...ATTACKED BY GIANT SPIDERS...
...OR HAD BAD JUJU THRUST UPON ME...
Come in We're OPEN
...UNTIL SAM HOOKER ENTERED MY LIFE.

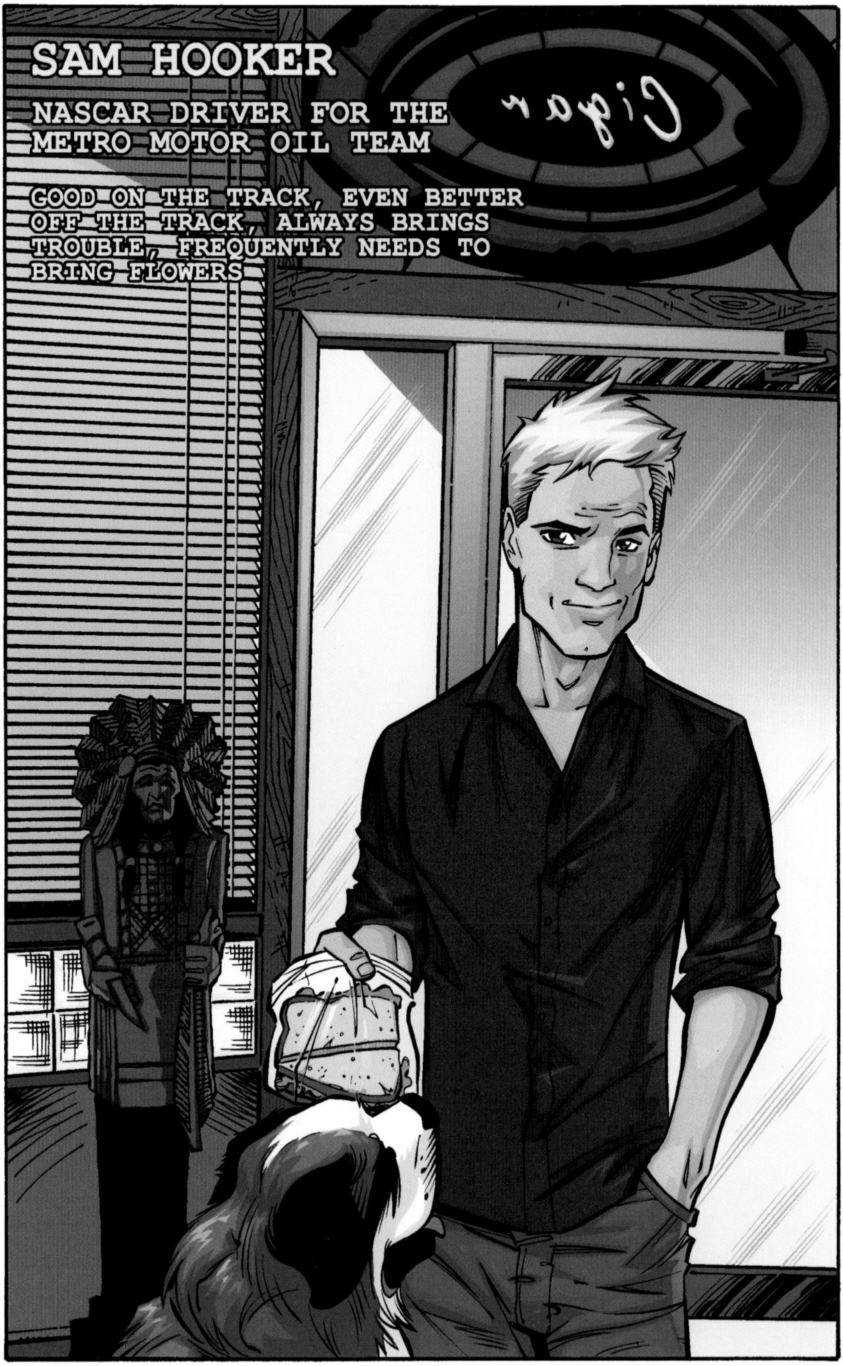
SAM HOOKER
NASCAR DRIVER FOR THE METRO MOTOR OIL TEAM
GOOD ON THE TRACK, EVEN BETTER OFF THE TRACK, ALWAYS BRINGS TROUBLE, FREQUENTLY NEEDS TO BRING FLOWERS
Cigar

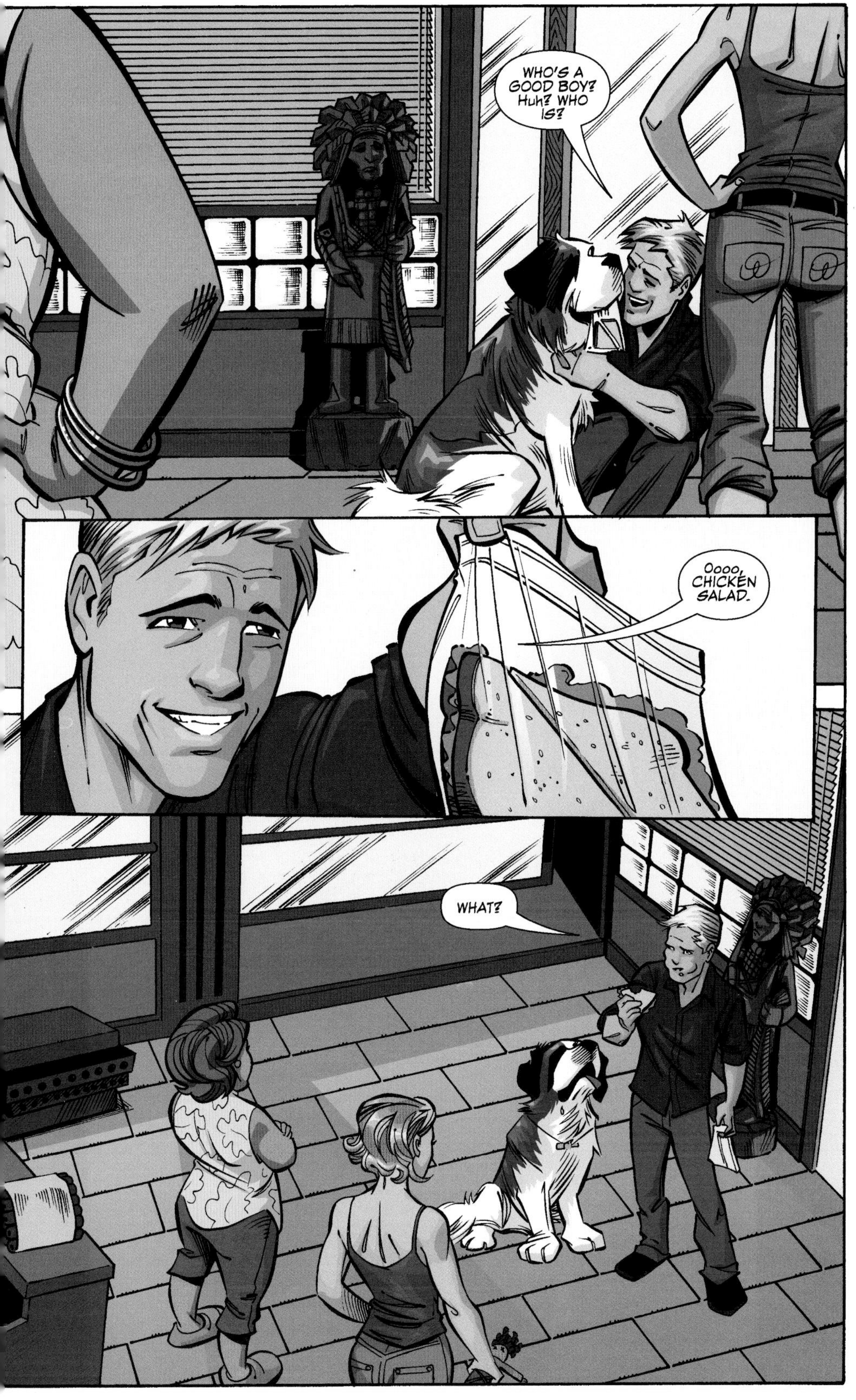
WHO'S A GOOD BOY? Huh? WHO IS?
Oooo, CHICKEN SALAD.
WHAT?

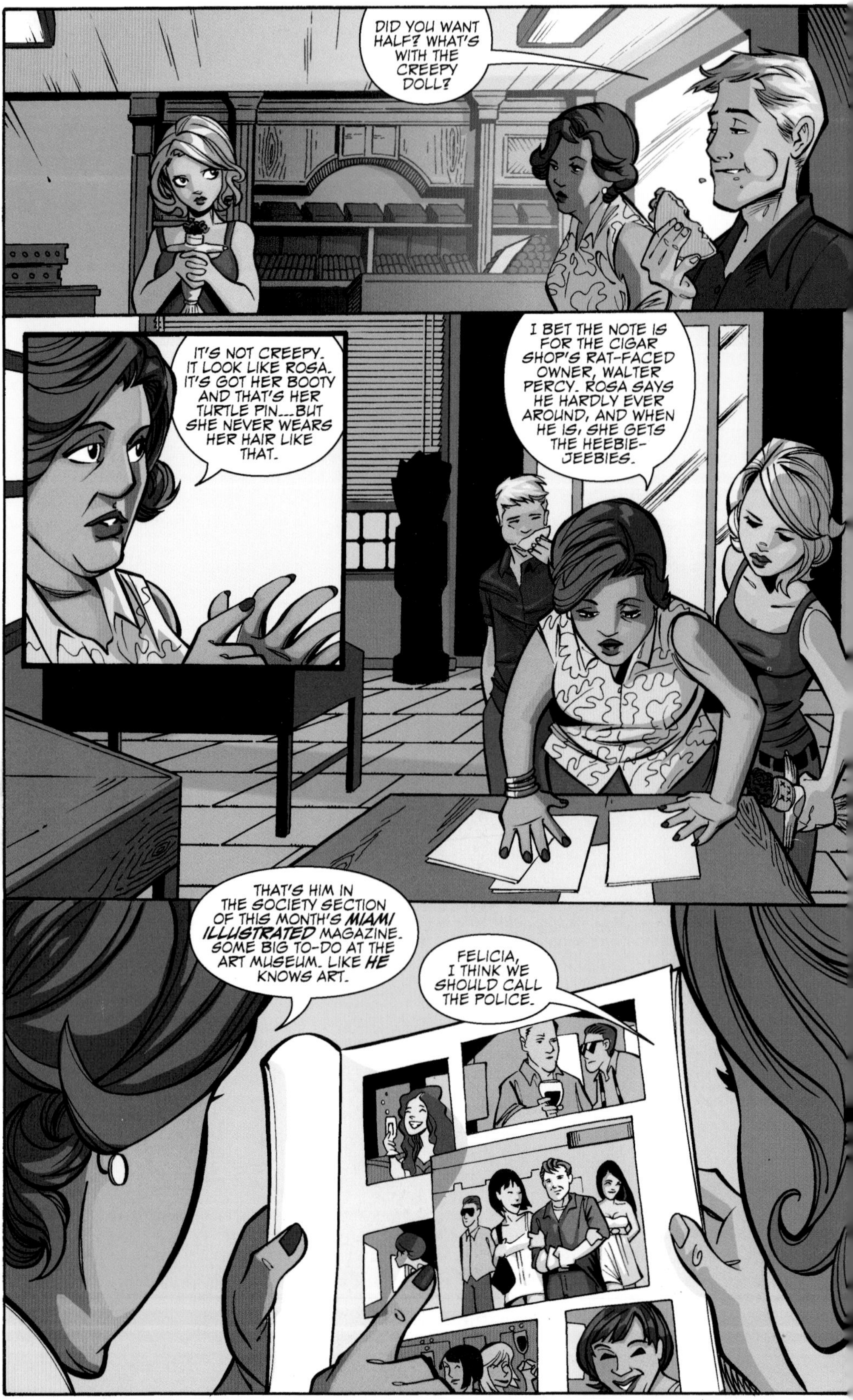
DID YOU WANT HALF? WHAT'S WITH THE CREEPY DOLL?
IT'S NOT CREEPY. IT LOOK LIKE ROSA. IT'S GOT HER BOOTY AND THAT'S HER TURTLE PIN...BUT SHE NEVER WEARS HER HAIR LIKE THAT.
I BET THE NOTE IS FOR THE CIGAR SHOP'S RAT-FACED OWNER, WALTER PERCY. ROSA SAYS HE HARDLY EVER AROUND, AND WHEN HE IS, SHE GETS THE HEEBIE-JEEBIES.
THAT'S HIM IN THE SOCIETY SECTION OF THIS MONTH'S MIAMI ILLUSTRATED MAGAZINE. SOME BIG TO-DO AT THE ART MUSEUM. LIKE HE KNOWS ART.
FELICIA, I THINK WE SHOULD CALL THE POLICE.

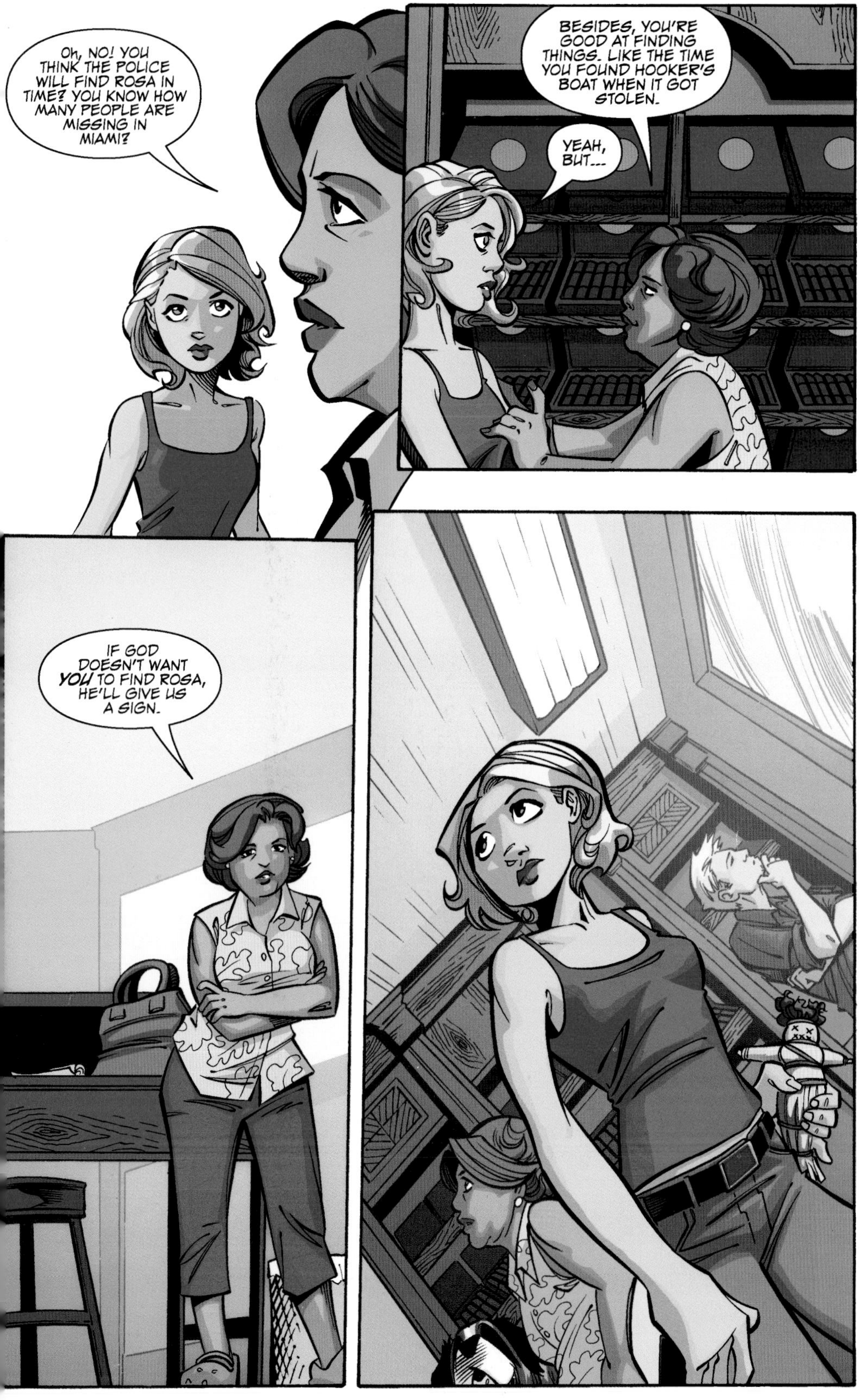
Oh, NO! YOU THINK THE POLICE WILL FIND ROSA IN TIME? YOU KNOW HOW MANY PEOPLE ARE MISSING IN MIAMI?
BESIDES, YOU'RE GOOD AT FINDING THINGS. LIKE THE TIME YOU FOUND HOOKER'S BOAT WHEN IT GOT STOLEN.
YEAH, BUT...
IF GOD DOESN'T WANT *YOU* TO FIND ROSA, HE'LL GIVE US A SIGN.

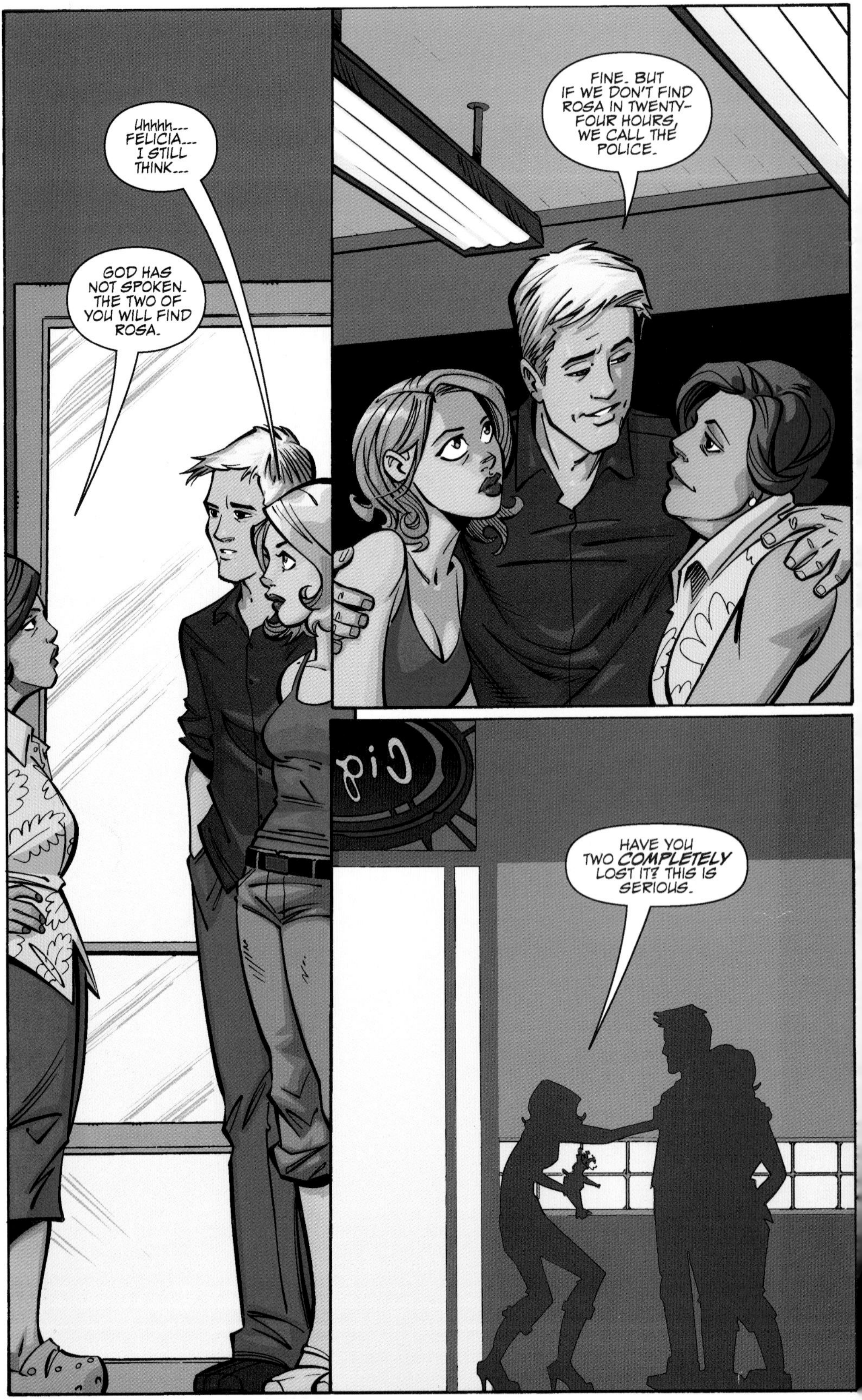
Uhhhh... FELICIA... I STILL THINK...
GOD HAS NOT SPOKEN. THE TWO OF YOU WILL FIND ROSA.
FINE. BUT IF WE DON'T FIND ROSA IN TWENTY-FOUR HOURS, WE CALL THE POLICE.
HAVE YOU TWO COMPLETELY LOST IT? THIS IS SERIOUS.

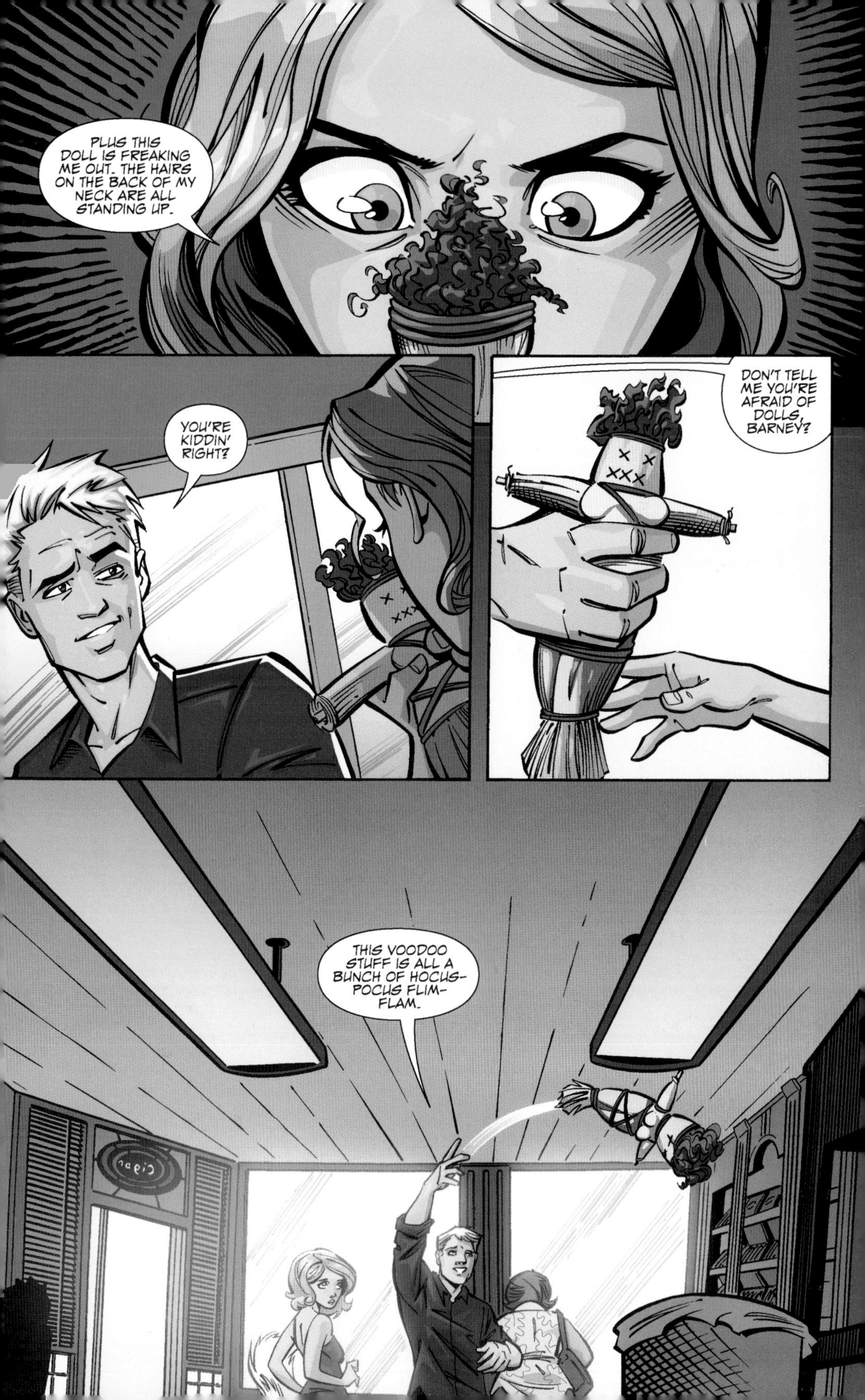
PLUS THIS DOLL IS FREAKING ME OUT. THE HAIRS ON THE BACK OF MY NECK ARE ALL STANDING UP.
YOU'RE KIDDIN' RIGHT?
DON'T TELL ME YOU'RE AFRAID OF DOLLS, BARNEY?
THIS VOODOO STUFF IS ALL A BUNCH OF HOCUS-POCUS FLIM-FLAM.

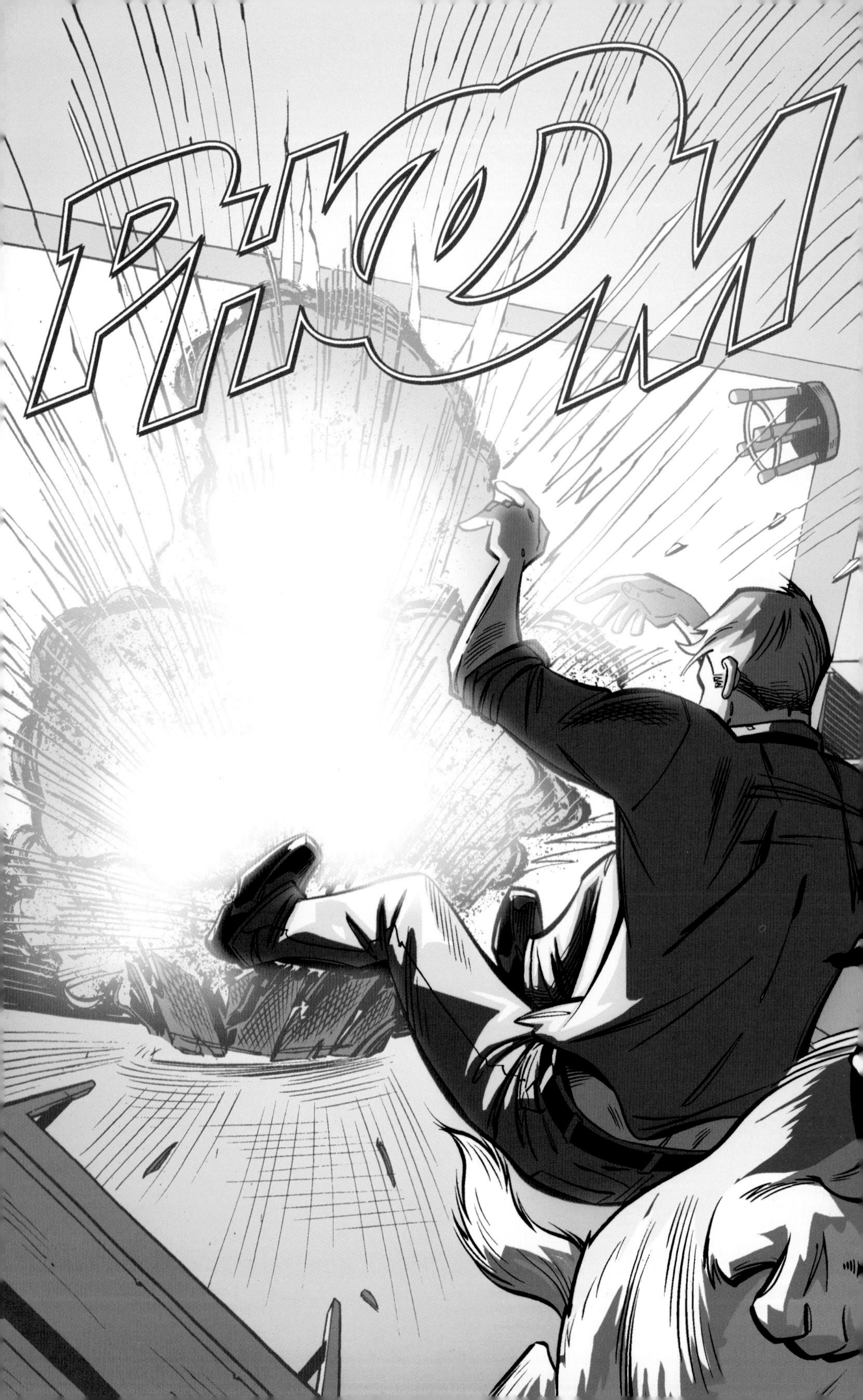

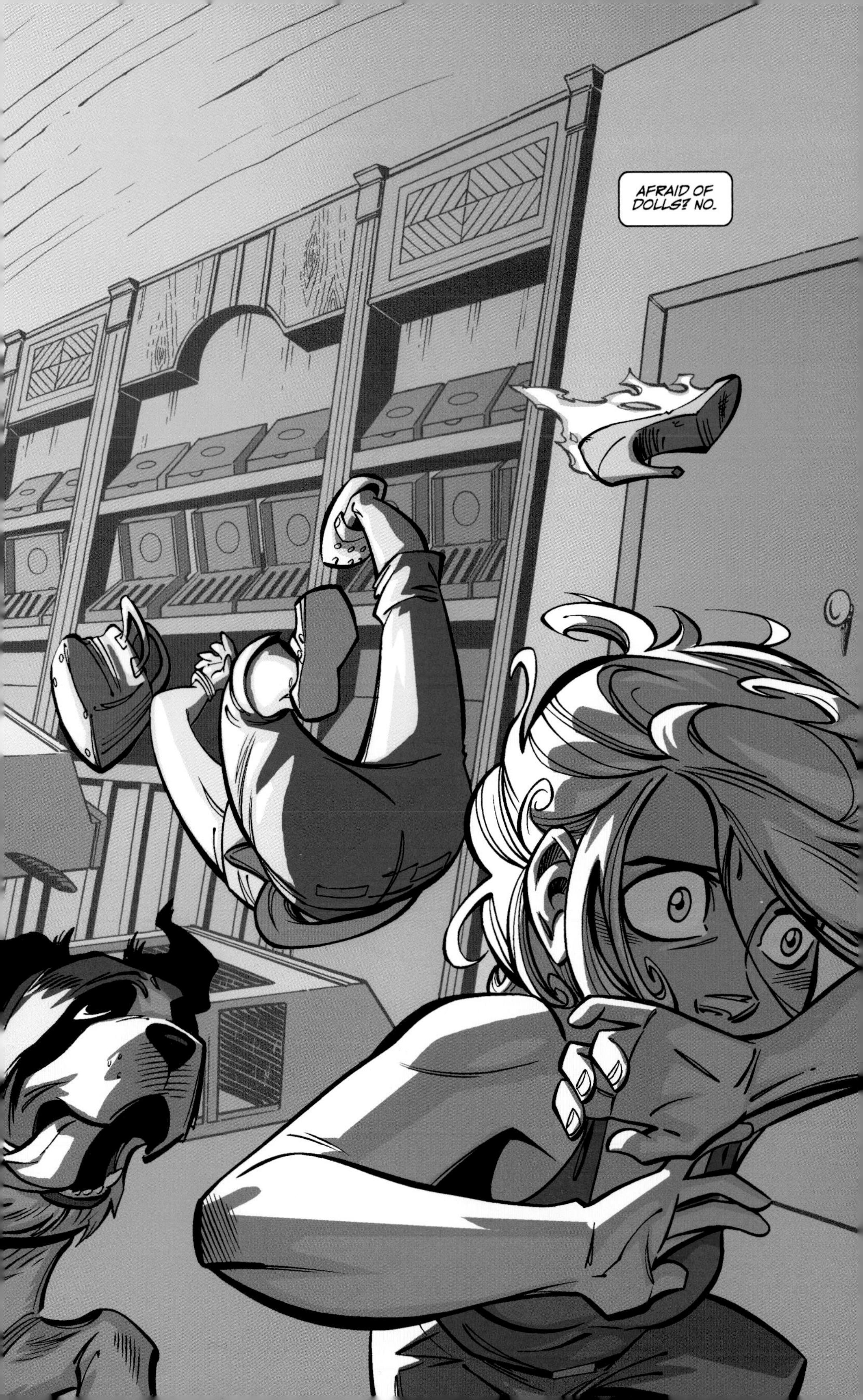
AFRAID OF DOLLS? NO.

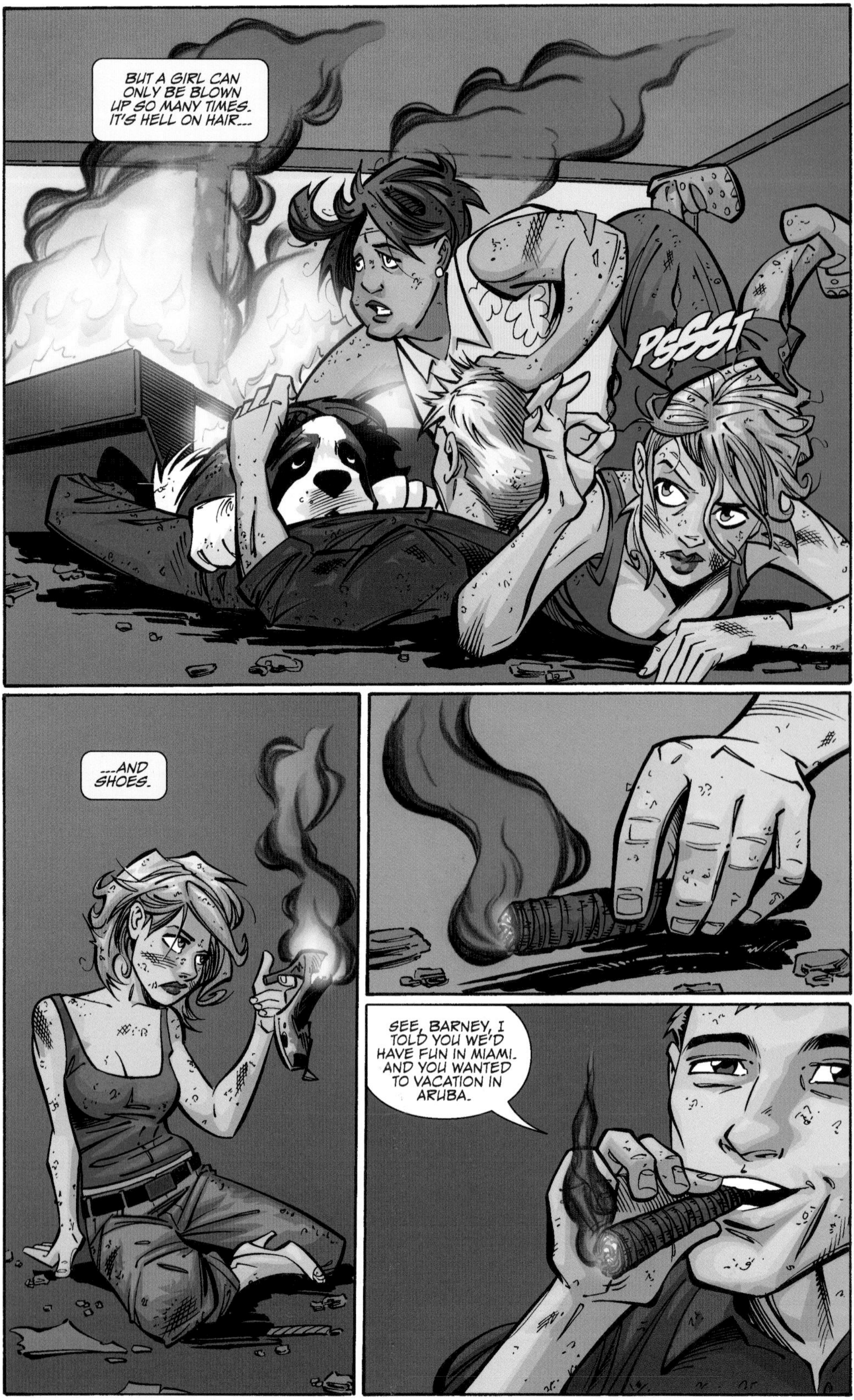
BUT A GIRL CAN ONLY BE BLOWN UP SO MANY TIMES. IT'S HELL ON HAIR...
PSSST
...AND SHOES.
SEE, BARNEY, I TOLD YOU WE'D HAVE FUN IN MIAMI. AND YOU WANTED TO VACATION IN ARUBA.

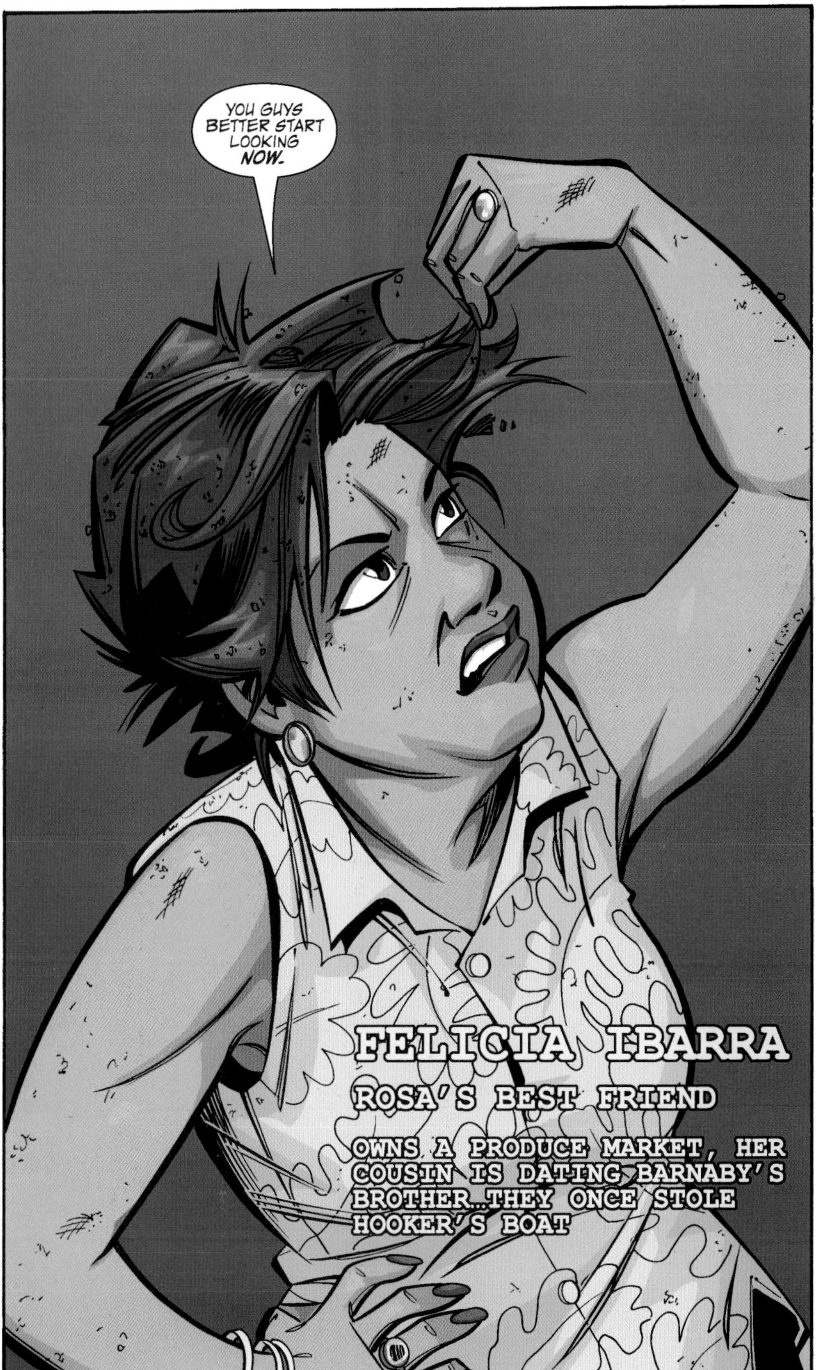
YOU GUYS BETTER START LOOKING NOW.
FELICIA IBARRA
ROSA'S BEST FRIEND
OWNS A PRODUCE MARKET, HER COUSIN IS DATING BARNABY'S BROTHER...THEY ONCE STOLE HOOKER'S BOAT

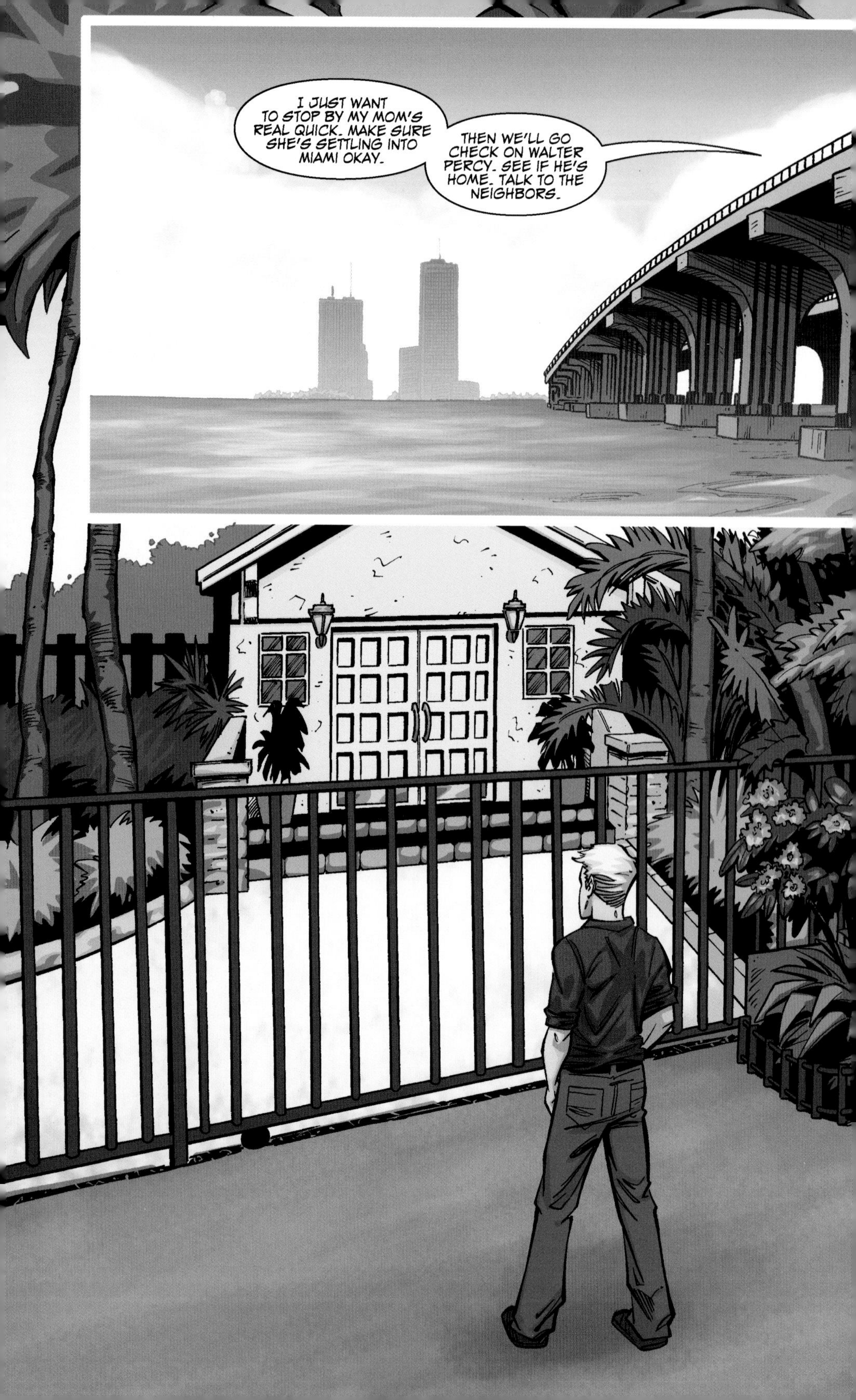
I JUST WANT TO STOP BY MY MOM'S REAL QUICK. MAKE SURE SHE'S SETTLING INTO MIAMI OKAY.
THEN WE'LL GO CHECK ON WALTER PERCY. SEE IF HE'S HOME. TALK TO THE NEIGHBORS.

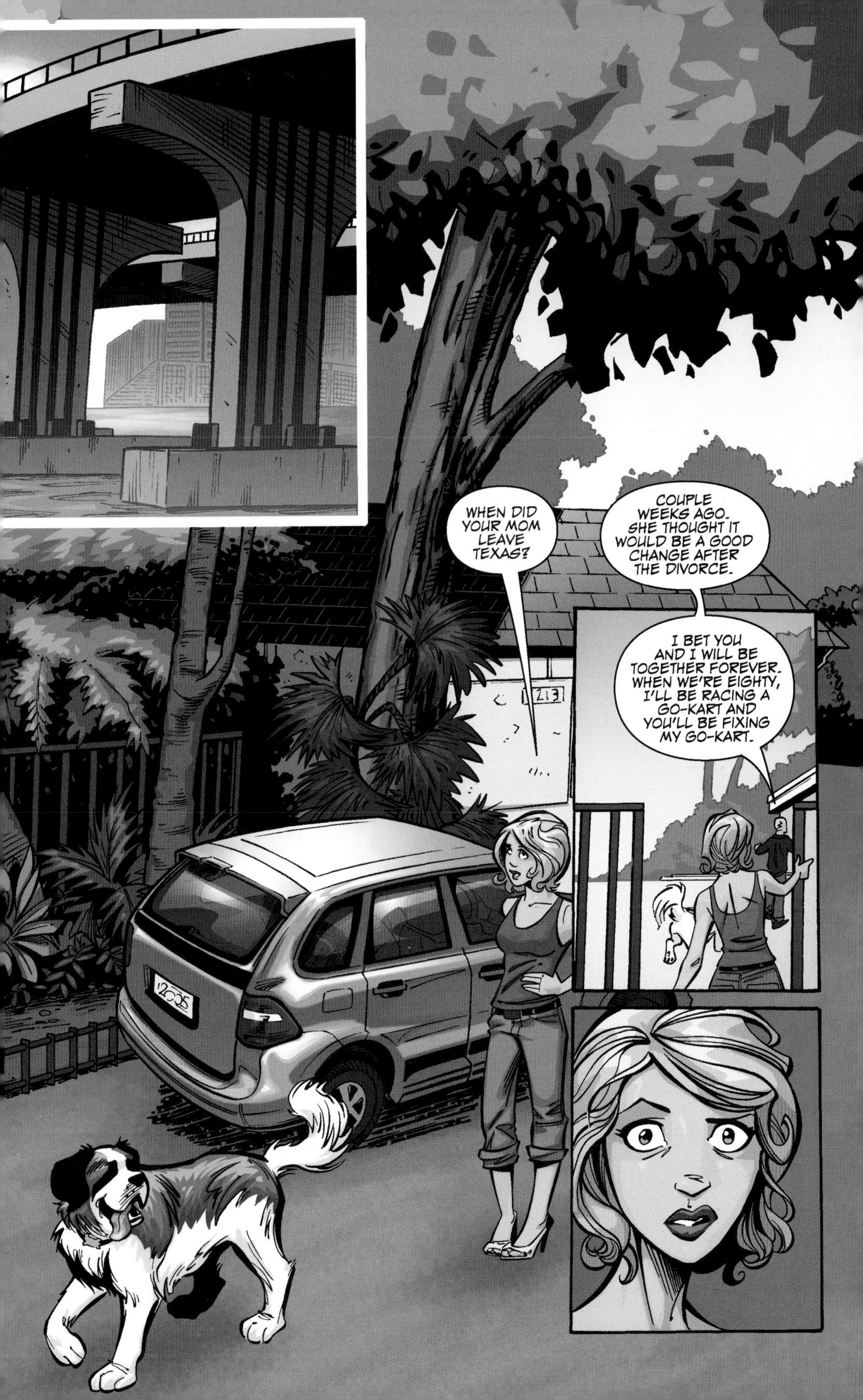
WHEN DID YOUR MOM LEAVE TEXAS?
COUPLE WEEKS AGO. SHE THOUGHT IT WOULD BE A GOOD CHANGE AFTER THE DIVORCE.
I BET YOU AND I WILL BE TOGETHER FOREVER. WHEN WE'RE EIGHTY, I'LL BE RACING A GO-KART AND YOU'LL BE FIXING MY GO-KART.

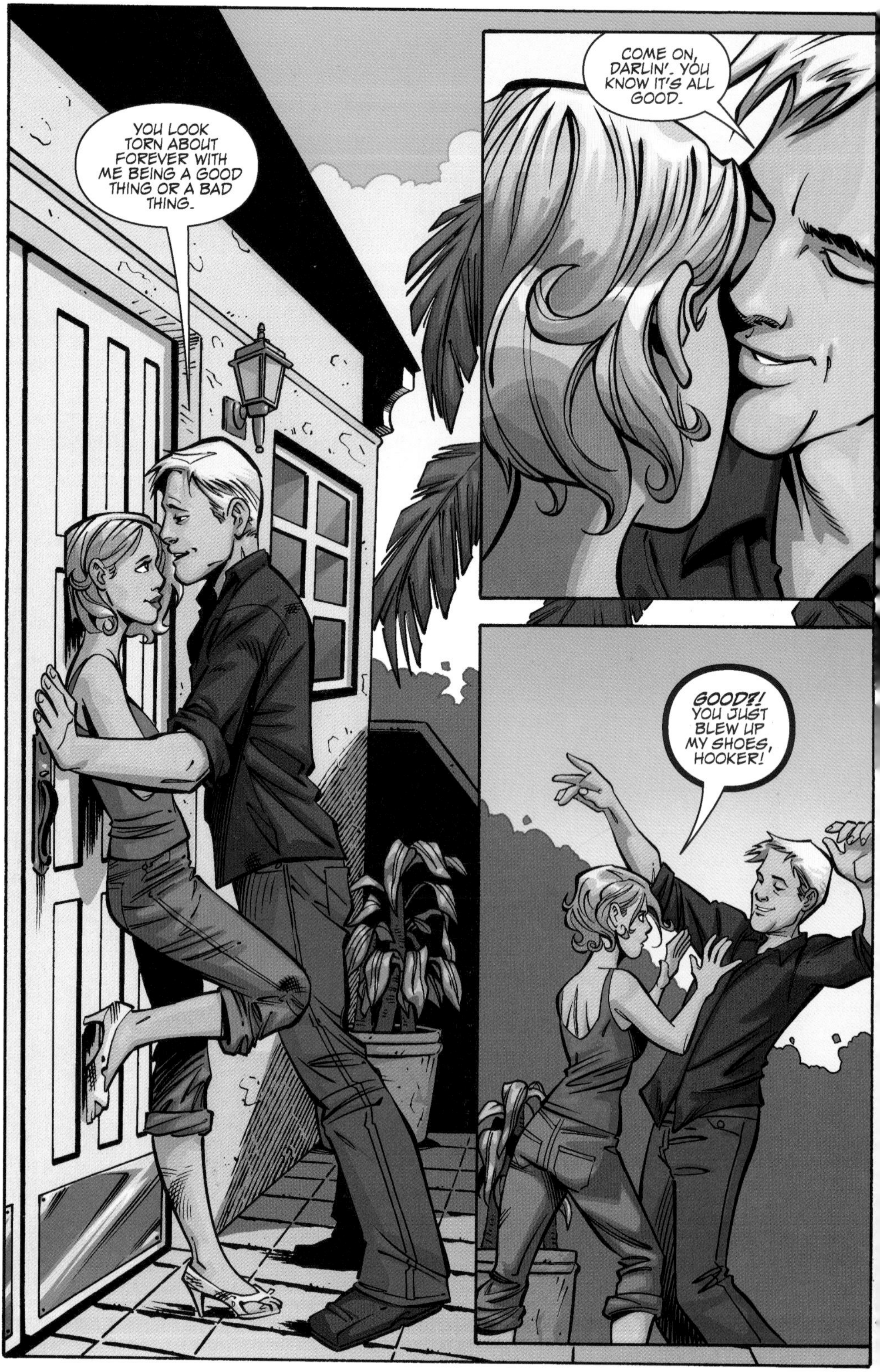
YOU LOOK TORN ABOUT FOREVER WITH ME BEING A GOOD THING OR A BAD THING.
COME ON, DARLIN'. YOU KNOW IT'S ALL GOOD.
GOOD?! YOU JUST BLEW UP MY SHOES, HOOKER!

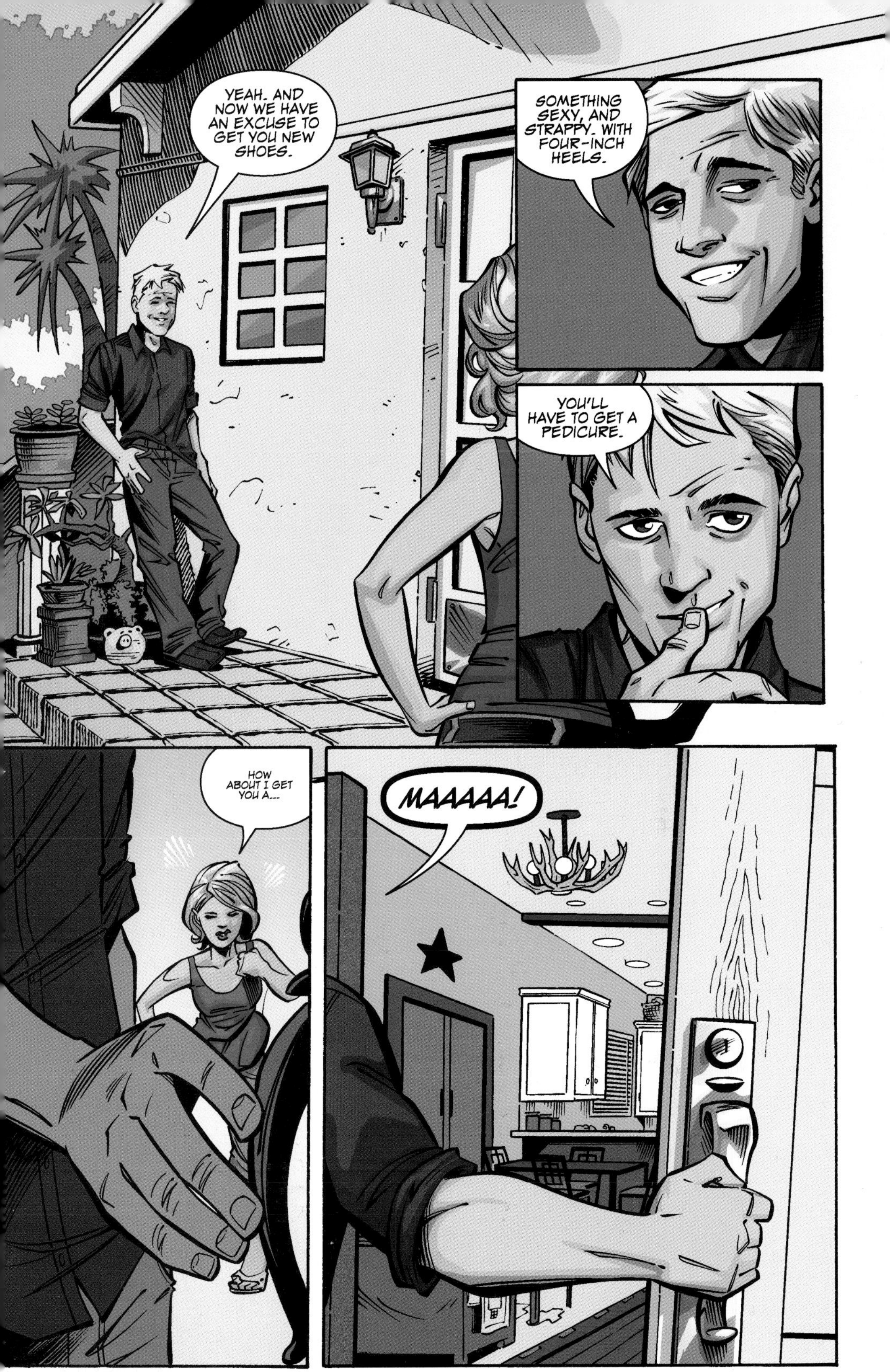
YEAH. AND NOW WE HAVE AN EXCUSE TO GET YOU NEW SHOES.
SOMETHING SEXY, AND STRAPPY. WITH FOUR-INCH HEELS.
YOU'LL HAVE TO GET A PEDICURE.
HOW ABOUT I GET YOU A...
MAAAAA!

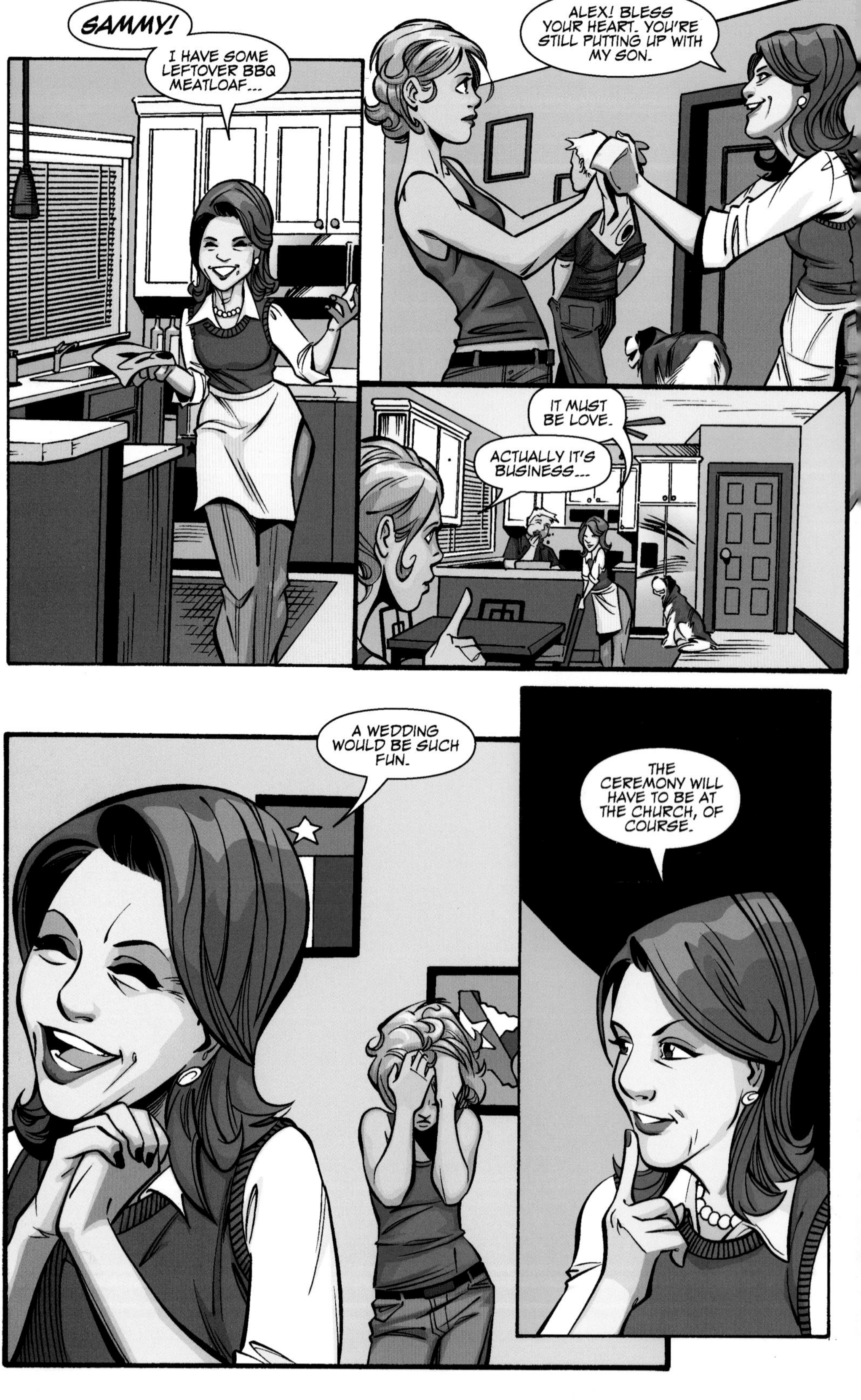
SAMMY!
I HAVE SOME LEFTOVER BBQ MEATLOAF...
ALEX! BLESS YOUR HEART. YOU'RE STILL PUTTING UP WITH MY SON.
IT MUST BE LOVE.
ACTUALLY IT'S BUSINESS...
A WEDDING WOULD BE SUCH FUN.
THE CEREMONY WILL HAVE TO BE AT THE CHURCH, OF COURSE.

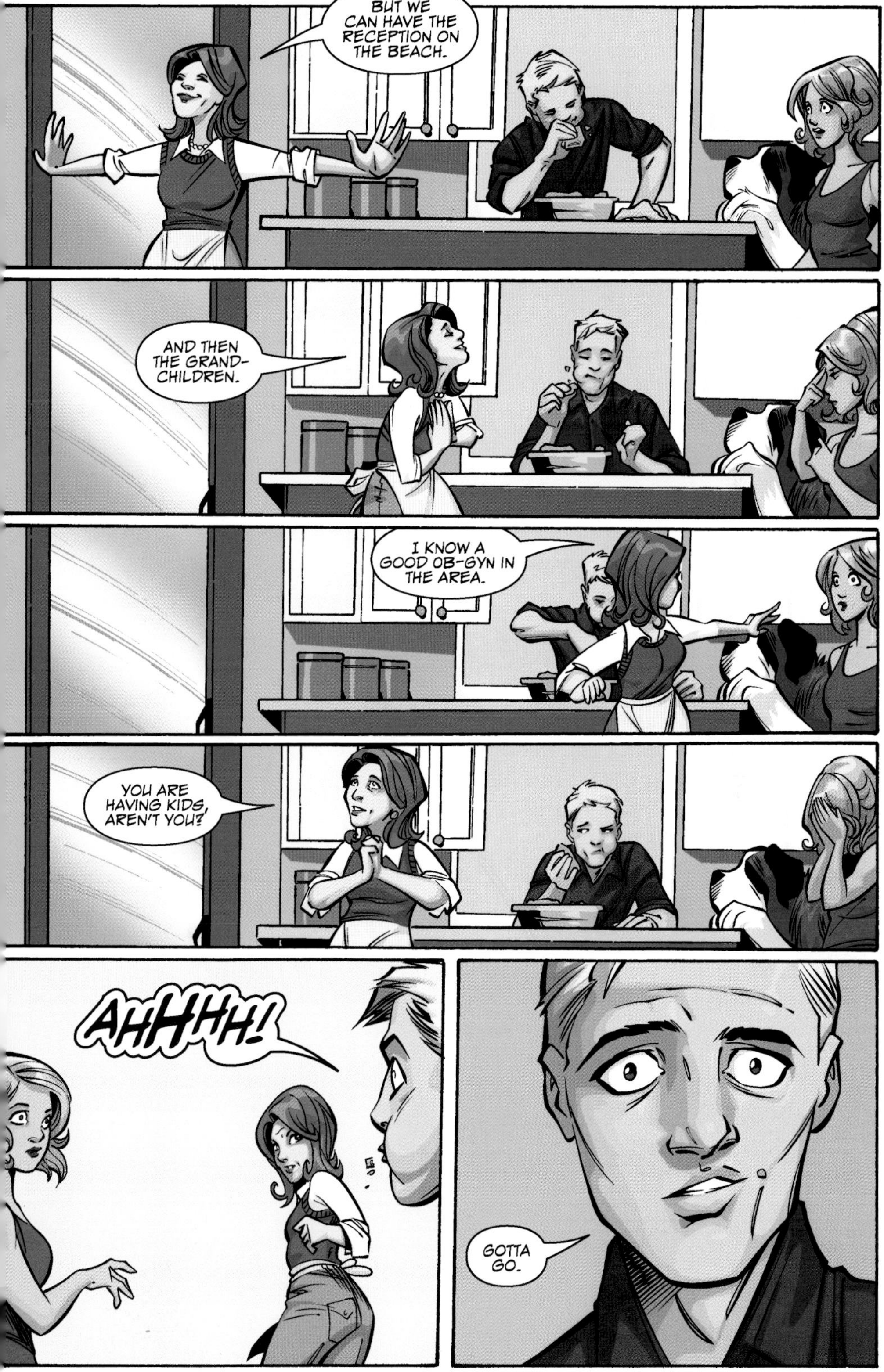
BUT WE CAN HAVE THE RECEPTION ON THE BEACH.
AND THEN THE GRAND-CHILDREN.
I KNOW A GOOD OB-GYN IN THE AREA.
YOU ARE HAVING KIDS, AREN'T YOU?
AHHHH!
GOTTA GO.

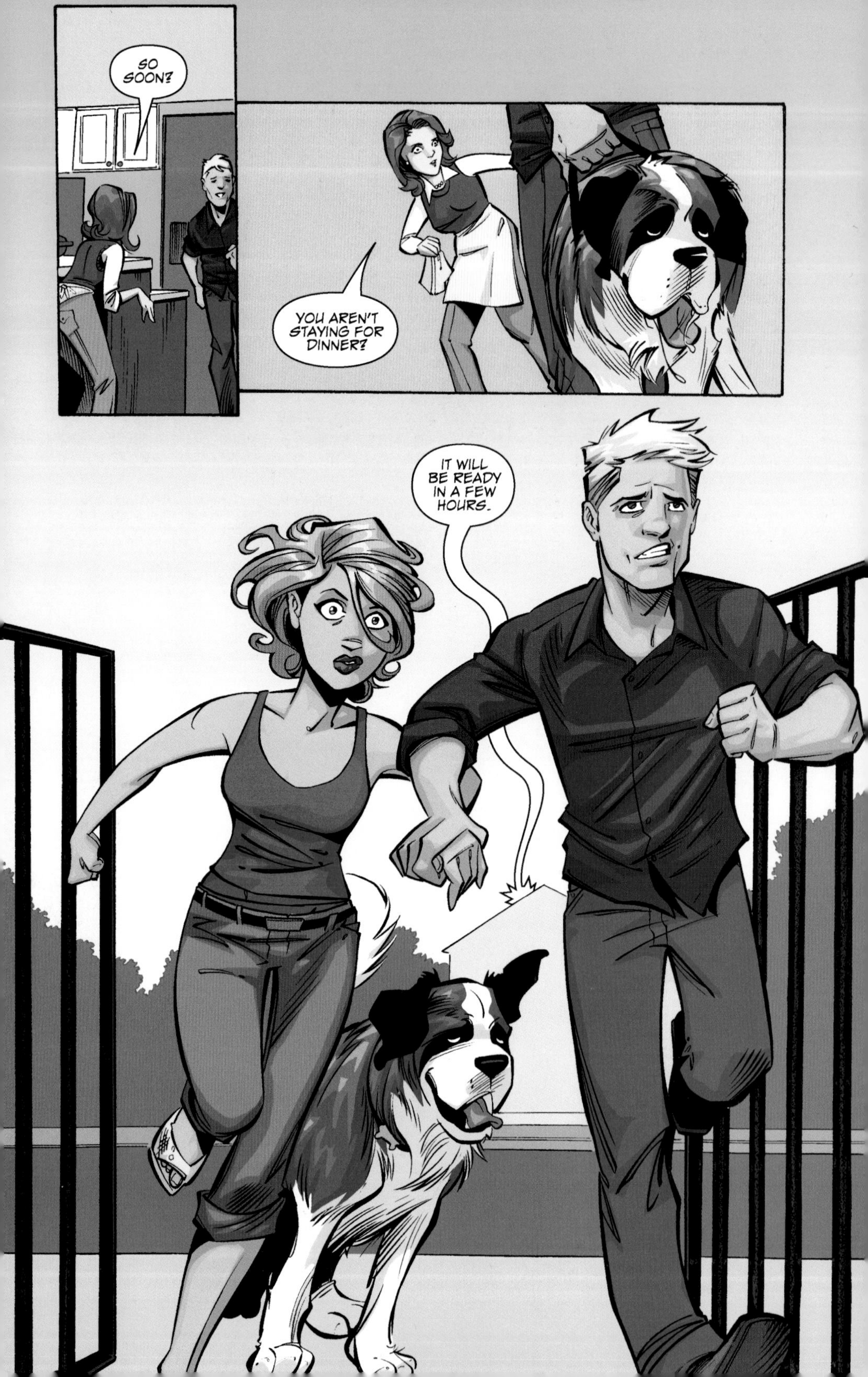
SO SOON?
YOU AREN'T STAYING FOR DINNER?
IT WILL BE READY IN A FEW HOURS.

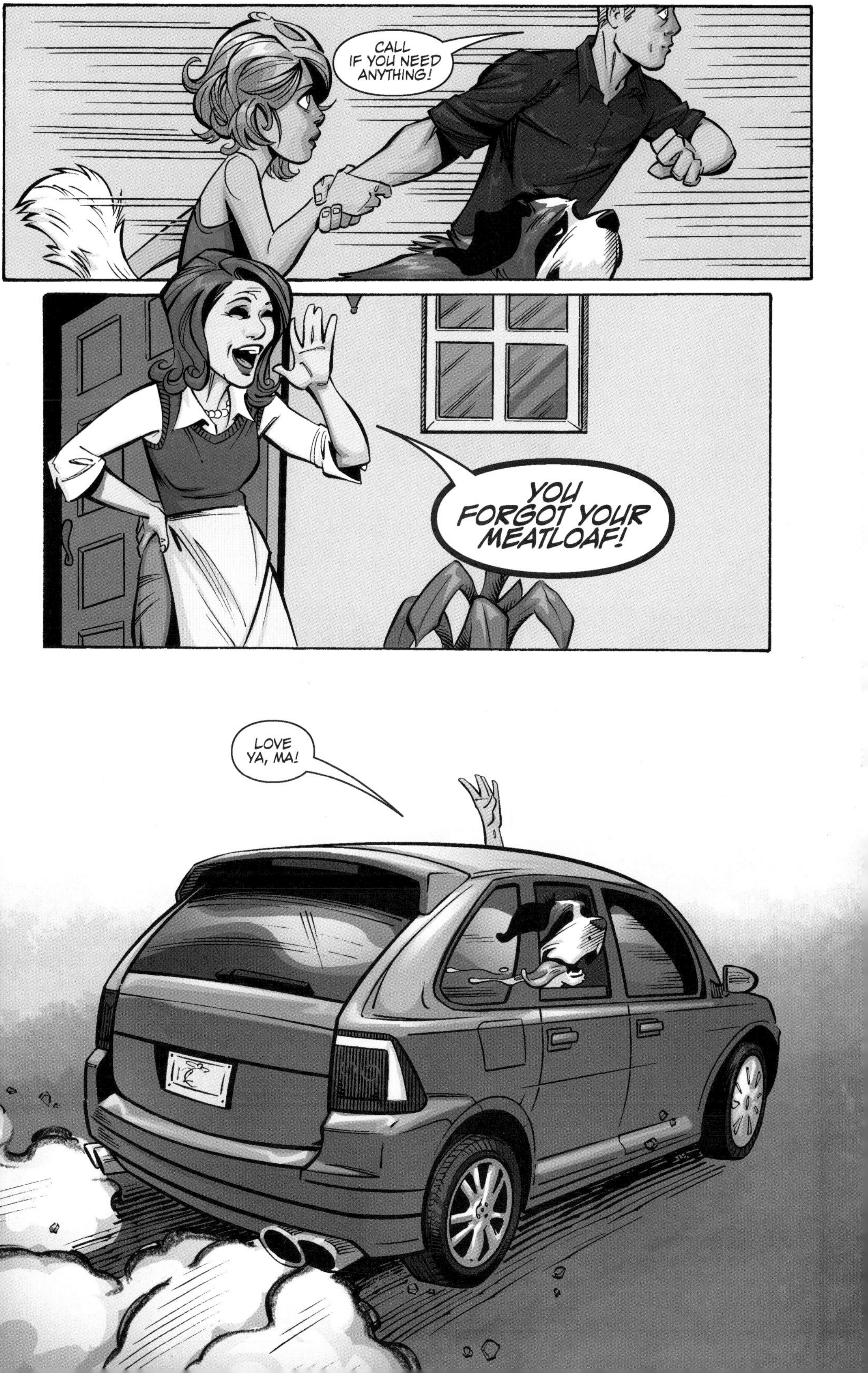
CALL IF YOU NEED ANYTHING!
YOU FORGOT YOUR MEATLOAF!
LOVE YA, MA!

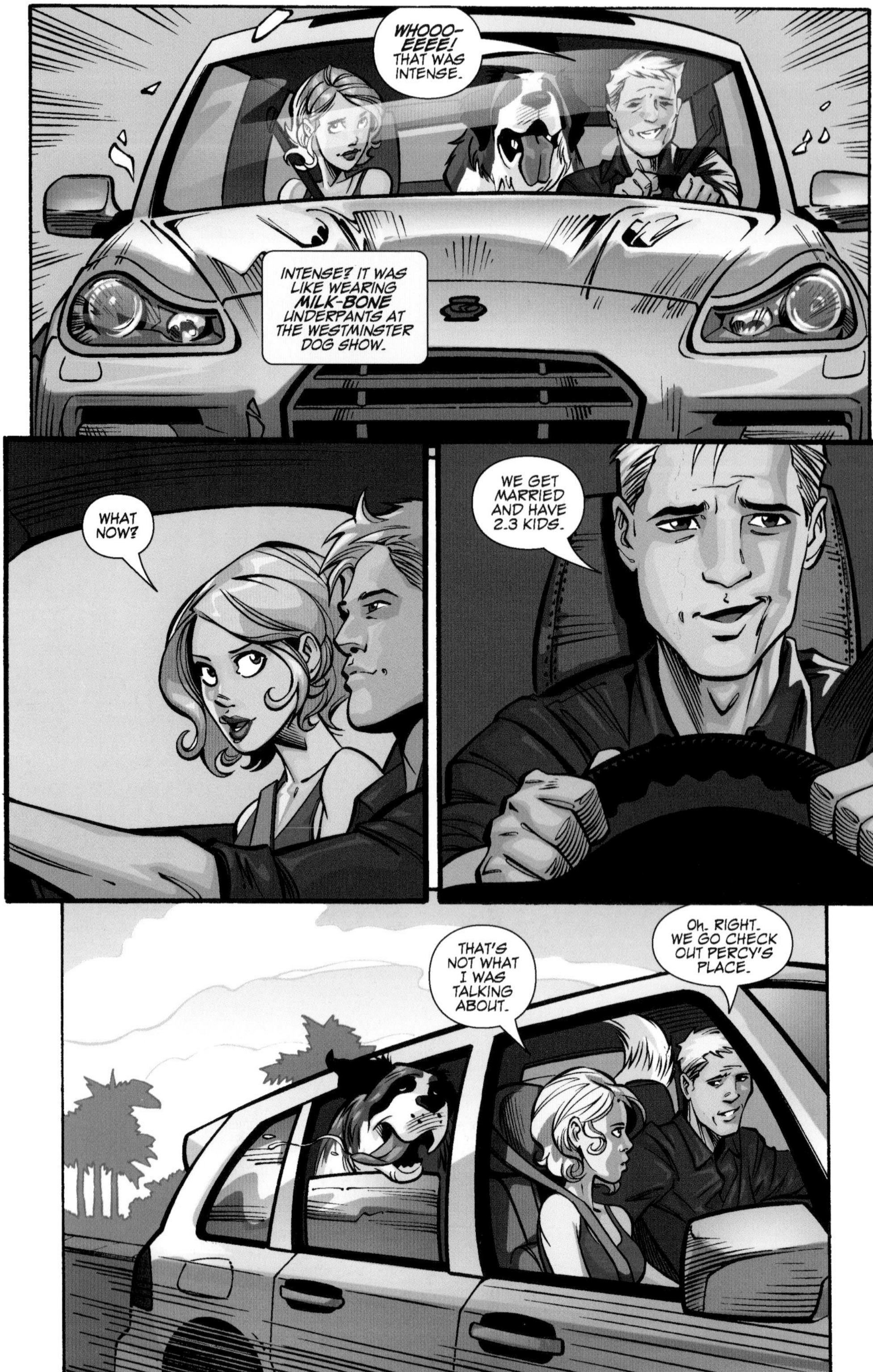
WHOOO-EEEE! THAT WAS INTENSE.
INTENSE? IT WAS LIKE WEARING MILK-BONE UNDERPANTS AT THE WESTMINSTER DOG SHOW.
WHAT NOW?
WE GET MARRIED AND HAVE 2.3 KIDS.
THAT'S NOT WHAT I WAS TALKING ABOUT.
Oh. RIGHT. WE GO CHECK OUT PERCY'S PLACE.

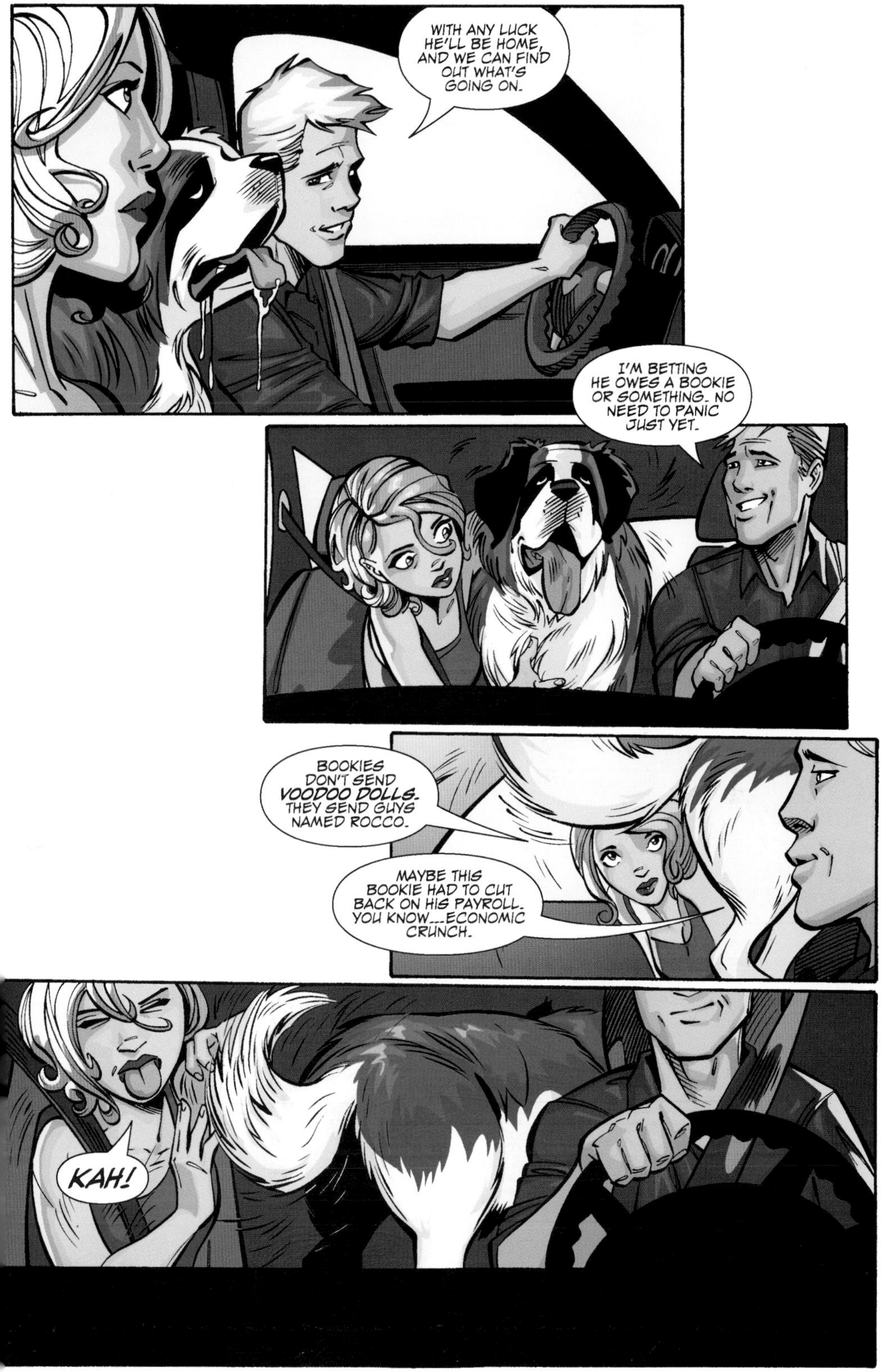
WITH ANY LUCK HE'LL BE HOME, AND WE CAN FIND OUT WHAT'S GOING ON.
I'M BETTING HE OWES A BOOKIE OR SOMETHING. NO NEED TO PANIC JUST YET.
BOOKIES DON'T SEND *VOODOO DOLLS.* THEY SEND GUYS NAMED ROCCO.
MAYBE THIS BOOKIE HAD TO CUT BACK ON HIS PAYROLL. YOU KNOW... ECONOMIC CRUNCH.
KAH!

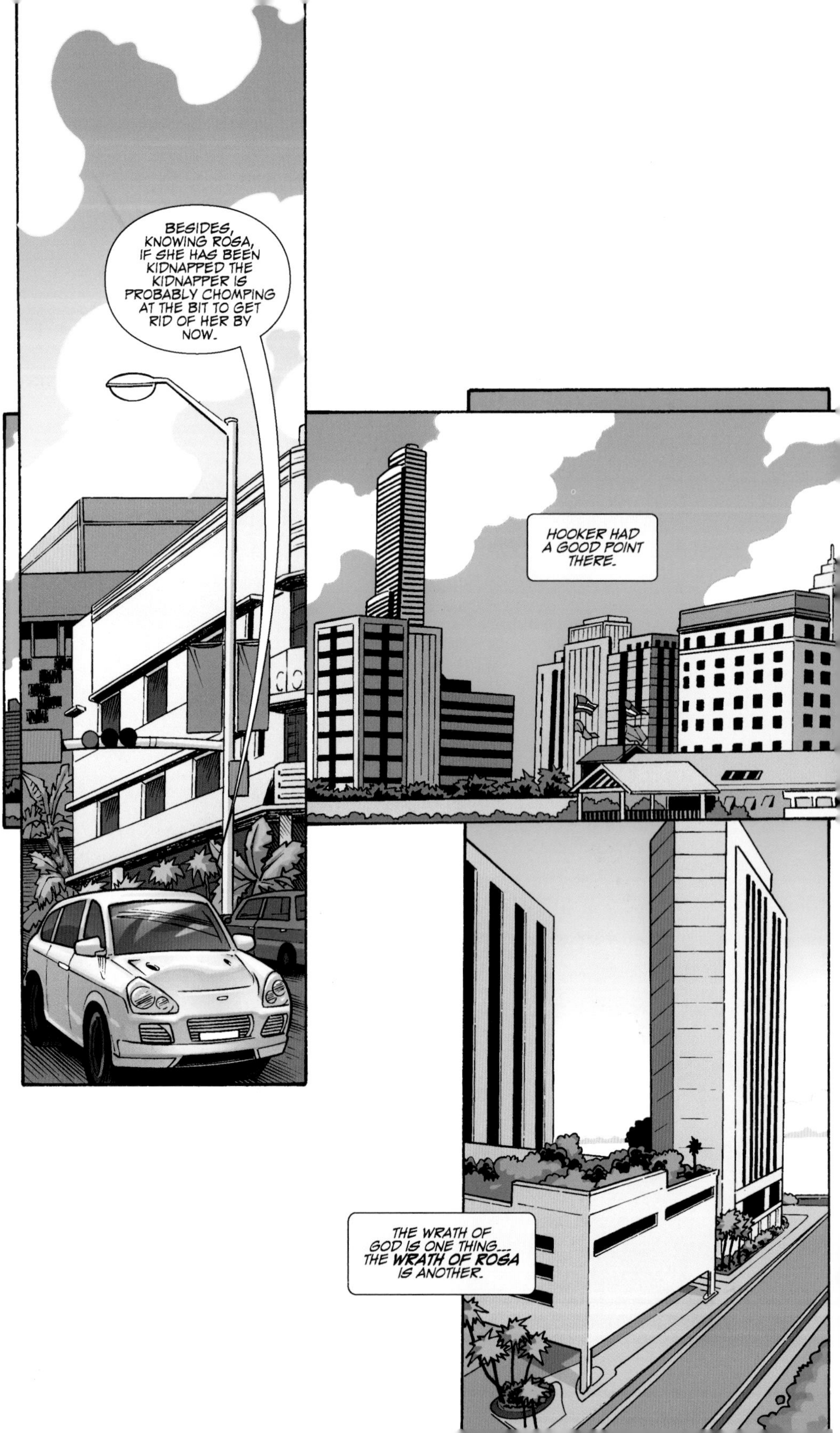
BESIDES, KNOWING ROSA, IF SHE HAS BEEN KIDNAPPED THE KIDNAPPER IS PROBABLY CHOMPING AT THE BIT TO GET RID OF HER BY NOW.
HOOKER HAD A GOOD POINT THERE.
THE WRATH OF GOD IS ONE THING... THE WRATH OF ROSA IS ANOTHER.

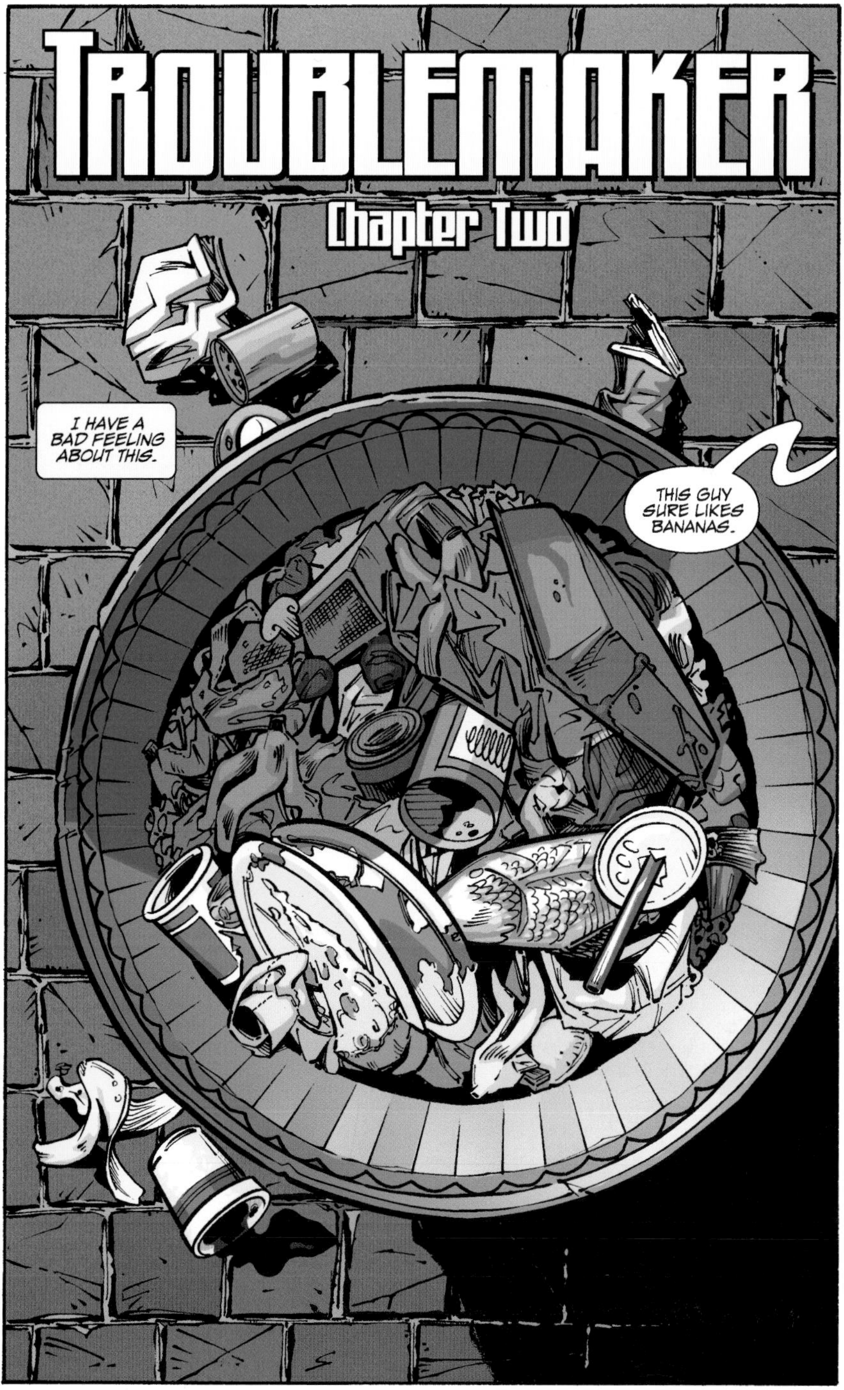
TROUBLEMAKER
Chapter Two
I HAVE A BAD FEELING ABOUT THIS.
THIS GUY SURE LIKES BANANAS.

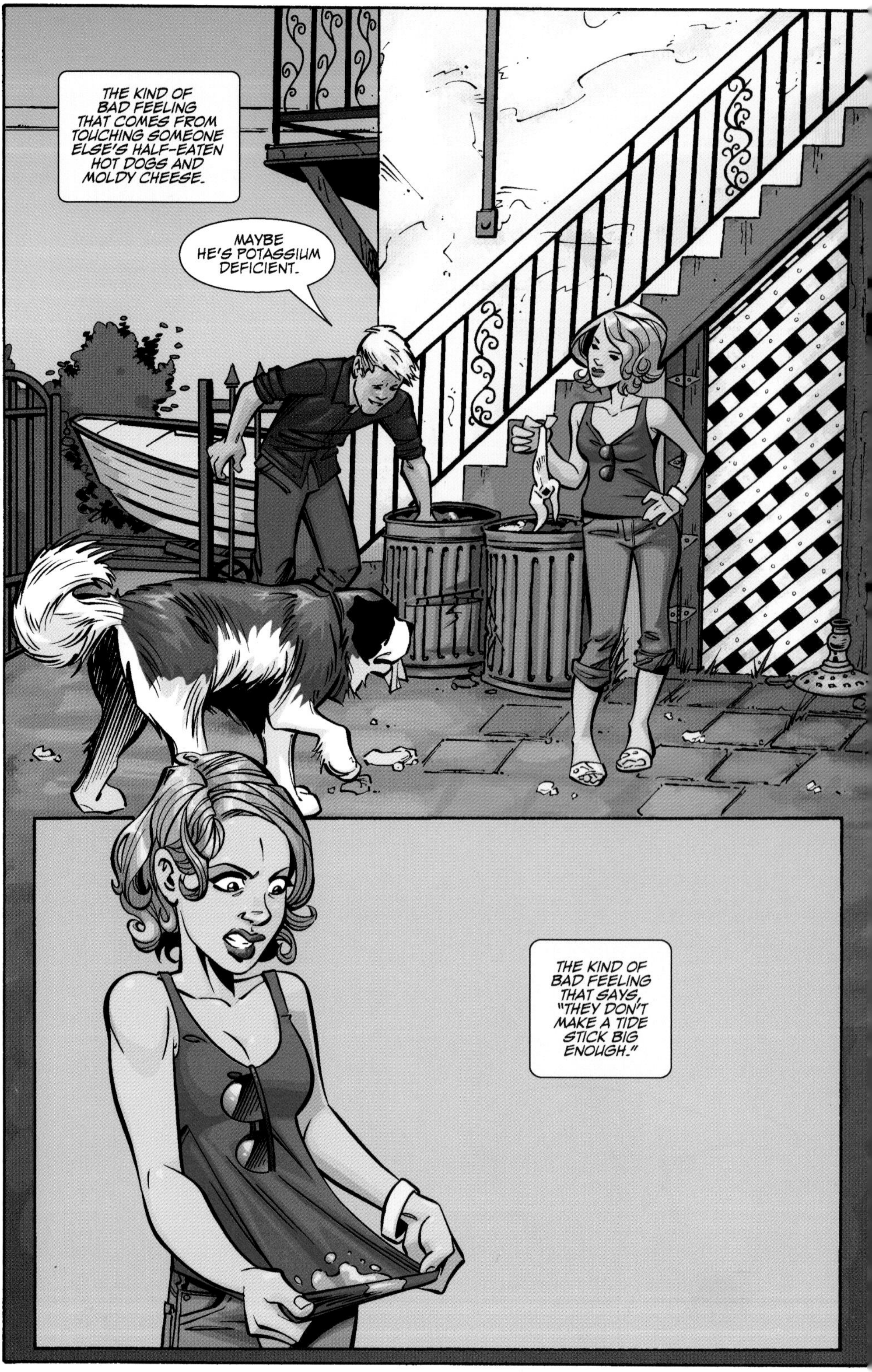
THE KIND OF BAD FEELING THAT COMES FROM TOUCHING SOMEONE ELSE'S HALF-EATEN HOT DOGS AND MOLDY CHEESE.
MAYBE HE'S POTASSIUM DEFICIENT.
THE KIND OF BAD FEELING THAT SAYS, "THEY DON'T MAKE A TIDE STICK BIG ENOUGH."

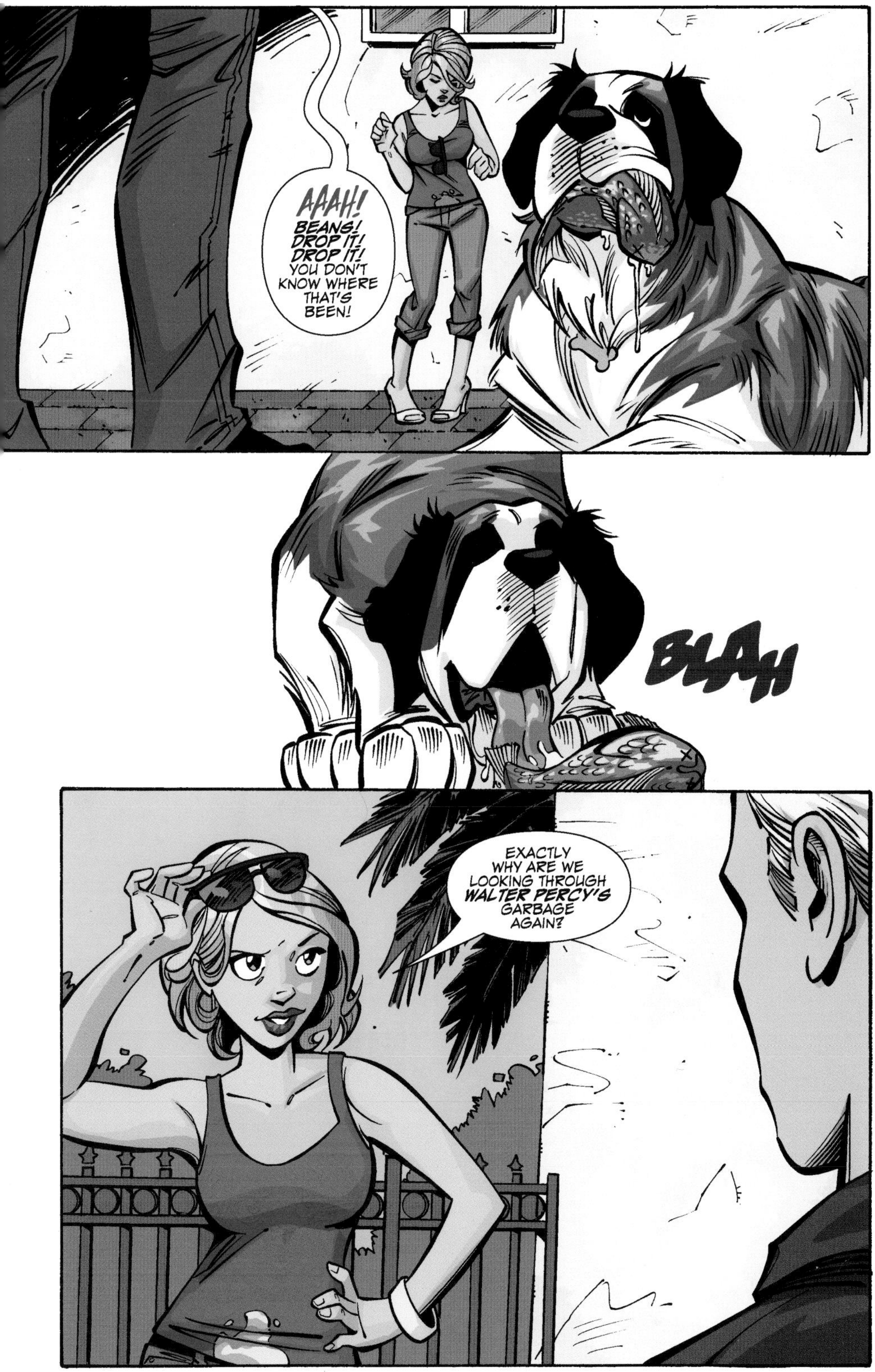
AAAH! BEANS! DROP IT! DROP IT! YOU DON'T KNOW WHERE THAT'S BEEN!
BLAH
EXACTLY WHY ARE WE LOOKING THROUGH WALTER PERCY'S GARBAGE AGAIN?

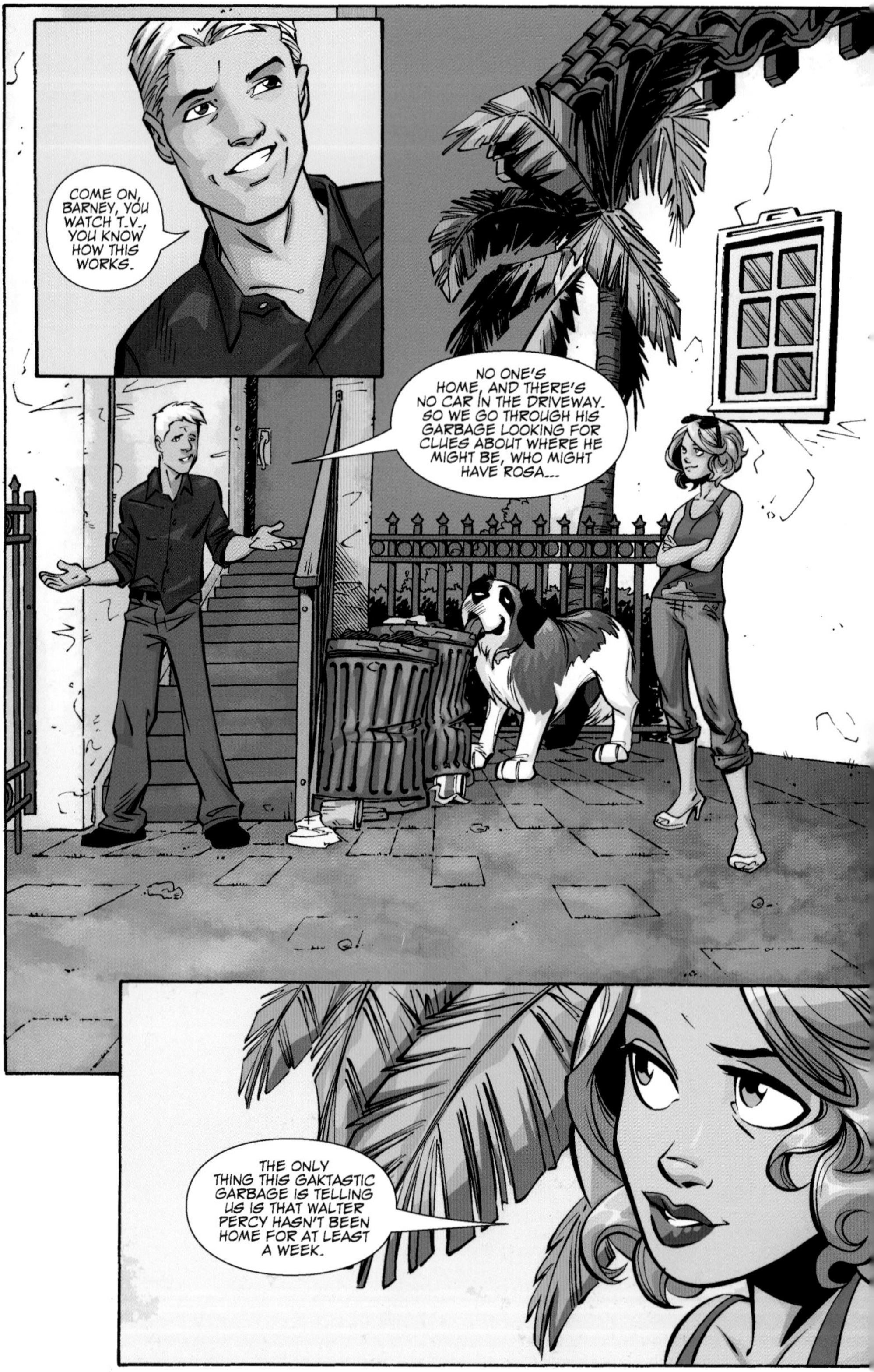
COME ON, BARNEY, YOU WATCH T.V., YOU KNOW HOW THIS WORKS.
NO ONE'S HOME, AND THERE'S NO CAR IN THE DRIVEWAY. SO WE GO THROUGH HIS GARBAGE LOOKING FOR CLUES ABOUT WHERE HE MIGHT BE, WHO MIGHT HAVE ROSA...
THE ONLY THING THIS GAKTASTIC GARBAGE IS TELLING US IS THAT WALTER PERCY HASN'T BEEN HOME FOR AT LEAST A WEEK.

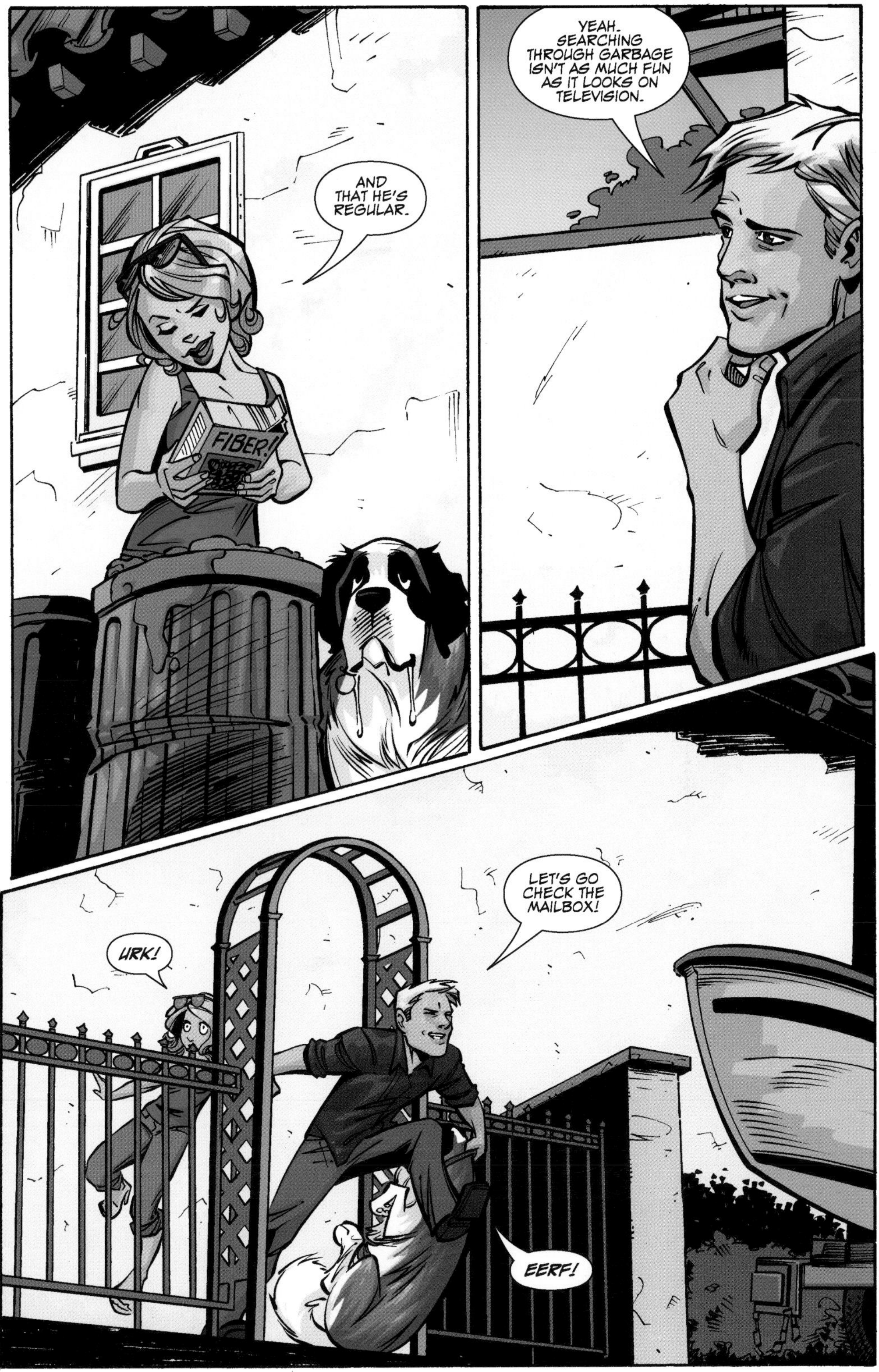
AND THAT HE'S REGULAR.
FIBER!
YEAH. SEARCHING THROUGH GARBAGE ISN'T AS MUCH FUN AS IT LOOKS ON TELEVISION.
URK!
LET'S GO CHECK THE MAILBOX!
EERF!

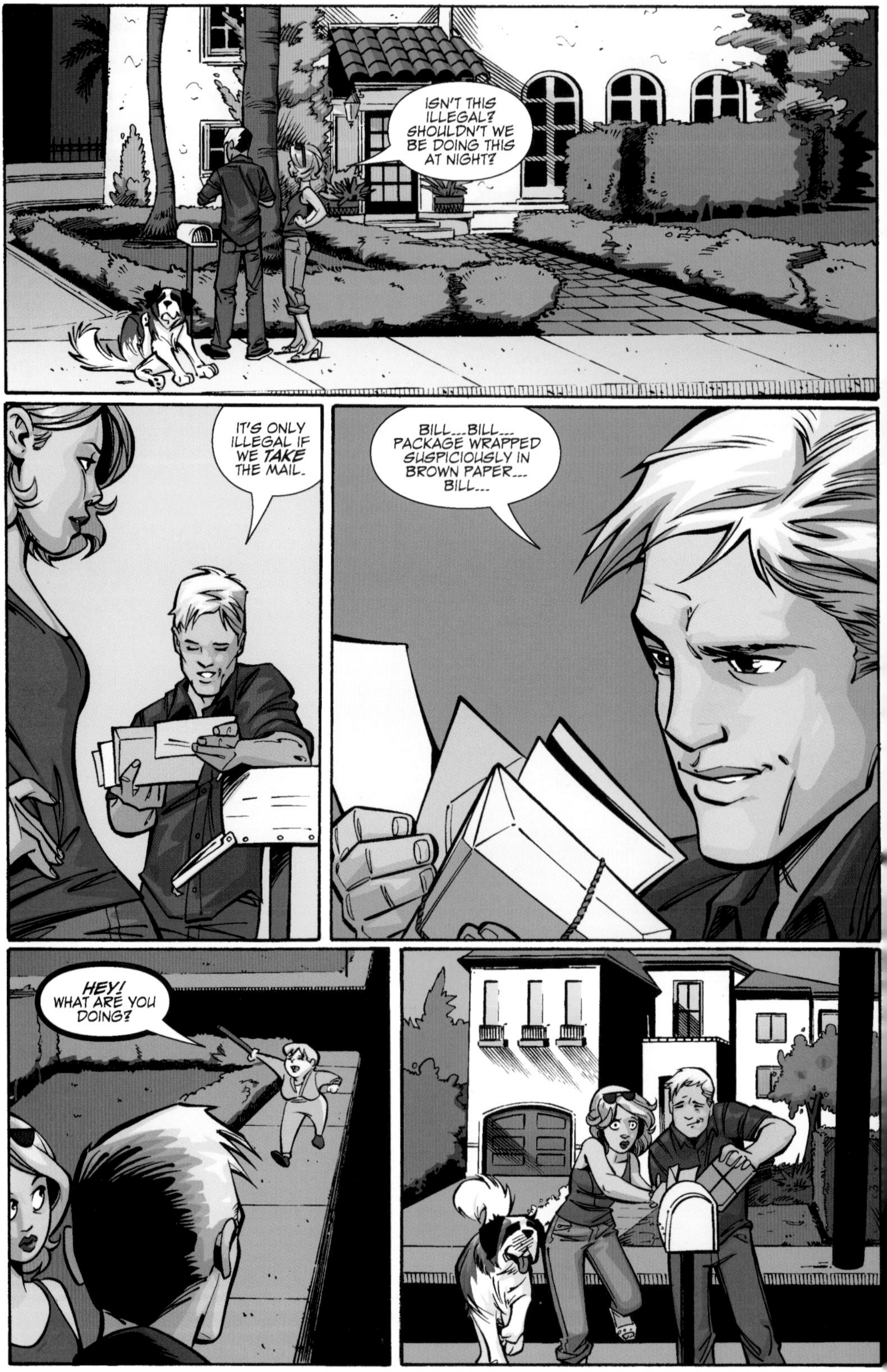
ISN'T THIS ILLEGAL? SHOULDN'T WE BE DOING THIS AT NIGHT?
IT'S ONLY ILLEGAL IF WE TAKE THE MAIL.
BILL... BILL... PACKAGE WRAPPED SUSPICIOUSLY IN BROWN PAPER... BILL...
HEY! WHAT ARE YOU DOING?

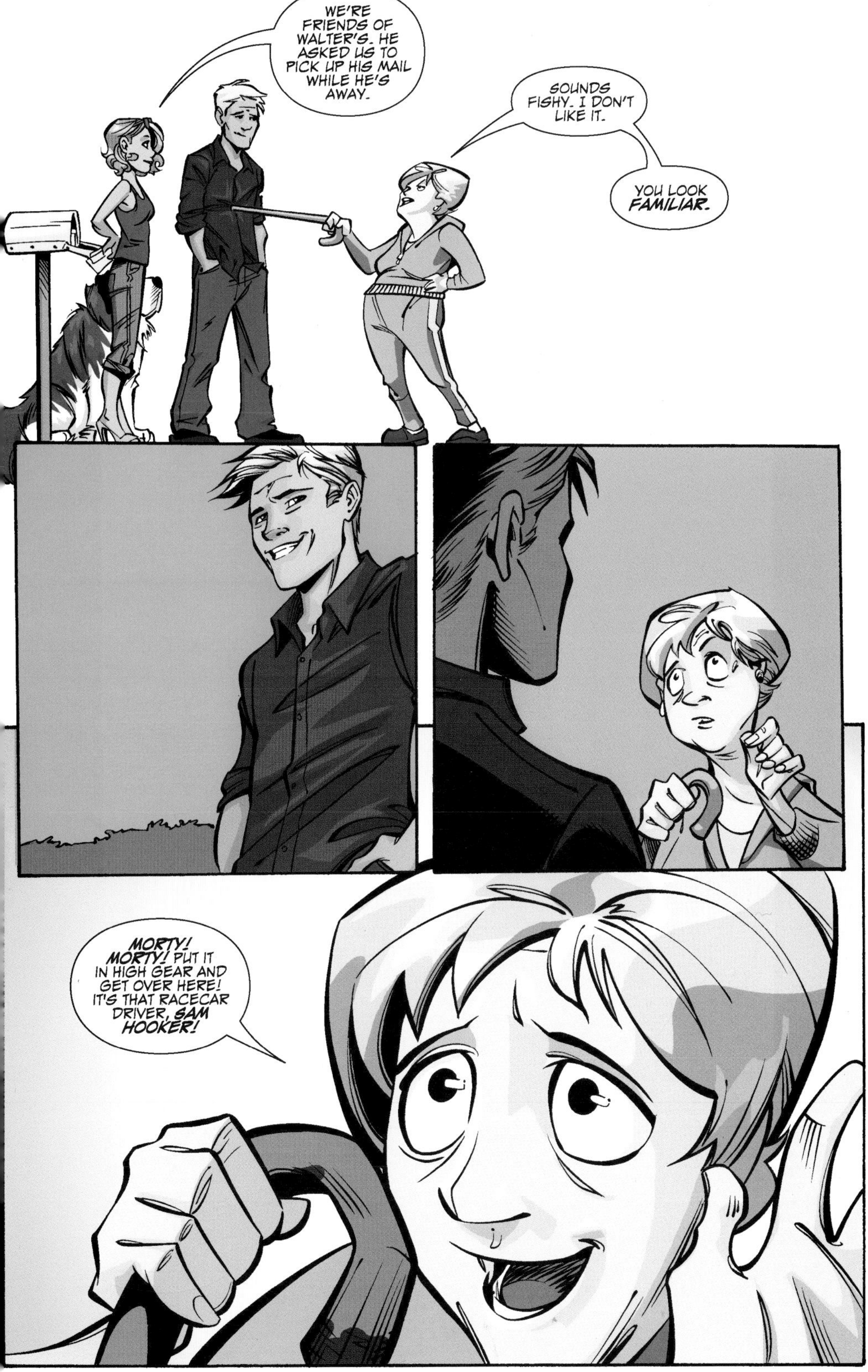
WE'RE FRIENDS OF WALTER'S. HE ASKED US TO PICK UP HIS MAIL WHILE HE'S AWAY.
SOUNDS FISHY. I DON'T LIKE IT.
YOU LOOK FAMILIAR.
MORTY! MORTY! PUT IT IN HIGH GEAR AND GET OVER HERE! IT'S THAT RACECAR DRIVER, SAM HOOKER!

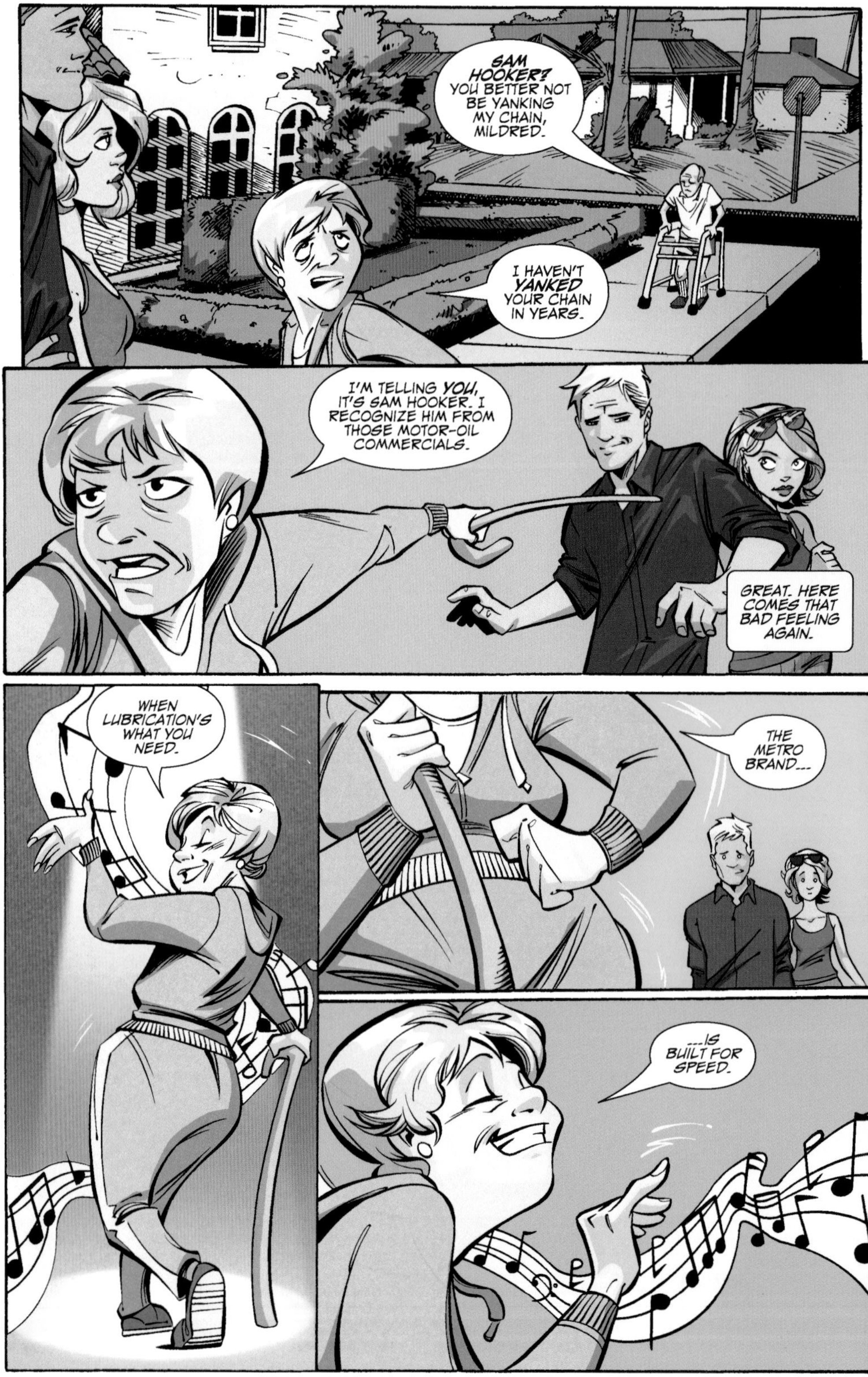
SAM HOOKER? YOU BETTER NOT BE YANKING MY CHAIN, MILDRED.
I HAVEN'T YANKED YOUR CHAIN IN YEARS.
I'M TELLING YOU, IT'S SAM HOOKER. I RECOGNIZE HIM FROM THOSE MOTOR-OIL COMMERCIALS.
GREAT. HERE COMES THAT BAD FEELING AGAIN.
WHEN LUBRICATION'S WHAT YOU NEED.
THE METRO BRAND...
...IS BUILT FOR SPEED.

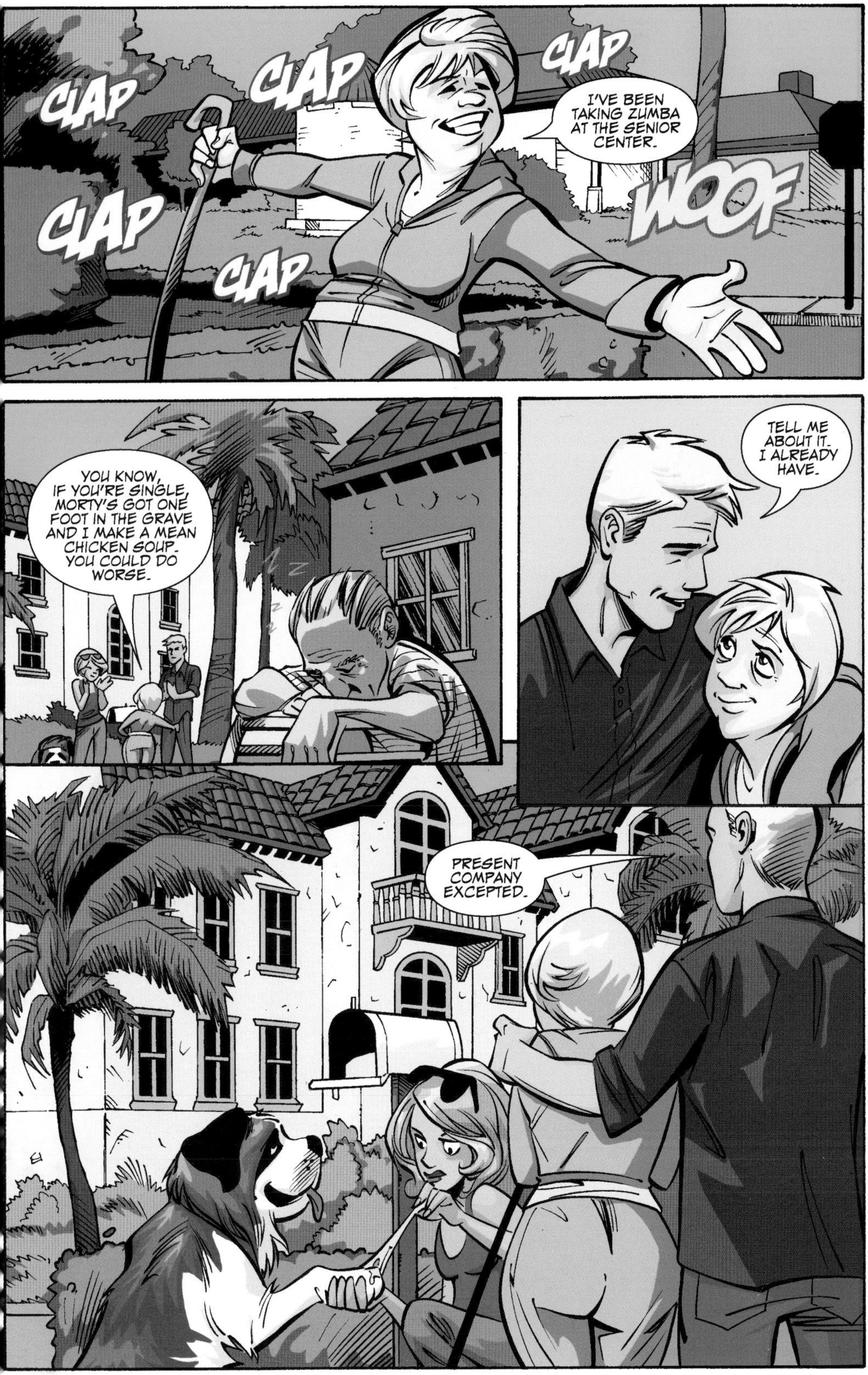
CLAP
CLAP
CLAP
I'VE BEEN TAKING ZUMBA AT THE SENIOR CENTER.
WOOF
CLAP
CLAP
YOU KNOW, IF YOU'RE SINGLE, MORTY'S GOT ONE FOOT IN THE GRAVE AND I MAKE A MEAN CHICKEN SOUP. YOU COULD DO WORSE.
TELL ME ABOUT IT. I ALREADY HAVE.
PRESENT COMPANY EXCEPTED.

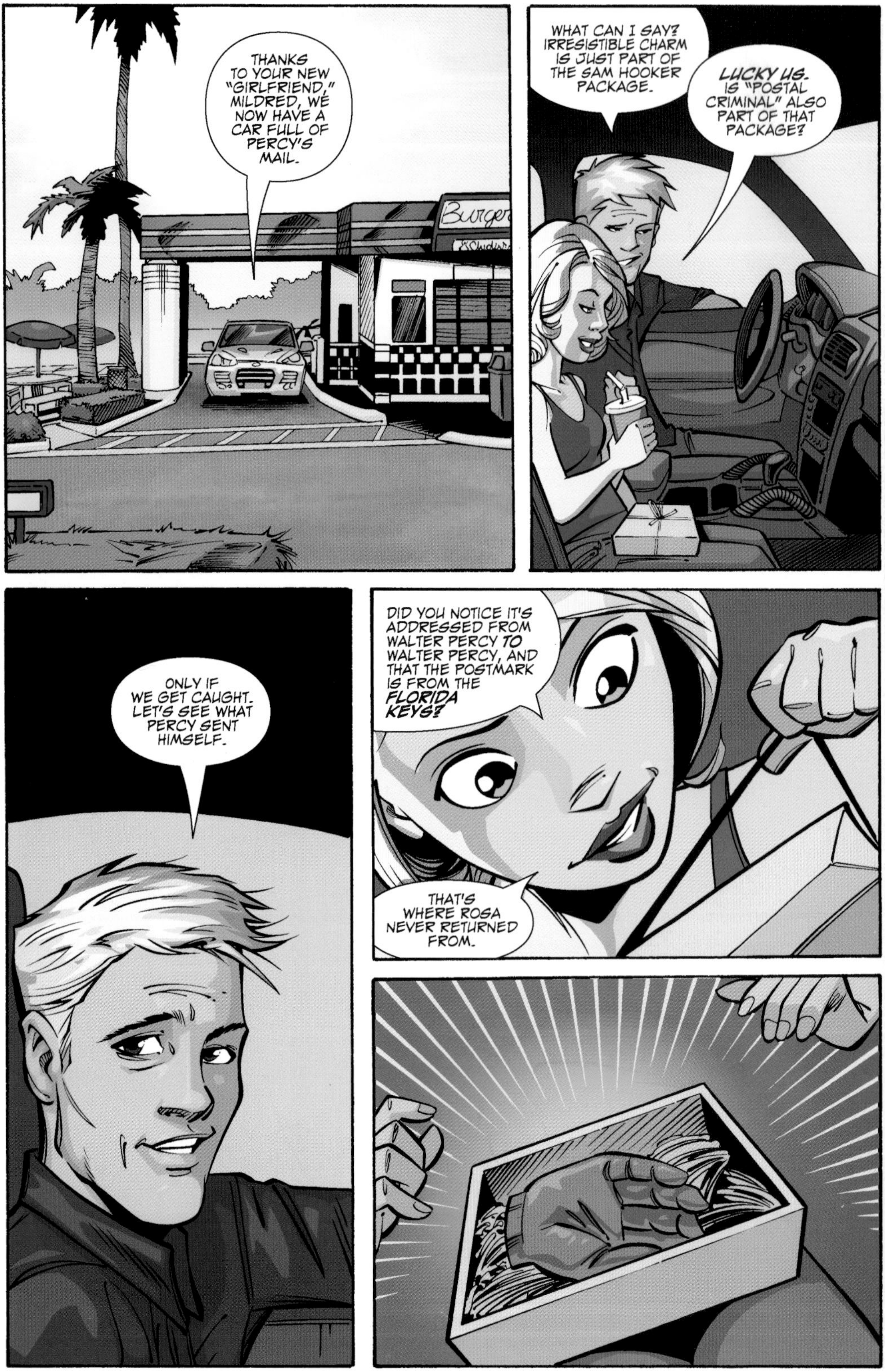
THANKS TO YOUR NEW "GIRLFRIEND," MILDRED, WE NOW HAVE A CAR FULL OF PERCY'S MAIL.
Burger
WHAT CAN I SAY? IRRESISTIBLE CHARM IS JUST PART OF THE SAM HOOKER PACKAGE.
LUCKY US. IS "POSTAL CRIMINAL" ALSO PART OF THAT PACKAGE?
ONLY IF WE GET CAUGHT. LET'S SEE WHAT PERCY SENT HIMSELF.
DID YOU NOTICE IT'S ADDRESSED FROM WALTER PERCY TO WALTER PERCY, AND THAT THE POSTMARK IS FROM THE FLORIDA KEYS?
THAT'S WHERE ROSA NEVER RETURNED FROM.

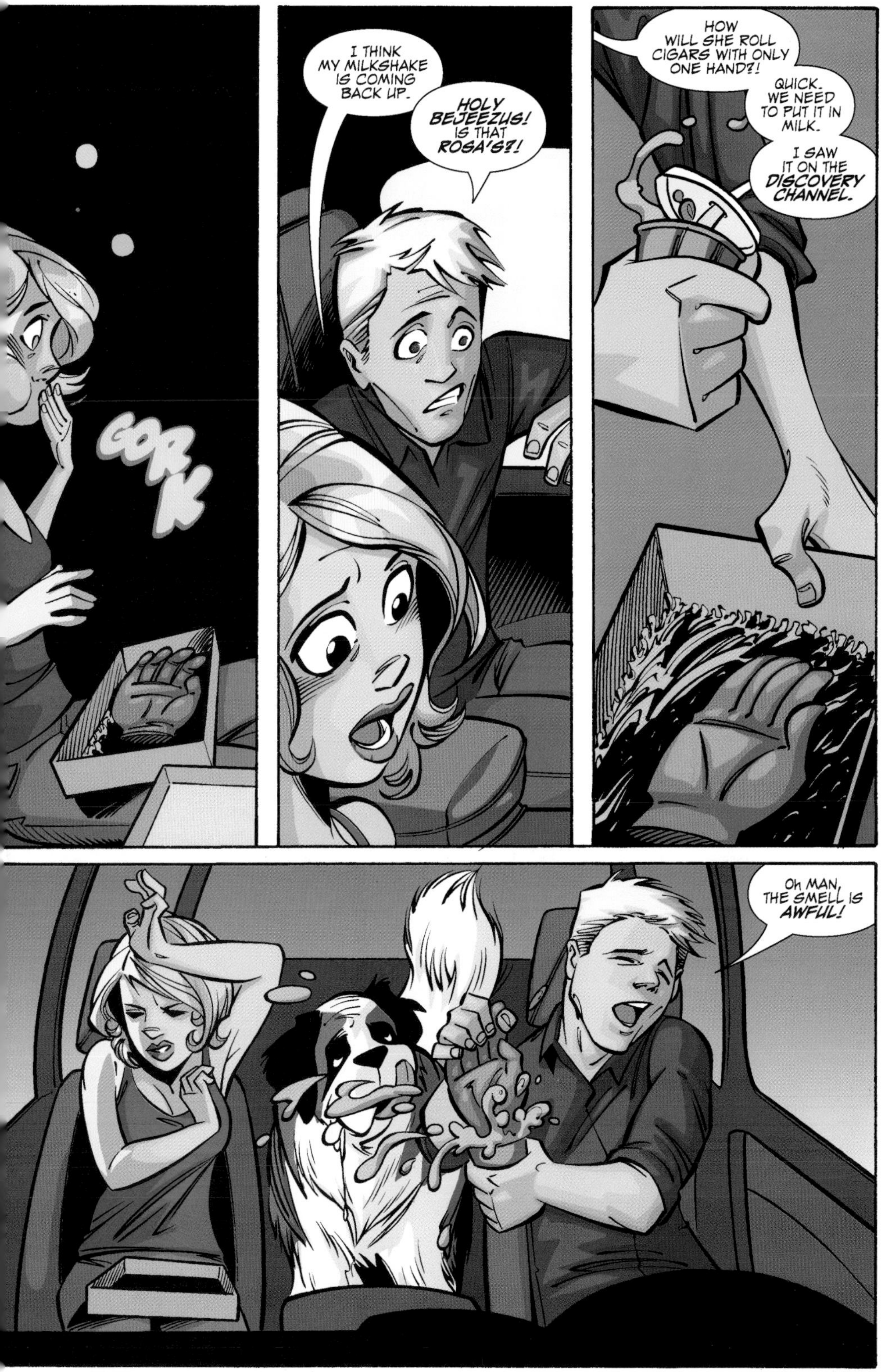
GORK
I THINK MY MILKSHAKE IS COMING BACK UP.
HOLY BEJEEZUS! IS THAT ROSA'S?!
HOW WILL SHE ROLL CIGARS WITH ONLY ONE HAND?!
QUICK. WE NEED TO PUT IT IN MILK.
I SAW IT ON THE DISCOVERY CHANNEL.
Oh MAN, THE SMELL IS AWFUL!

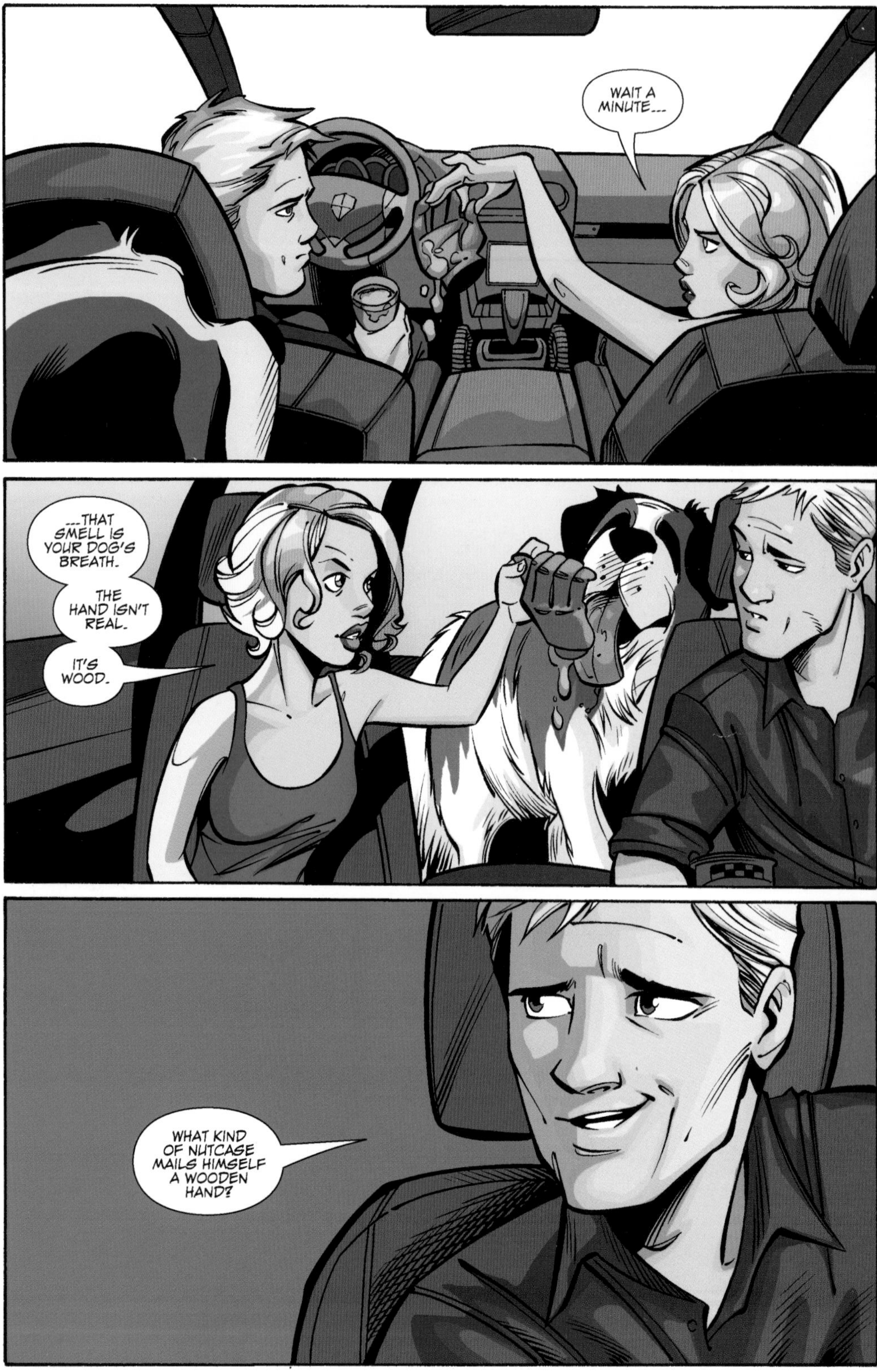
WAIT A MINUTE...
...THAT SMELL IS YOUR DOG'S BREATH.
THE HAND ISN'T REAL.
IT'S WOOD.
WHAT KIND OF NUTCASE MAILS HIMSELF A WOODEN HAND?

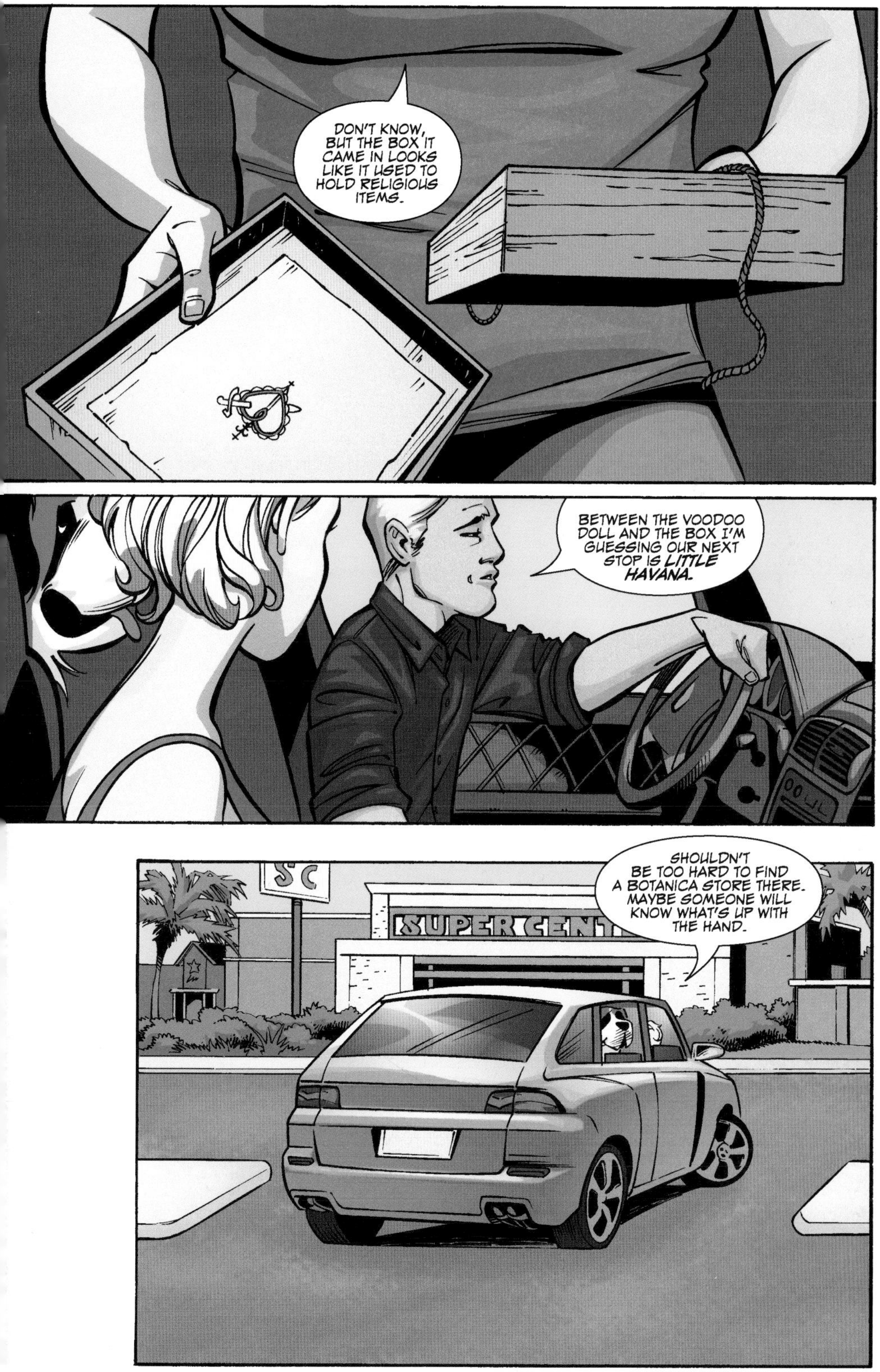
DON'T KNOW, BUT THE BOX IT CAME IN LOOKS LIKE IT USED TO HOLD RELIGIOUS ITEMS.
BETWEEN THE VOODOO DOLL AND THE BOX I'M GUESSING OUR NEXT STOP IS *LITTLE HAVANA.*
SUPER CENT
SHOULDN'T BE TOO HARD TO FIND A BOTANICA STORE THERE. MAYBE SOMEONE WILL KNOW WHAT'S UP WITH THE HAND.

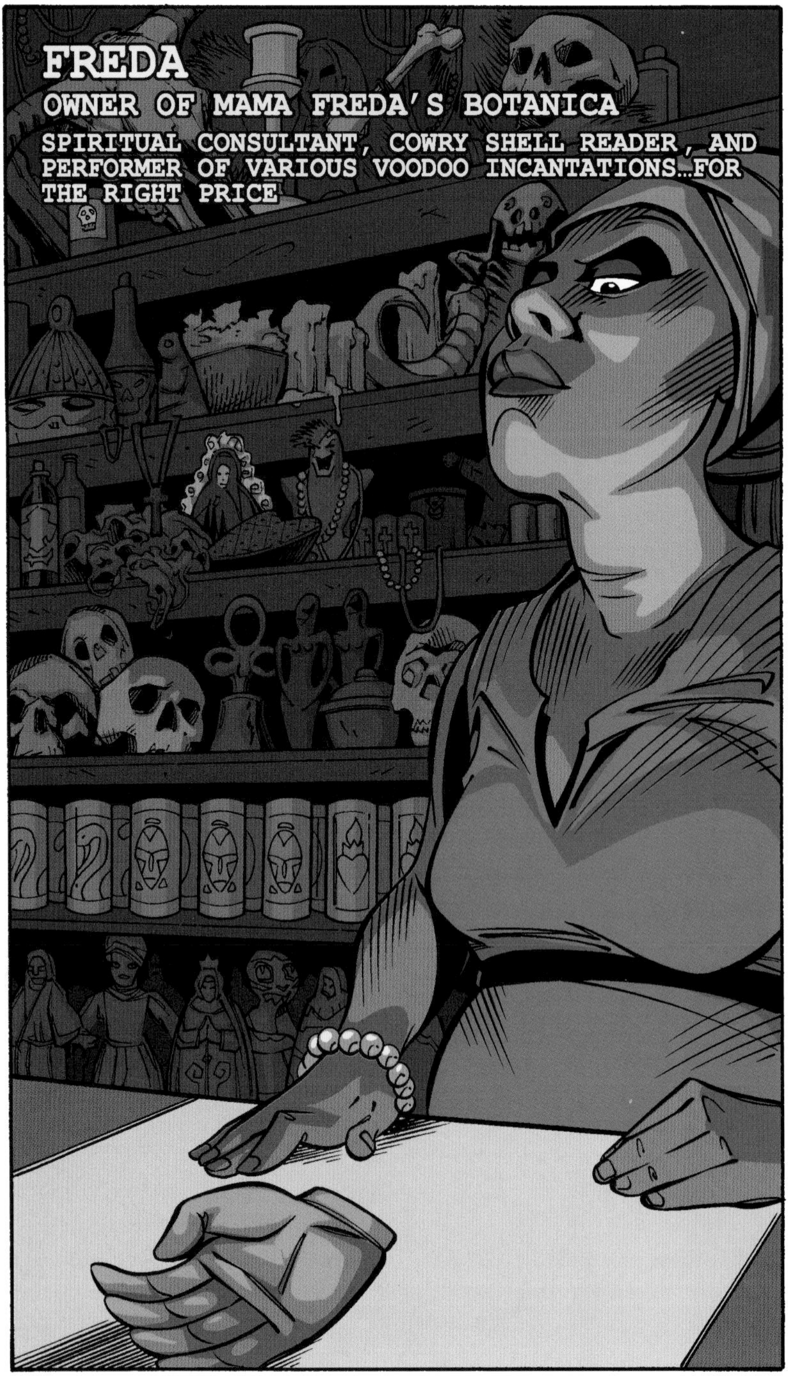
FREDA
OWNER OF MAMA FREDA'S BOTANICA
SPIRITUAL CONSULTANT, COWRY SHELL READER, AND PERFORMER OF VARIOUS VOODOO INCANTATIONS…FOR THE RIGHT PRICE

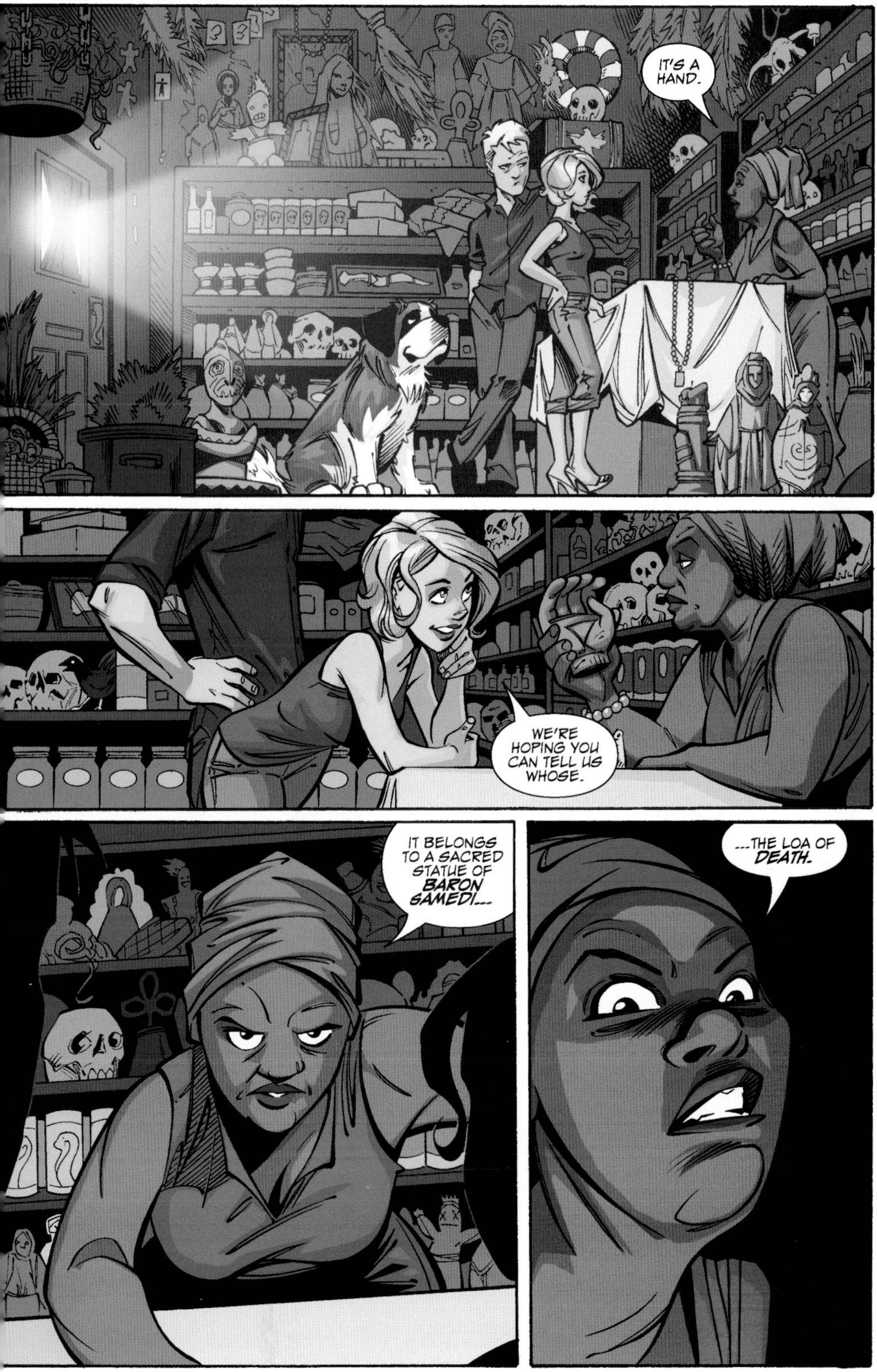
IT'S A HAND.
WE'RE HOPING YOU CAN TELL US WHOSE.
IT BELONGS TO A SACRED STATUE OF *BARON SAMEDI*...
...THE LOA OF *DEATH*.

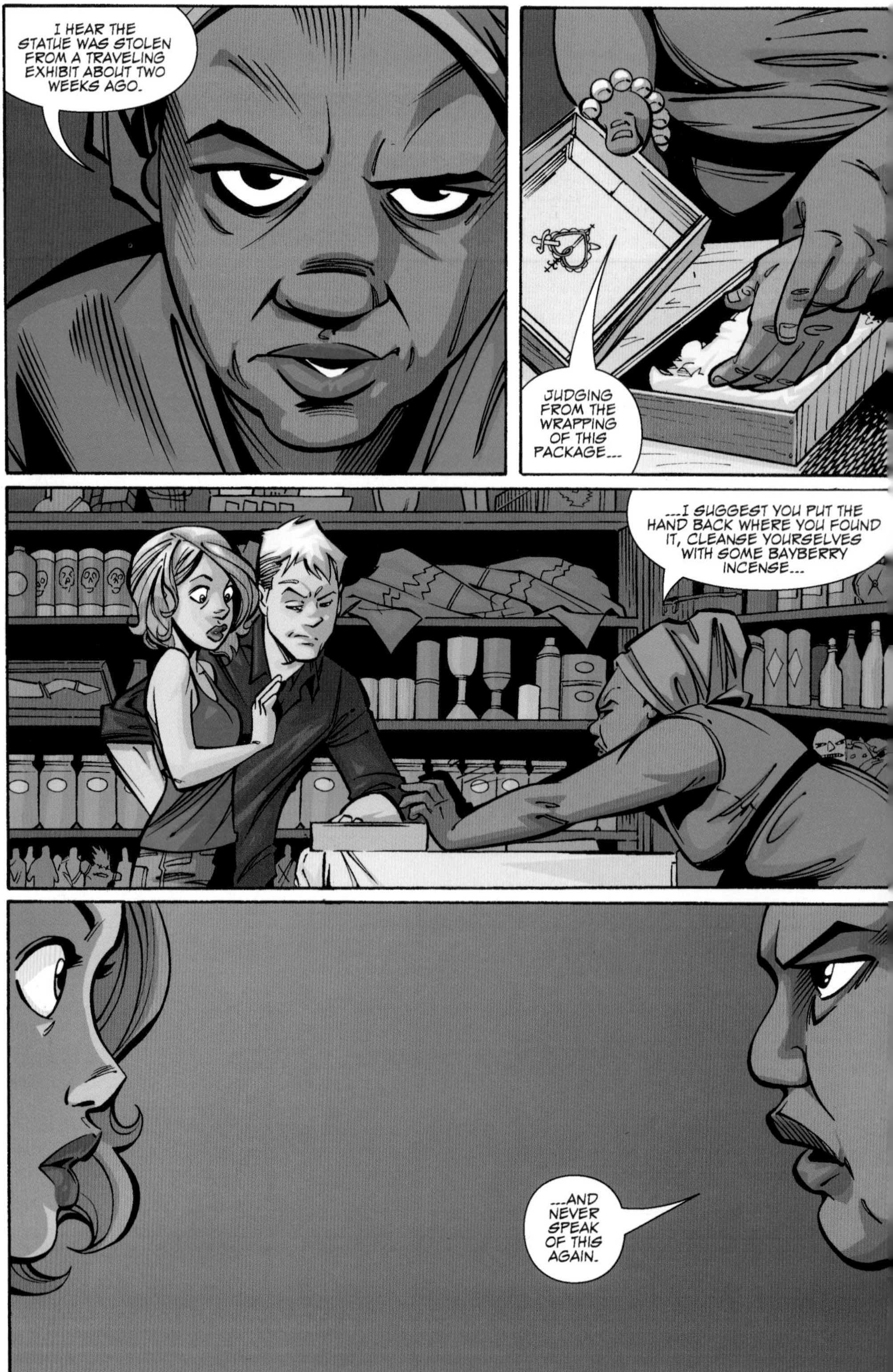
I HEAR THE STATUE WAS STOLEN FROM A TRAVELING EXHIBIT ABOUT TWO WEEKS AGO.
JUDGING FROM THE WRAPPING OF THIS PACKAGE...
...I SUGGEST YOU PUT THE HAND BACK WHERE YOU FOUND IT, CLEANSE YOURSELVES WITH SOME BAYBERRY INCENSE...
...AND NEVER SPEAK OF THIS AGAIN.

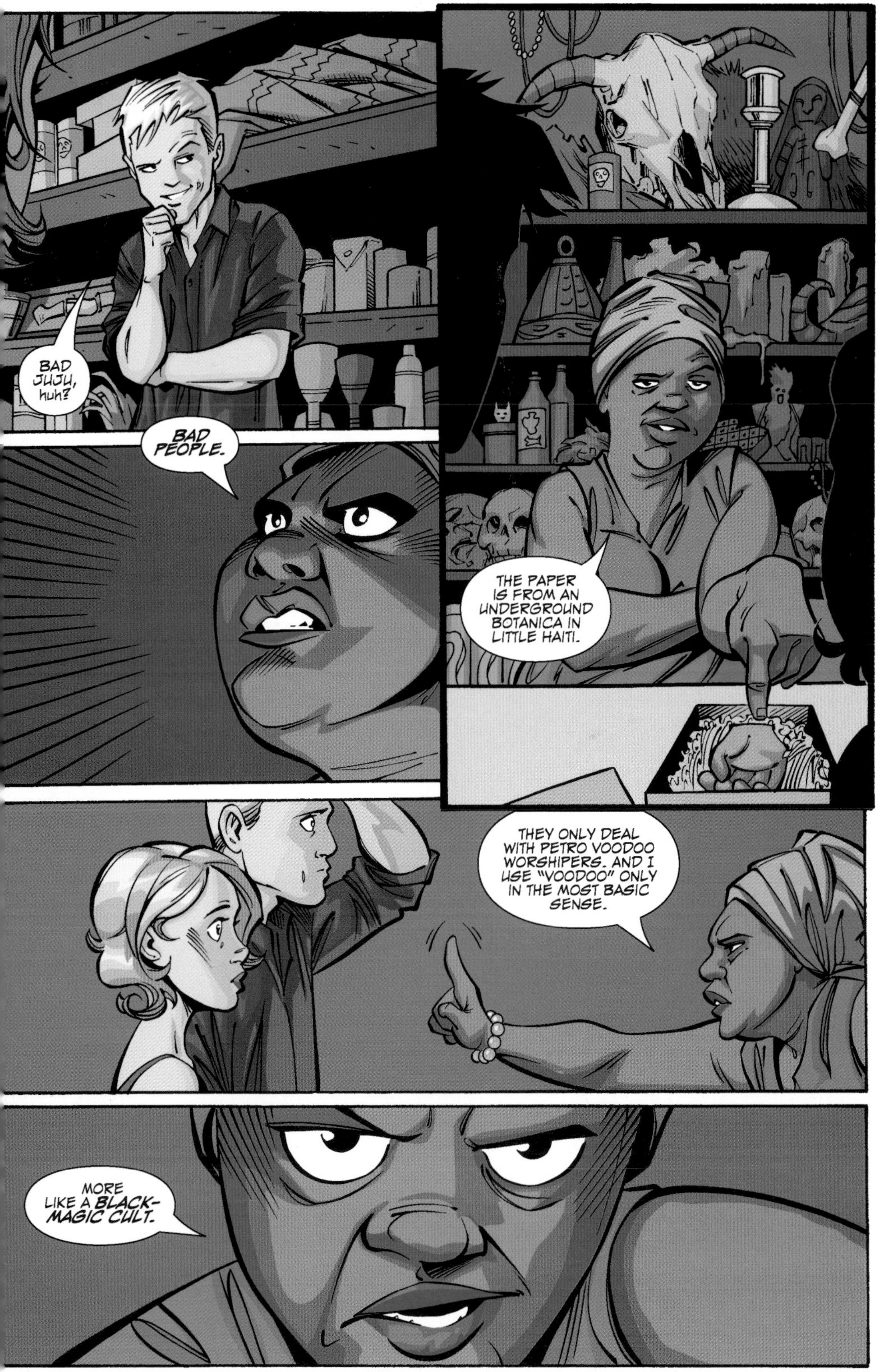

BAD JUJU, huh?
BAD PEOPLE.
THE PAPER IS FROM AN UNDERGROUND BOTANICA IN LITTLE HAITI.
THEY ONLY DEAL WITH PETRO VOODOO WORSHIPERS. AND I USE "VOODOO" ONLY IN THE MOST BASIC SENSE.
MORE LIKE A BLACK-MAGIC CULT.

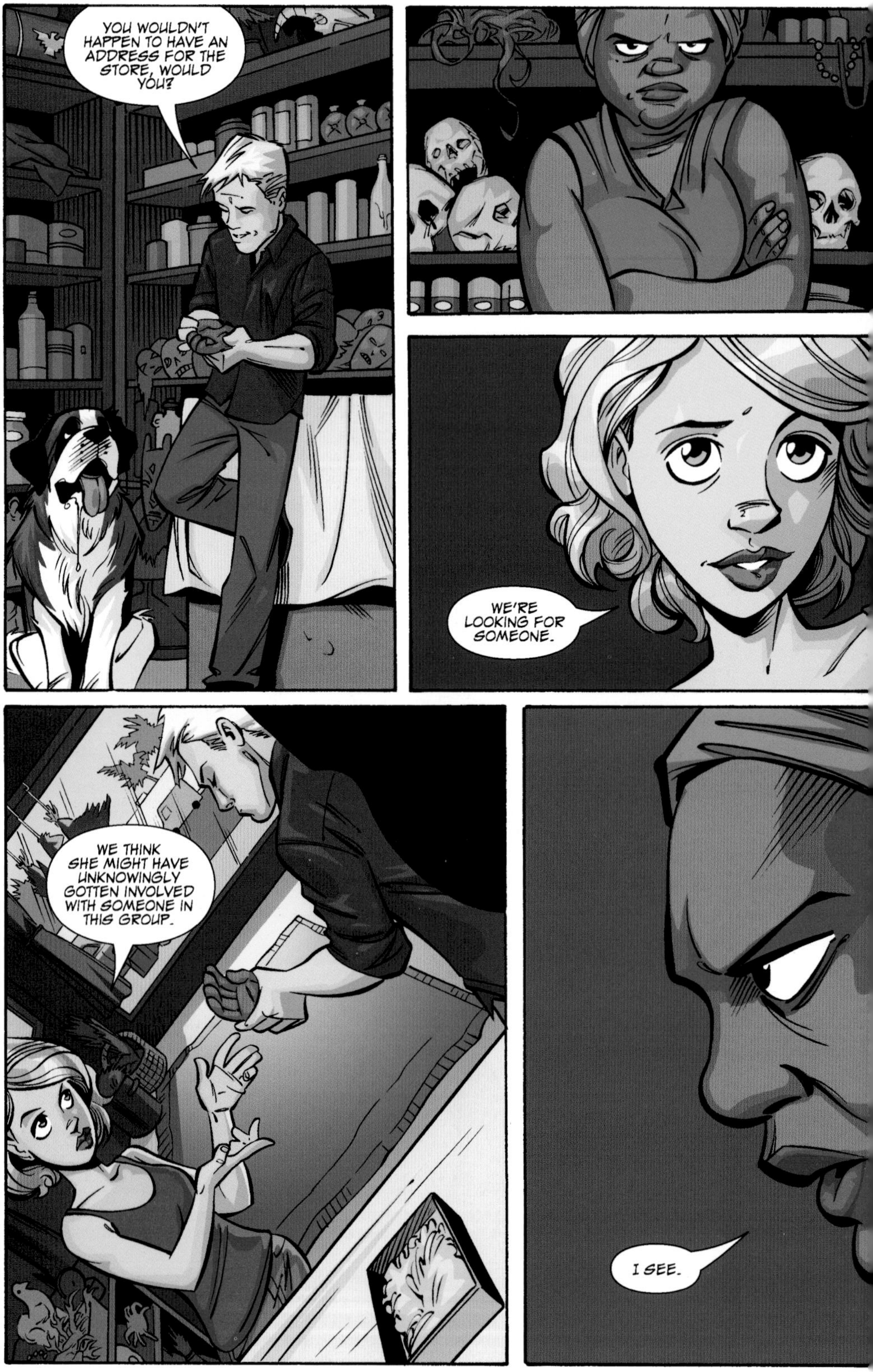
YOU WOULDN'T HAPPEN TO HAVE AN ADDRESS FOR THE STORE, WOULD YOU?
WE'RE LOOKING FOR SOMEONE.
WE THINK SHE MIGHT HAVE UNKNOWINGLY GOTTEN INVOLVED WITH SOMEONE IN THIS GROUP.
I SEE.

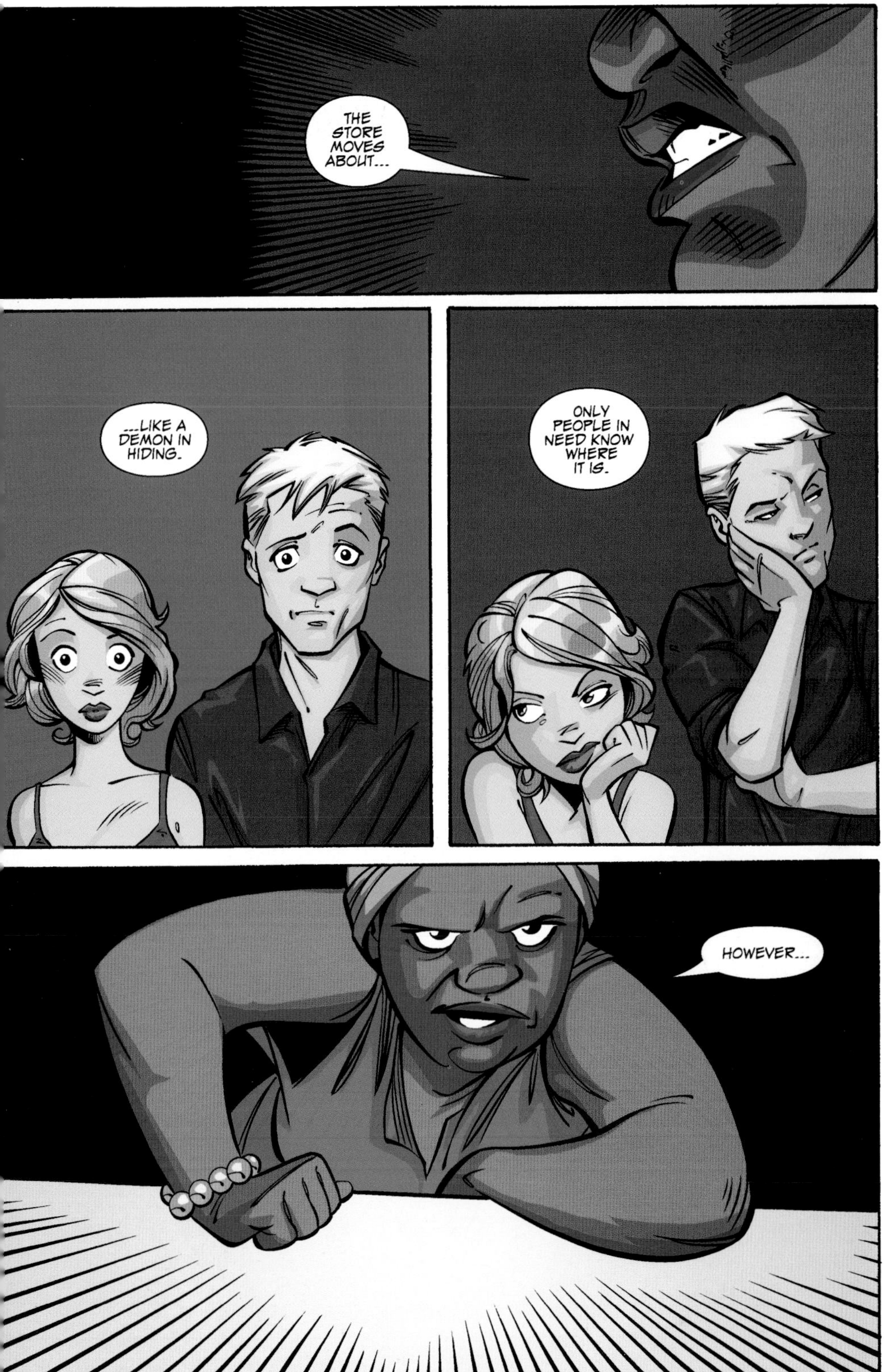
THE STORE MOVES ABOUT...
...LIKE A DEMON IN HIDING.
ONLY PEOPLE IN NEED KNOW WHERE IT IS.
HOWEVER...

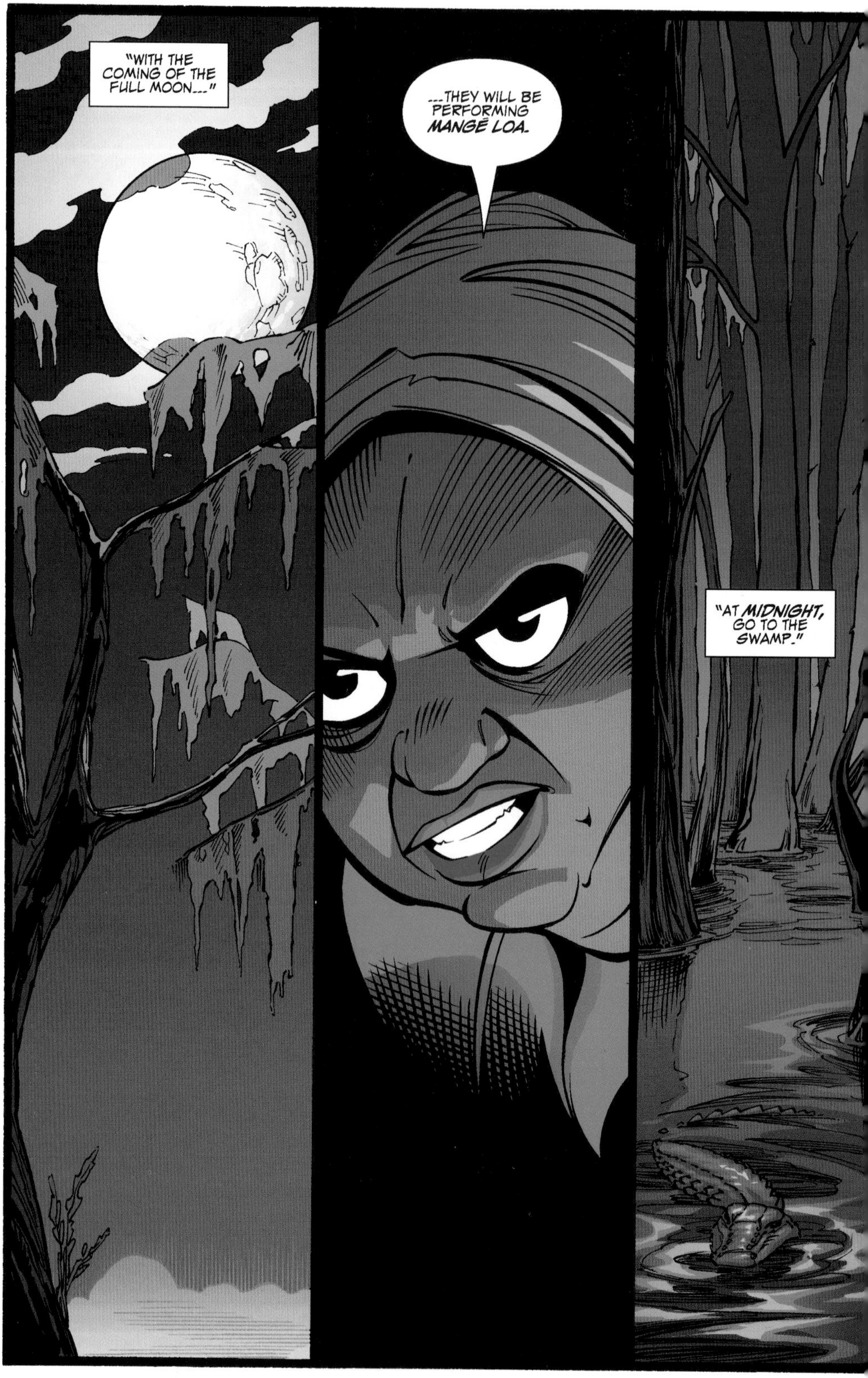
"WITH THE COMING OF THE FULL MOON..."
...THEY WILL BE PERFORMING *MANGÉ LOA*.
"AT *MIDNIGHT*, GO TO THE SWAMP."

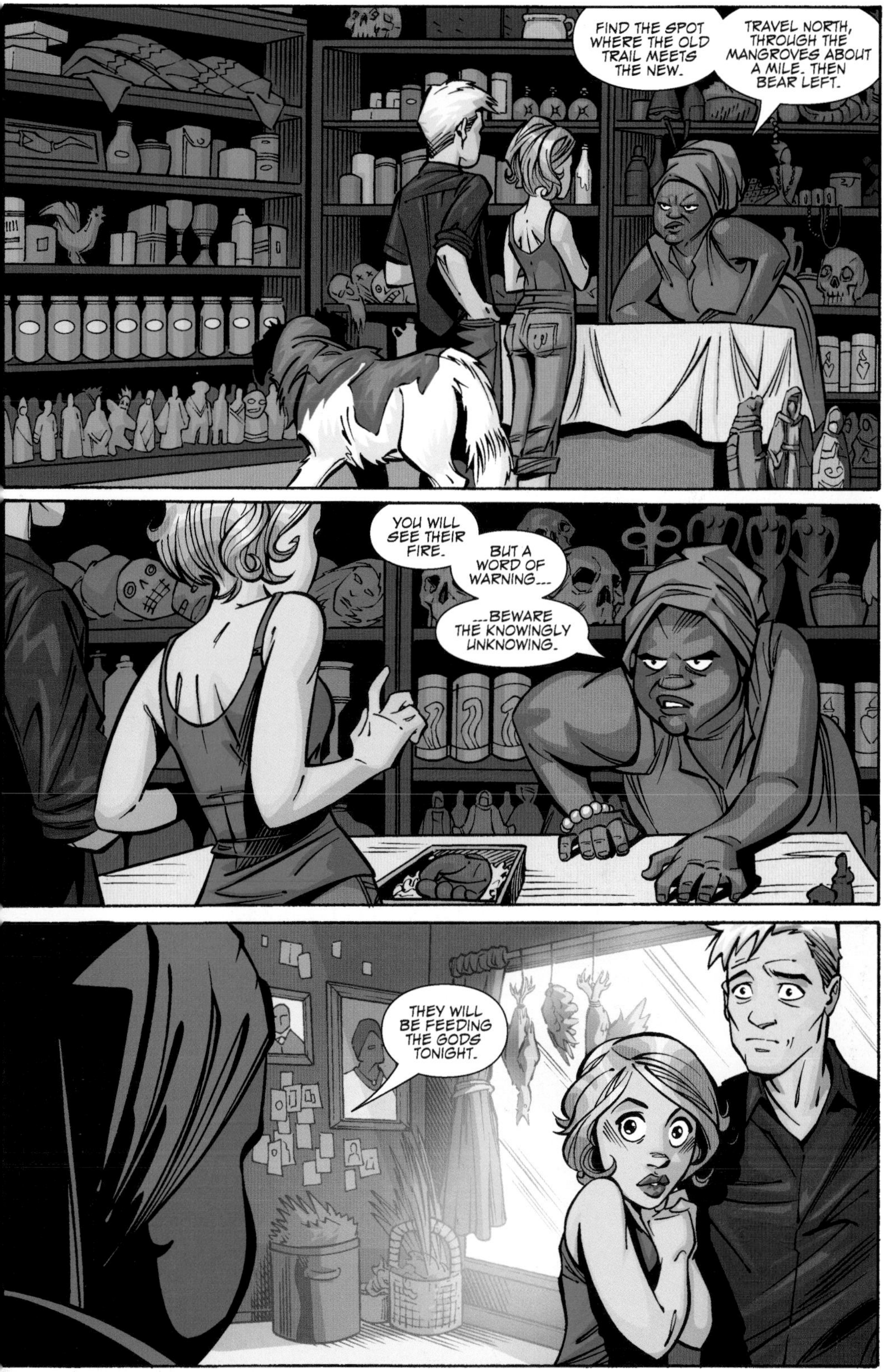
FIND THE SPOT WHERE THE OLD TRAIL MEETS THE NEW.
TRAVEL NORTH, THROUGH THE MANGROVES ABOUT A MILE. THEN BEAR LEFT.
YOU WILL SEE THEIR FIRE.
BUT A WORD OF WARNING...
...BEWARE THE KNOWINGLY UNKNOWING.
THEY WILL BE FEEDING THE GODS TONIGHT.

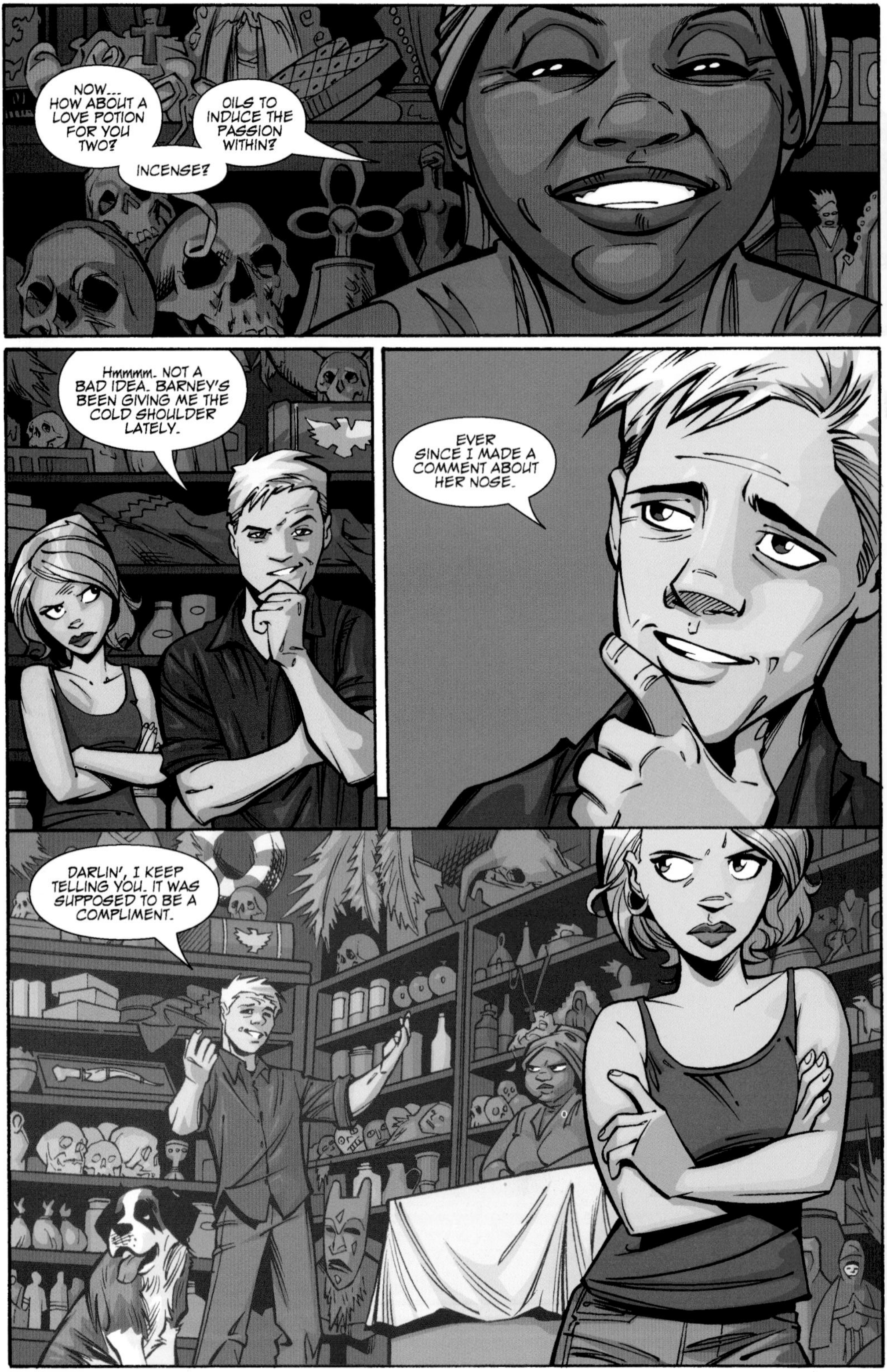
NOW... HOW ABOUT A LOVE POTION FOR YOU TWO?
INCENSE?
OILS TO INDUCE THE PASSION WITHIN?
Hmmmm. NOT A BAD IDEA. BARNEY'S BEEN GIVING ME THE COLD SHOULDER LATELY.
EVER SINCE I MADE A COMMENT ABOUT HER NOSE.
DARLIN', I KEEP TELLING YOU. IT WAS SUPPOSED TO BE A COMPLIMENT.

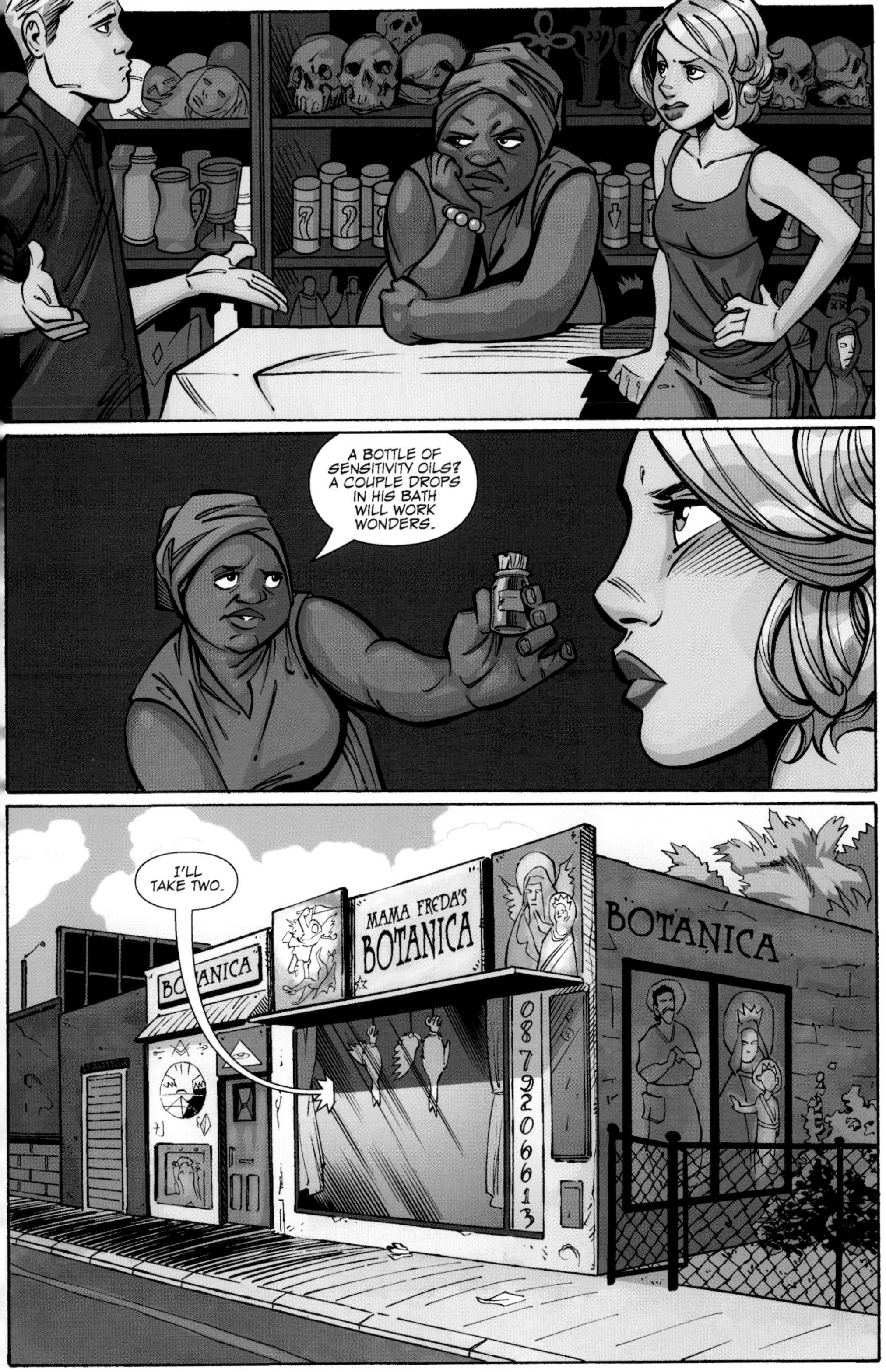
A BOTTLE OF SENSITIVITY OILS? A COUPLE DROPS IN HIS BATH WILL WORK WONDERS.
I'LL TAKE TWO.
MAMA FREDA'S BOTANICA
BOTANICA
BOTANICA
0879206613

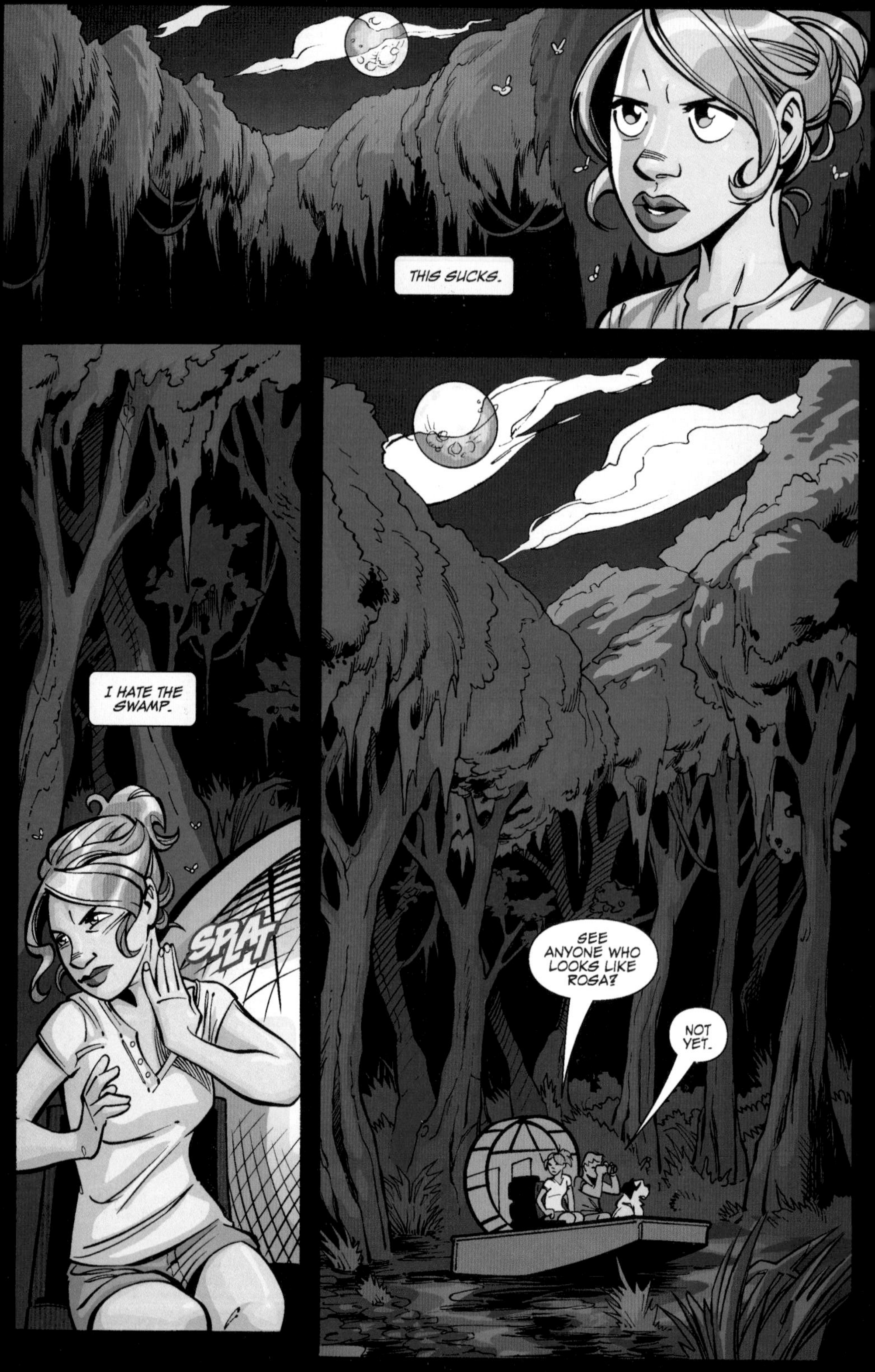
THIS SUCKS.
I HATE THE SWAMP.
SPLAT
SEE ANYONE WHO LOOKS LIKE ROSA?
NOT YET.

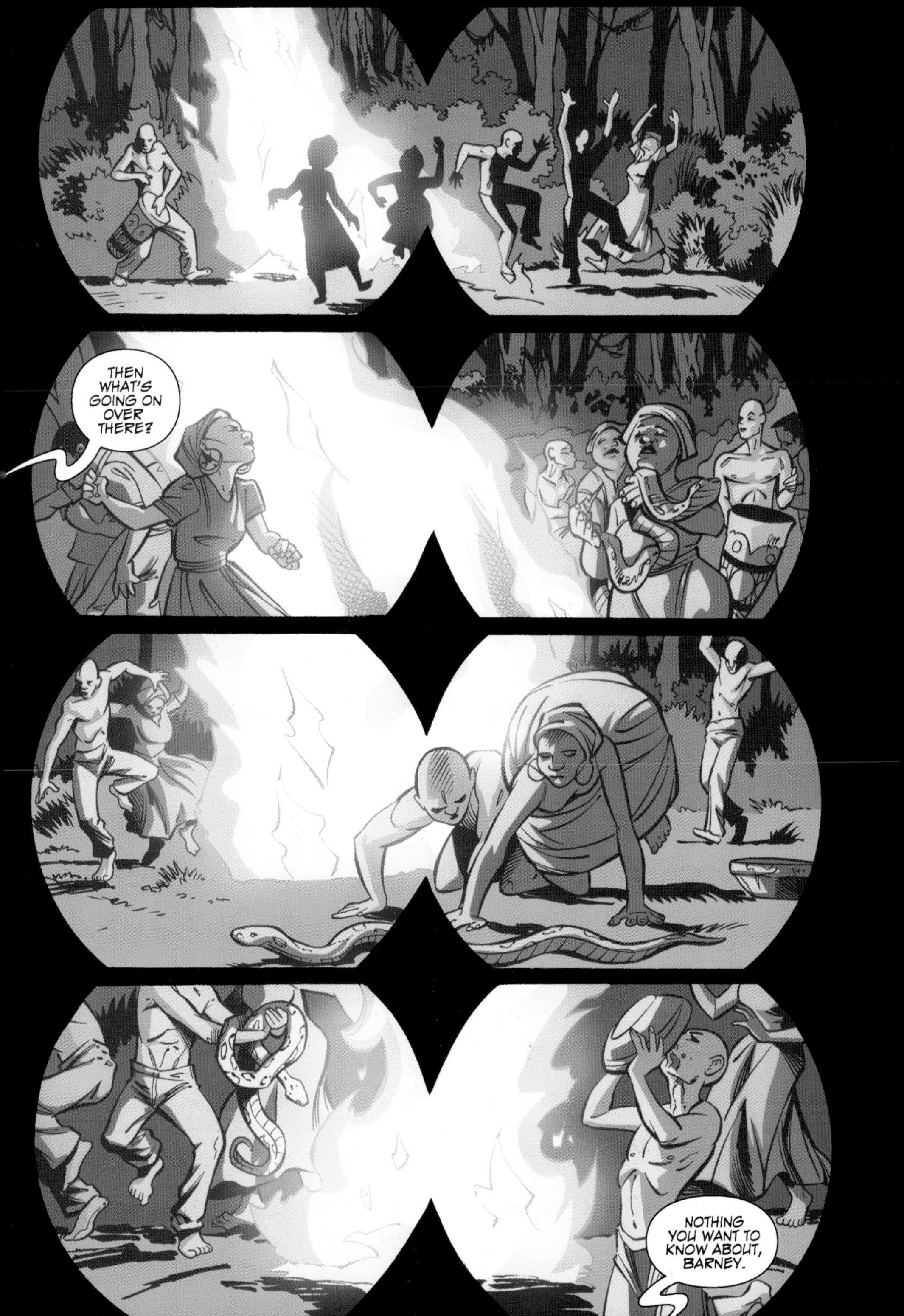
THEN WHAT'S GOING ON OVER THERE?
NOTHING YOU WANT TO KNOW ABOUT, BARNEY.

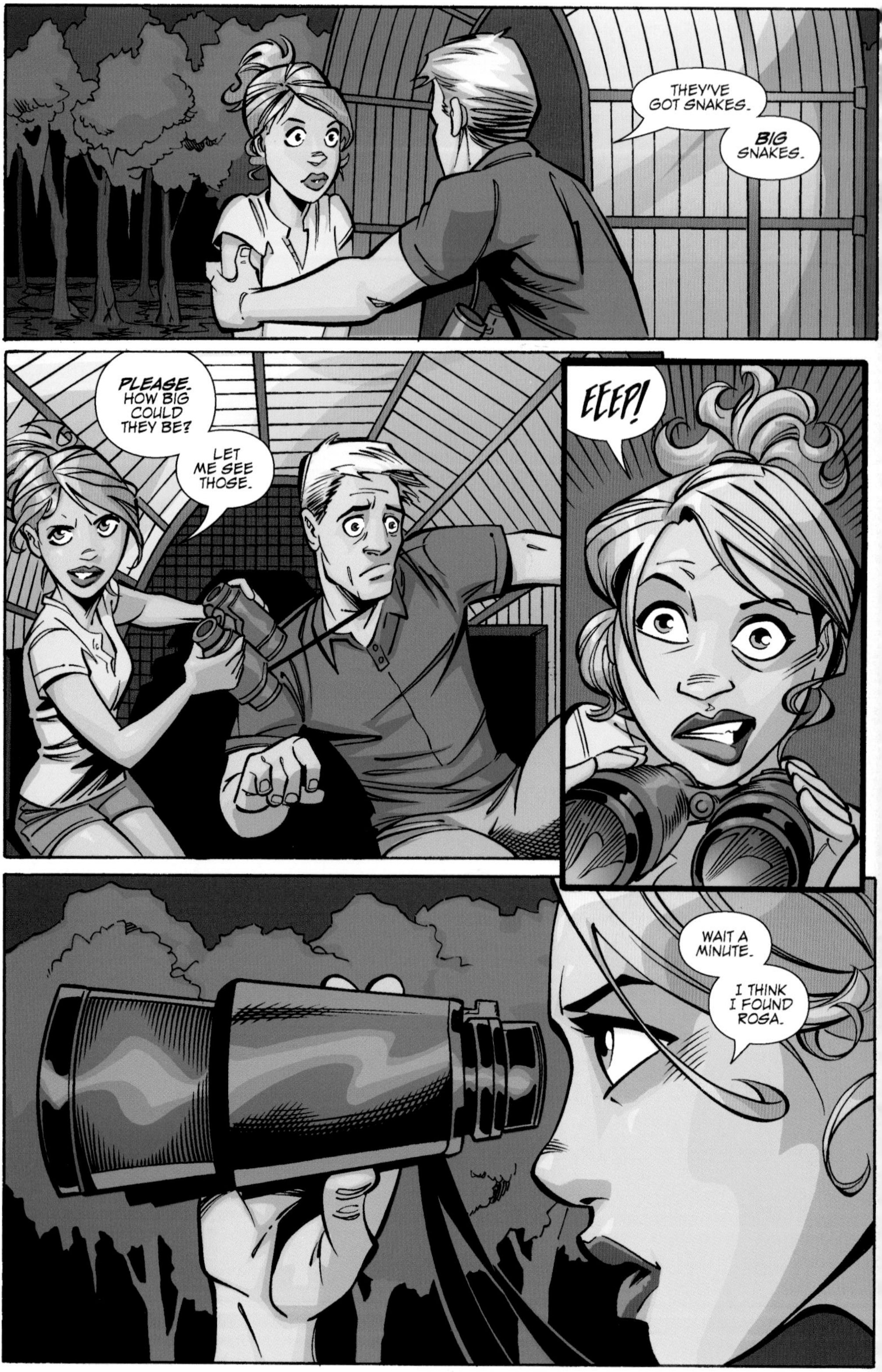
THEY'VE GOT SNAKES.
BIG SNAKES.
PLEASE. HOW BIG COULD THEY BE?
LET ME SEE THOSE.
EEEP!
WAIT A MINUTE.
I THINK I FOUND ROSA.

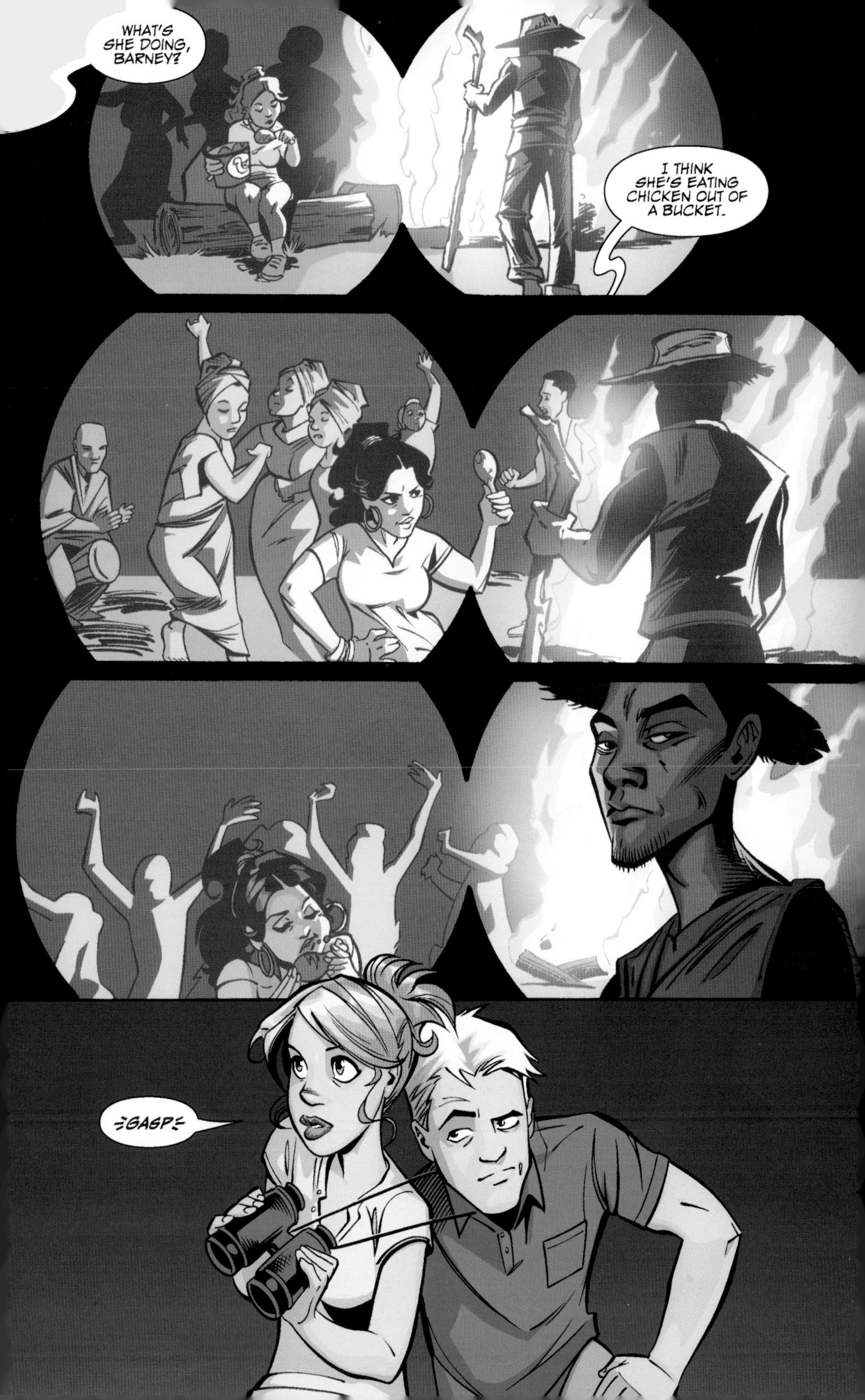
WHAT'S SHE DOING, BARNEY?
I THINK SHE'S EATING CHICKEN OUT OF A BUCKET.
=GASP=

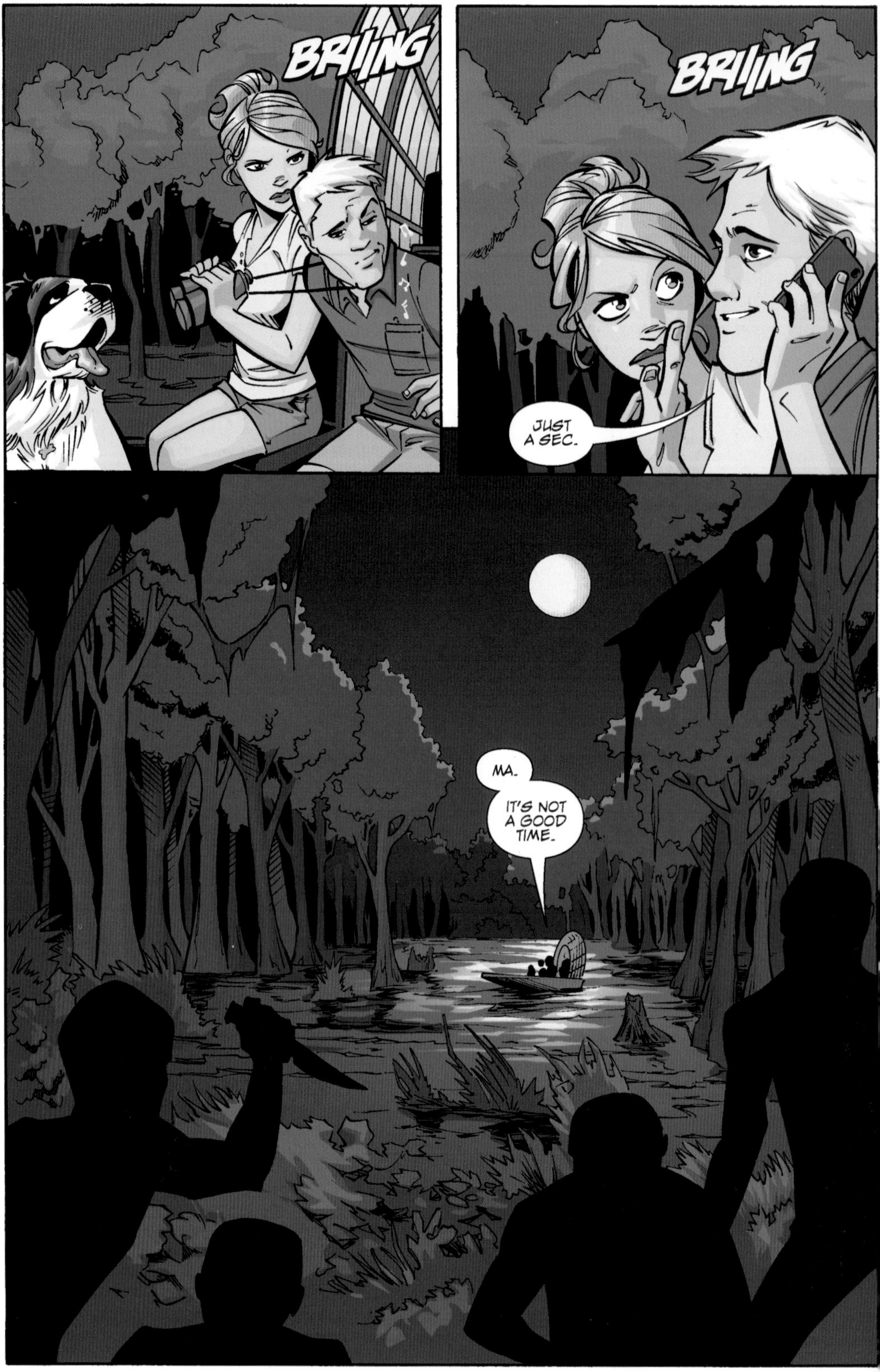
BRIIING
BRIIING
JUST A SEC.
MA.
IT'S NOT A GOOD TIME.

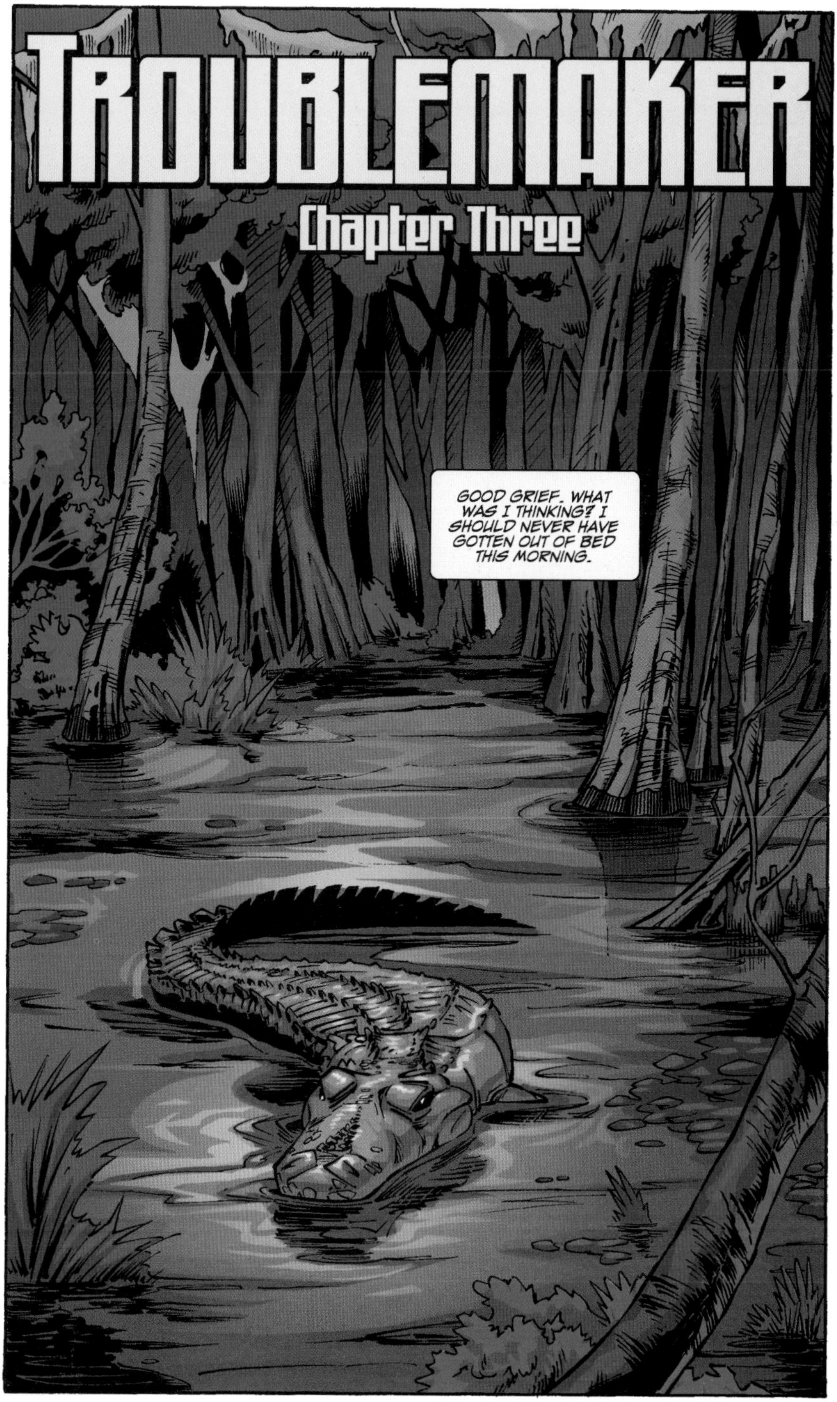
TROUBLEMAKER
Chapter Three
GOOD GRIEF. WHAT WAS I THINKING? I SHOULD NEVER HAVE GOTTEN OUT OF BED THIS MORNING.

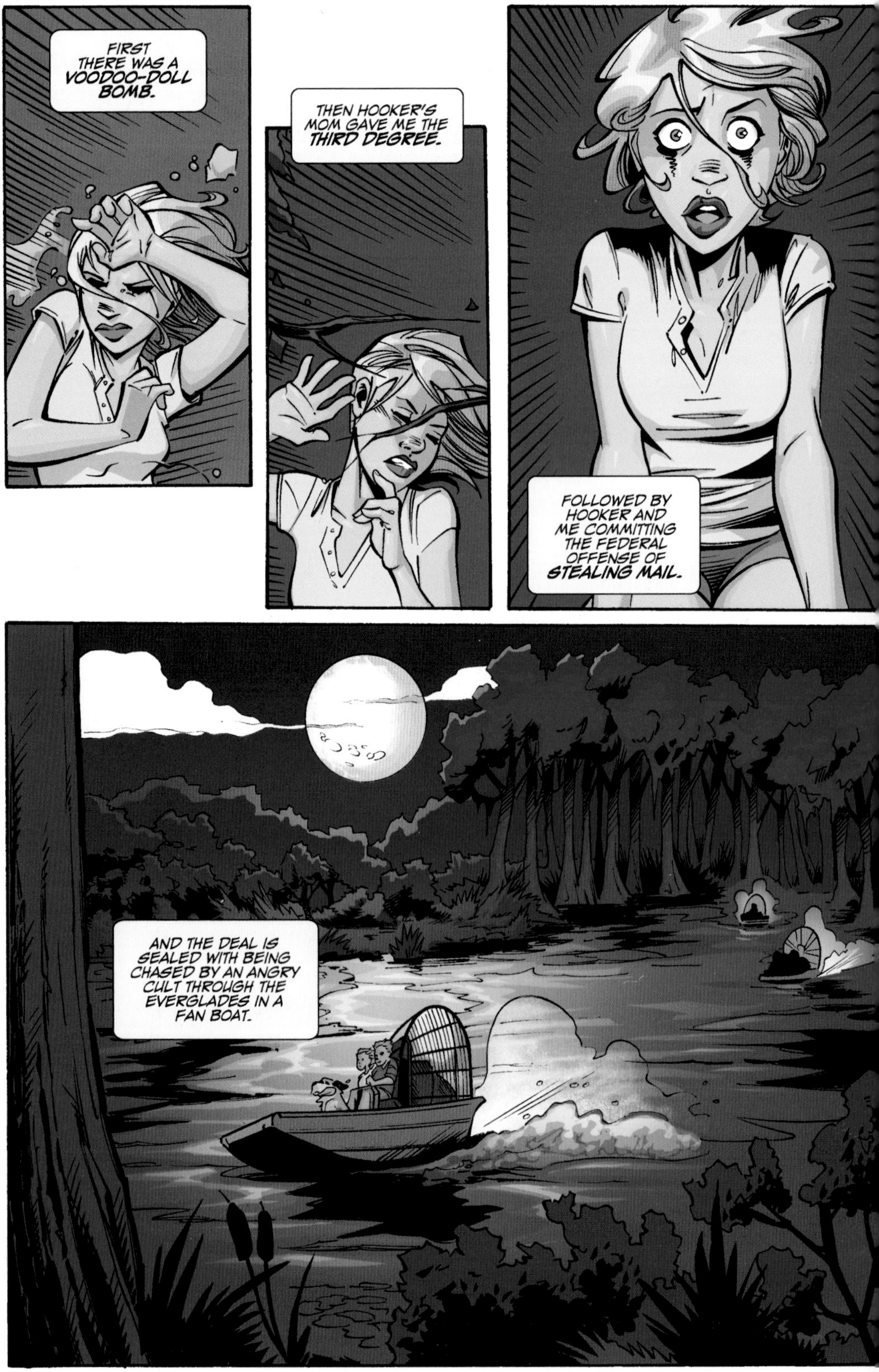
FIRST THERE WAS A VOODOO-DOLL BOMB.
THEN HOOKER'S MOM GAVE ME THE THIRD DEGREE.
FOLLOWED BY HOOKER AND ME COMMITTING THE FEDERAL OFFENSE OF STEALING MAIL.
AND THE DEAL IS SEALED WITH BEING CHASED BY AN ANGRY CULT THROUGH THE EVERGLADES IN A FAN BOAT.

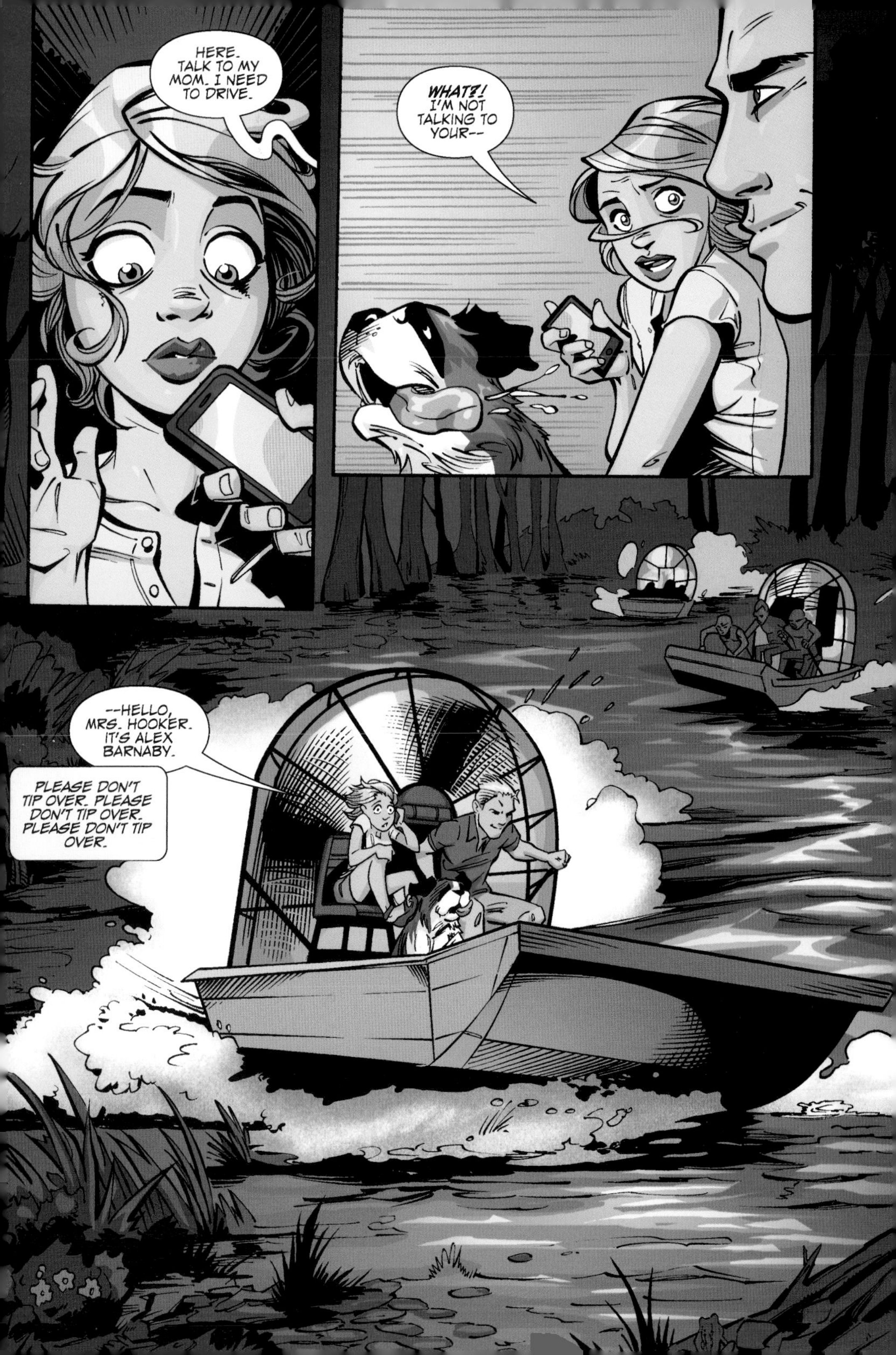
HERE. TALK TO MY MOM. I NEED TO DRIVE.
WHAT?! I'M NOT TALKING TO YOUR--
--HELLO, MRS. HOOKER. IT'S ALEX BARNABY.
PLEASE DON'T TIP OVER. PLEASE DON'T TIP OVER. PLEASE DON'T TIP OVER.

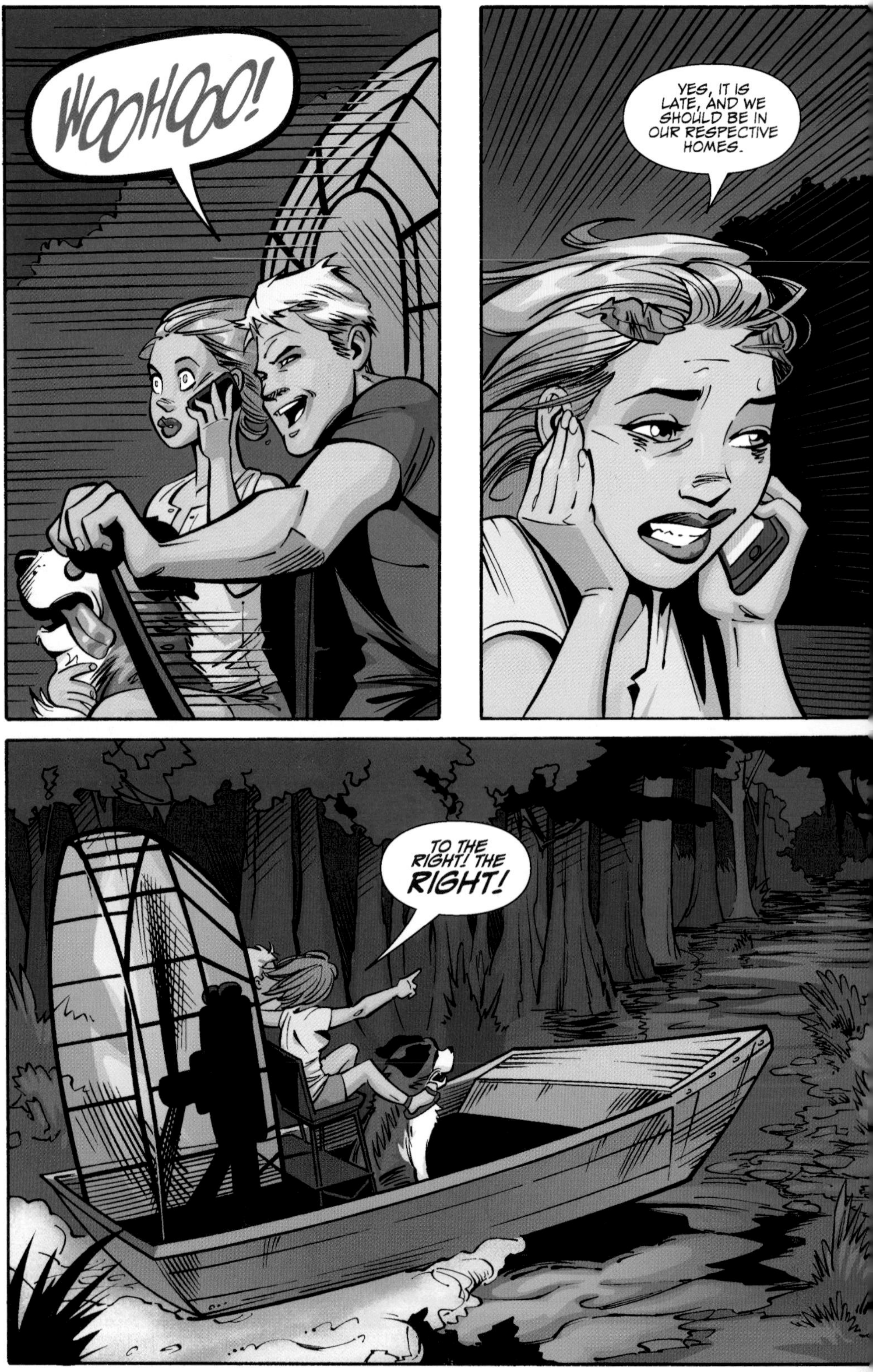
WOOHOOO!
YES, IT IS LATE, AND WE SHOULD BE IN OUR RESPECTIVE HOMES.
TO THE RIGHT! THE RIGHT!

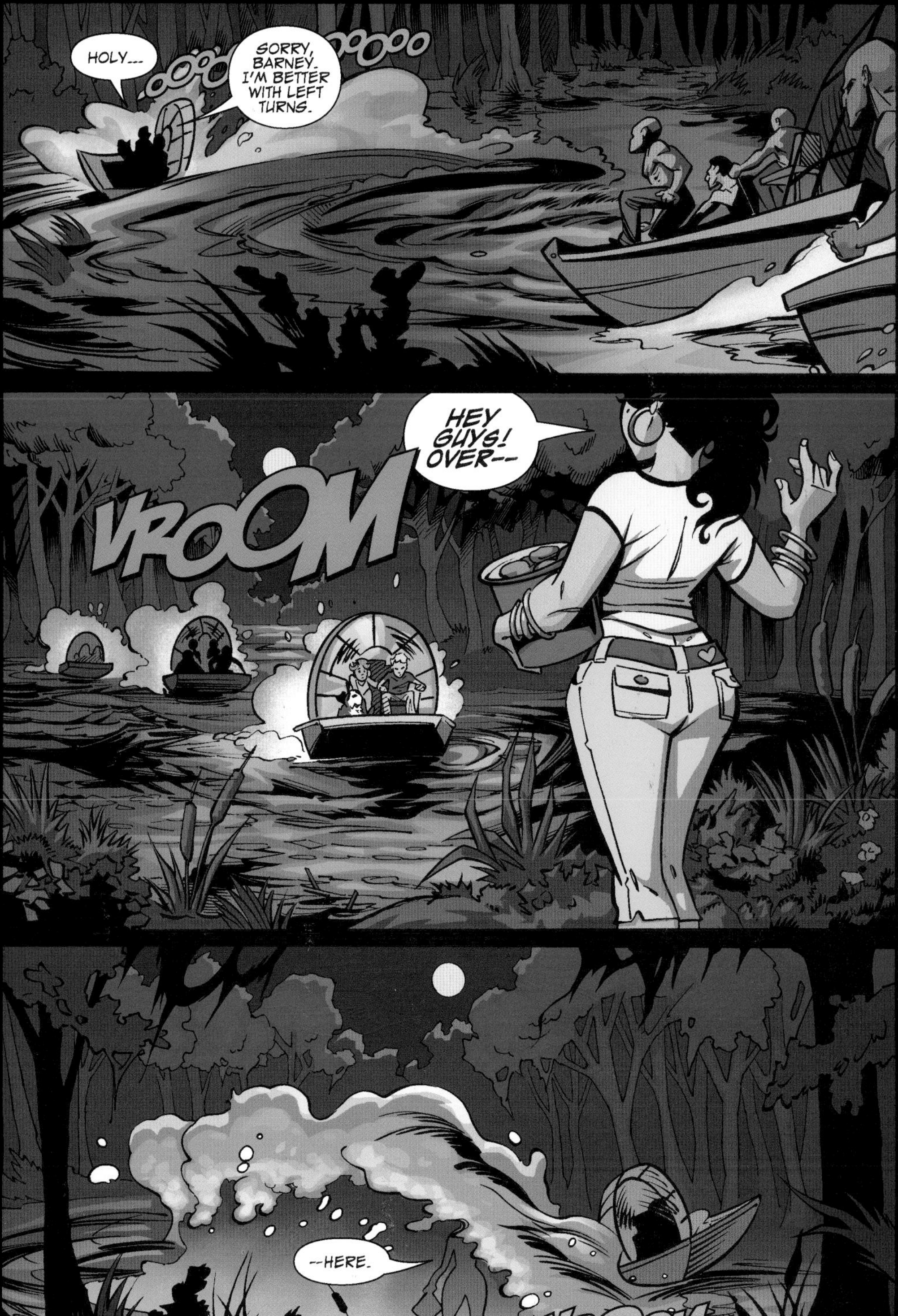
HOLY---
SORRY, BARNEY. I'M BETTER WITH LEFT TURNS.
HEY GUYS! OVER--
VROOM
--HERE.
VROOM

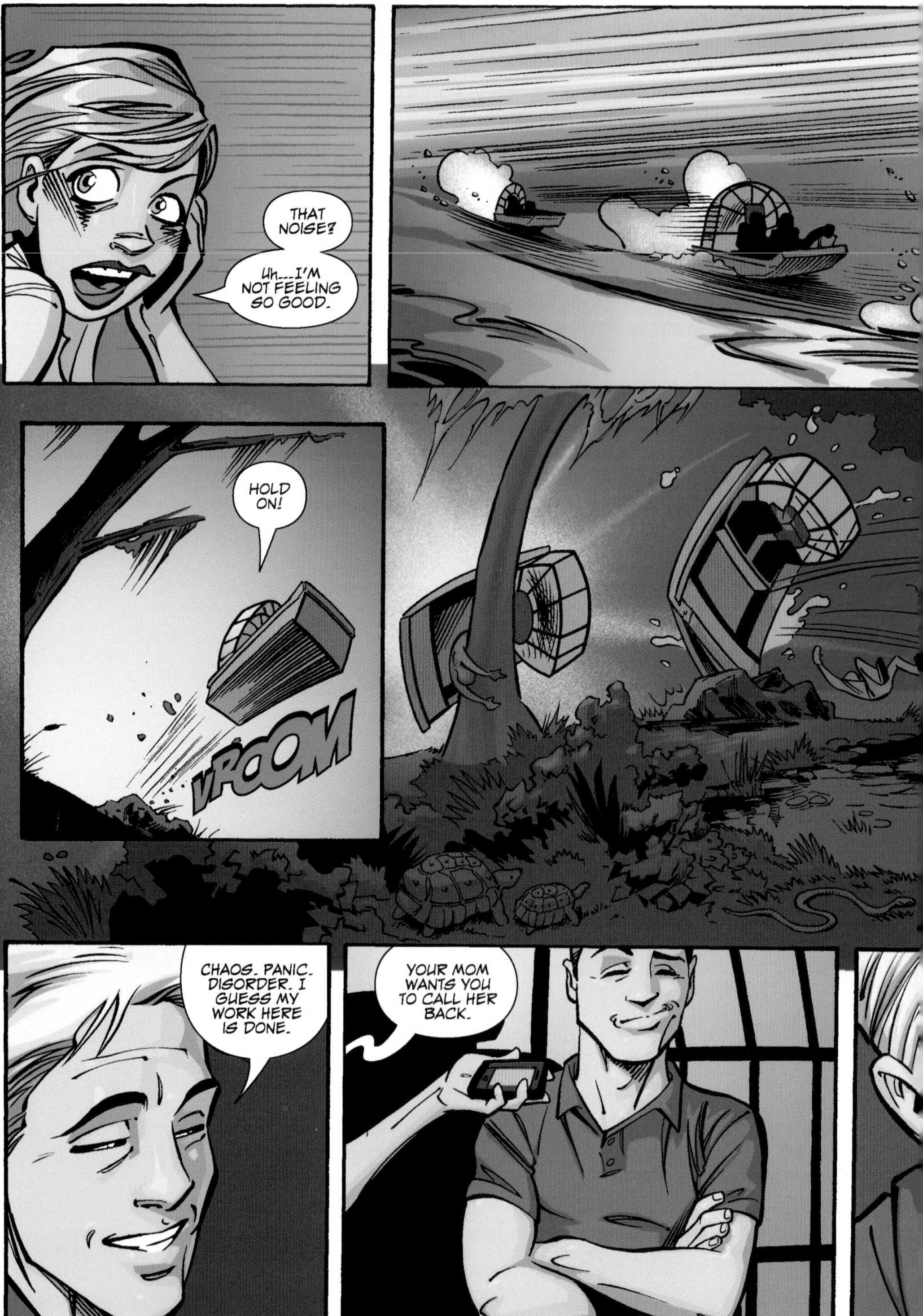
THAT NOISE?
Uh...I'M NOT FEELING SO GOOD.
HOLD ON!
VROOM
CHAOS. PANIC. DISORDER. I GUESS MY WORK HERE IS DONE.
YOUR MOM WANTS YOU TO CALL HER BACK.

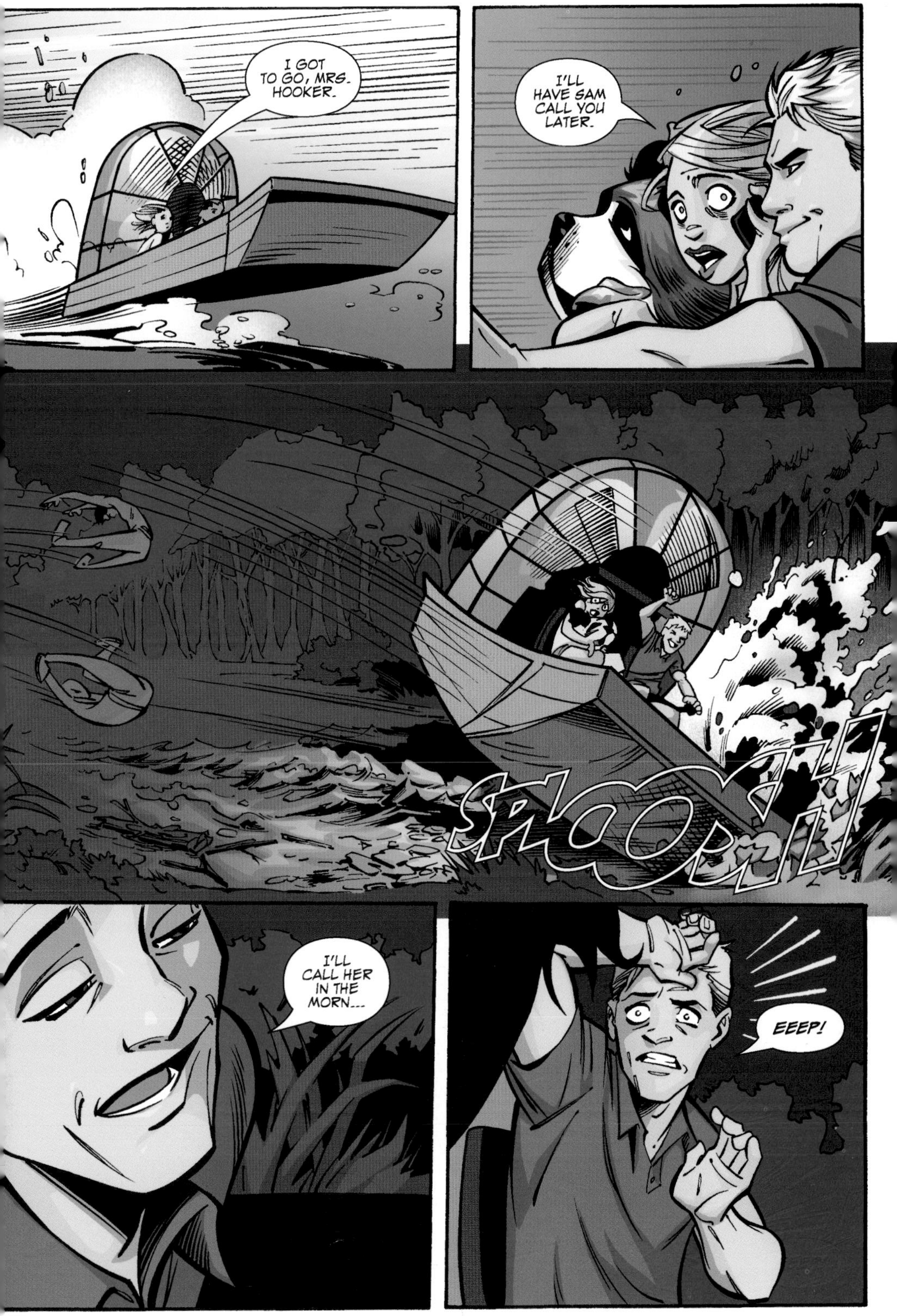
I GOT TO GO, MRS. HOOKER.
I'LL HAVE SAM CALL YOU LATER.
SPLOOSH!
I'LL CALL HER IN THE MORN...
EEEP!

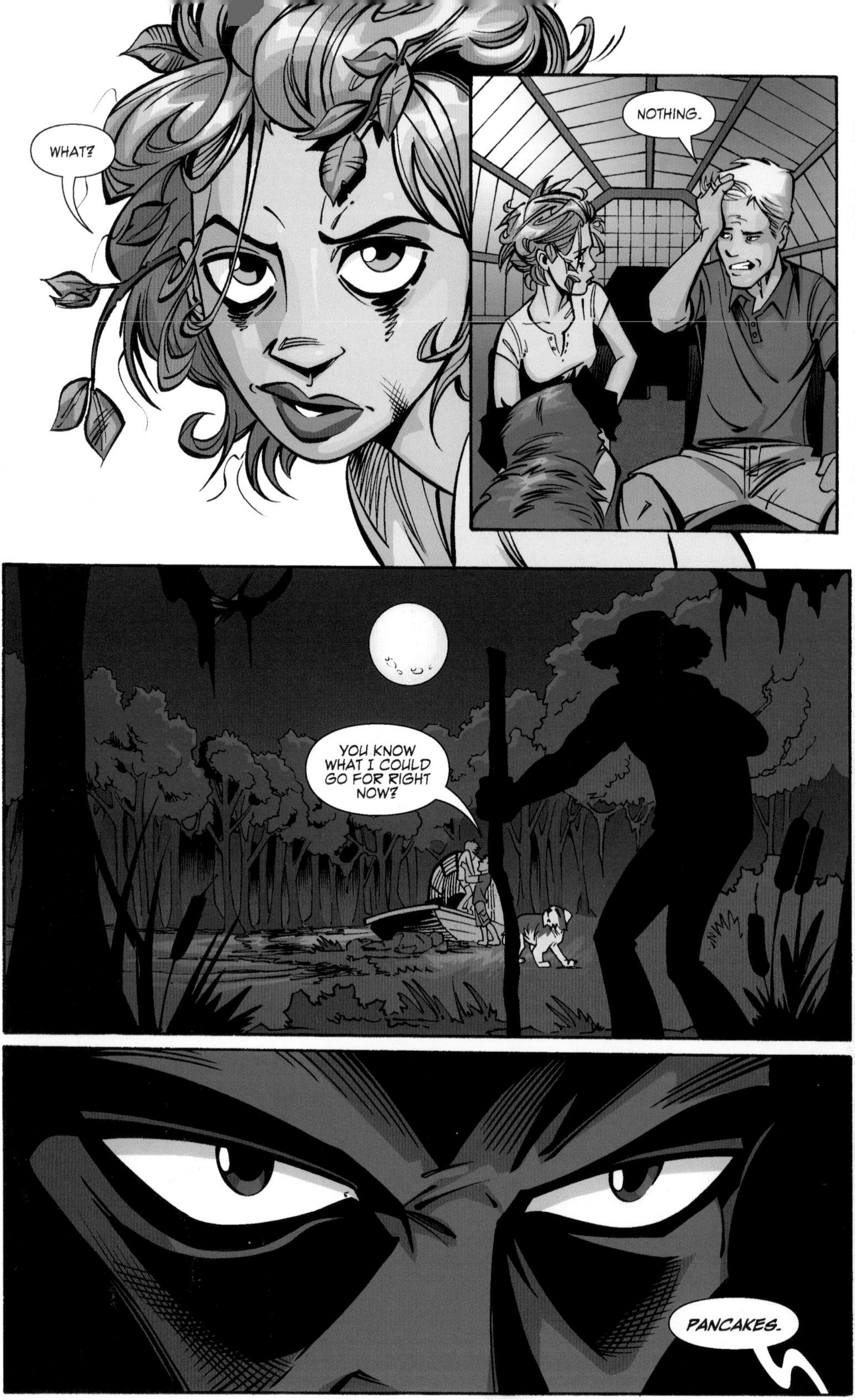
WHAT?
NOTHING.
YOU KNOW WHAT I COULD GO FOR RIGHT NOW?
PANCAKES.

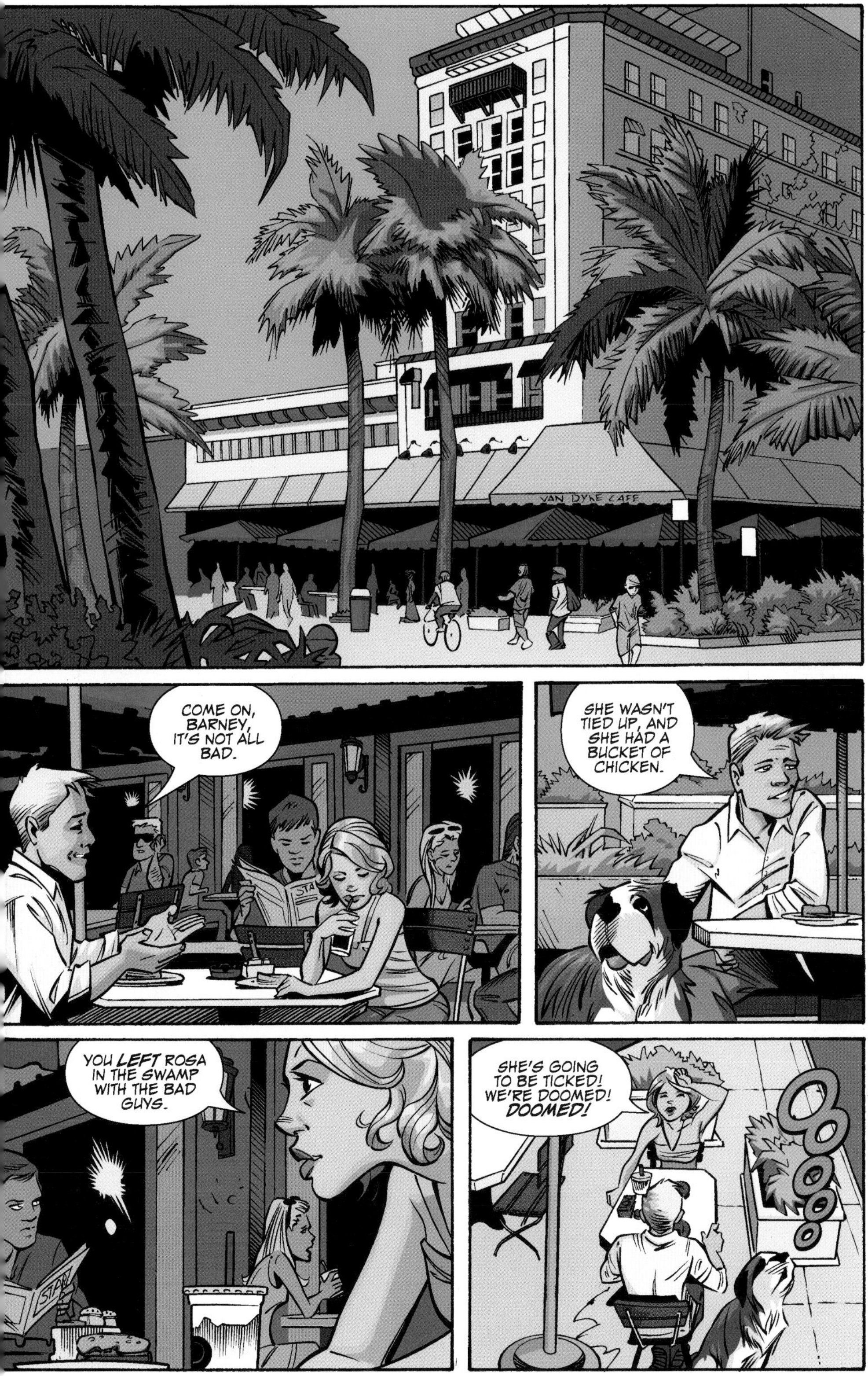
VAN DYKE CAFE
COME ON, BARNEY, IT'S NOT ALL BAD.
SHE WASN'T TIED UP, AND SHE HAD A BUCKET OF CHICKEN.
YOU *LEFT* ROSA IN THE SWAMP WITH THE BAD GUYS.
SHE'S GOING TO BE TICKED! WE'RE DOOMED! ***DOOMED!***

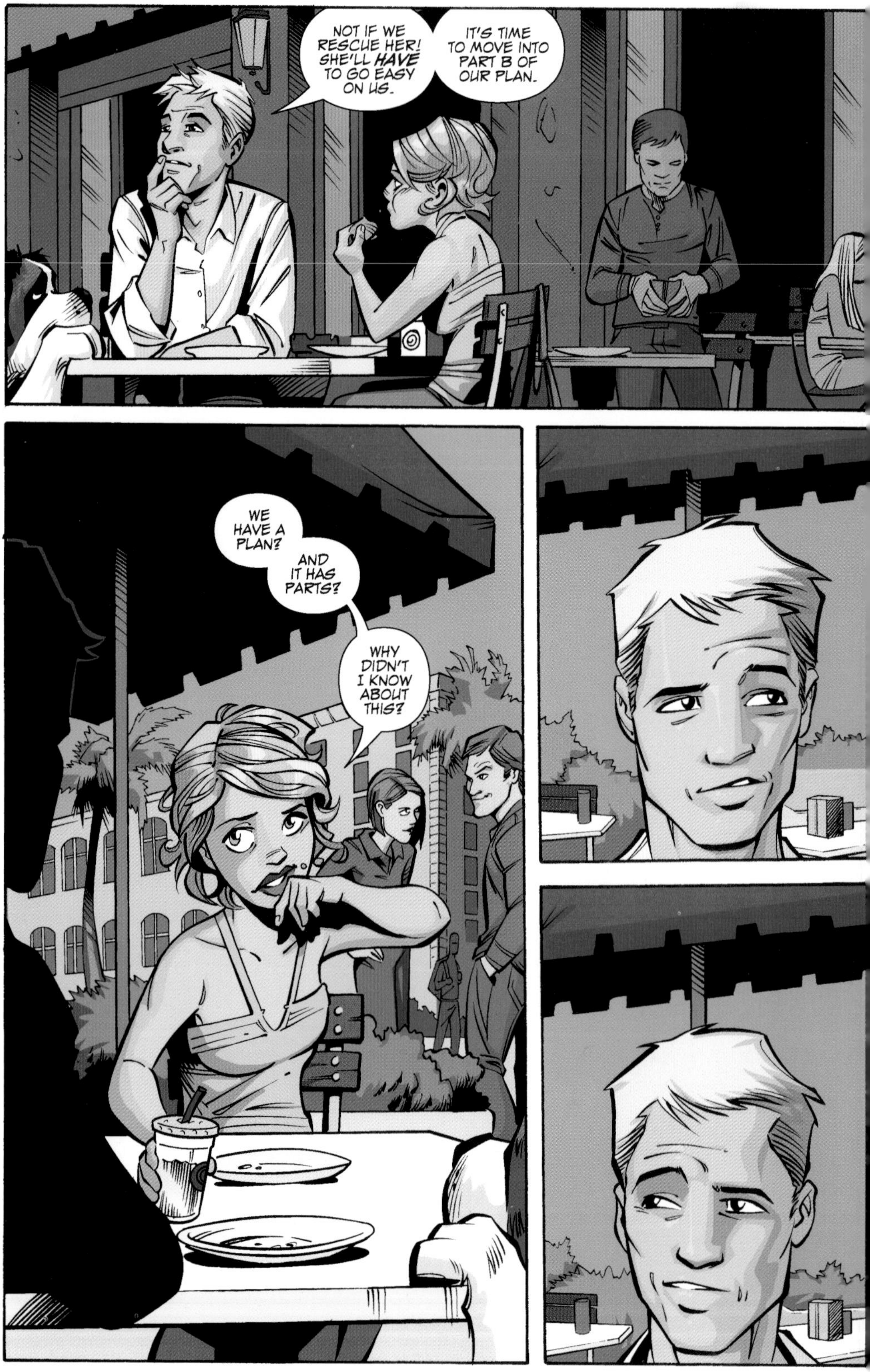
NOT IF WE RESCUE HER! SHE'LL HAVE TO GO EASY ON US.
IT'S TIME TO MOVE INTO PART B OF OUR PLAN.
WE HAVE A PLAN?
AND IT HAS PARTS?
WHY DIDN'T I KNOW ABOUT THIS?

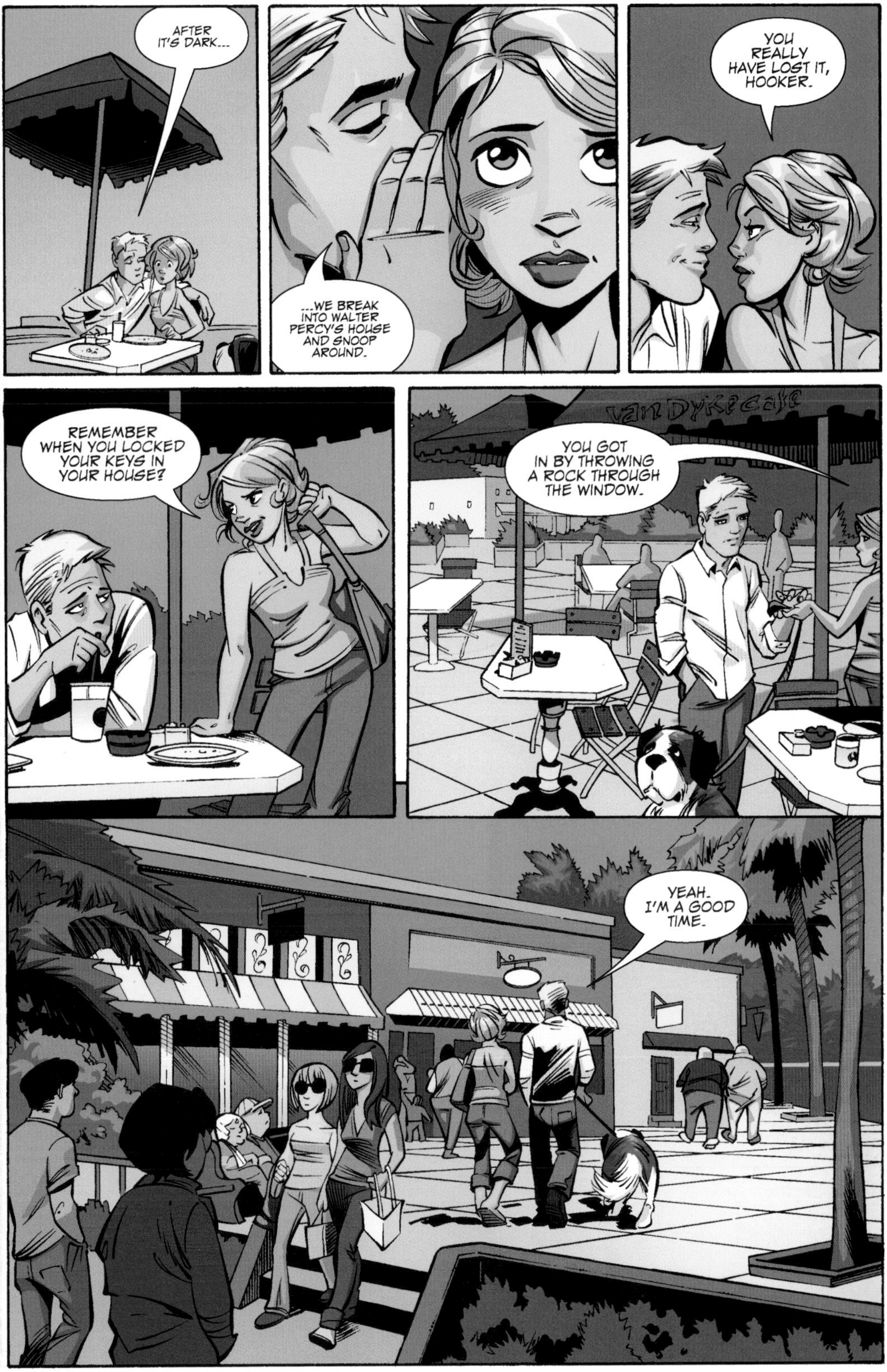
AFTER IT'S DARK...
...WE BREAK INTO WALTER PERCY'S HOUSE AND SNOOP AROUND.
YOU REALLY HAVE LOST IT, HOOKER.
REMEMBER WHEN YOU LOCKED YOUR KEYS IN YOUR HOUSE?
van Dyke cafe
YOU GOT IN BY THROWING A ROCK THROUGH THE WINDOW.
YEAH. I'M A GOOD TIME.

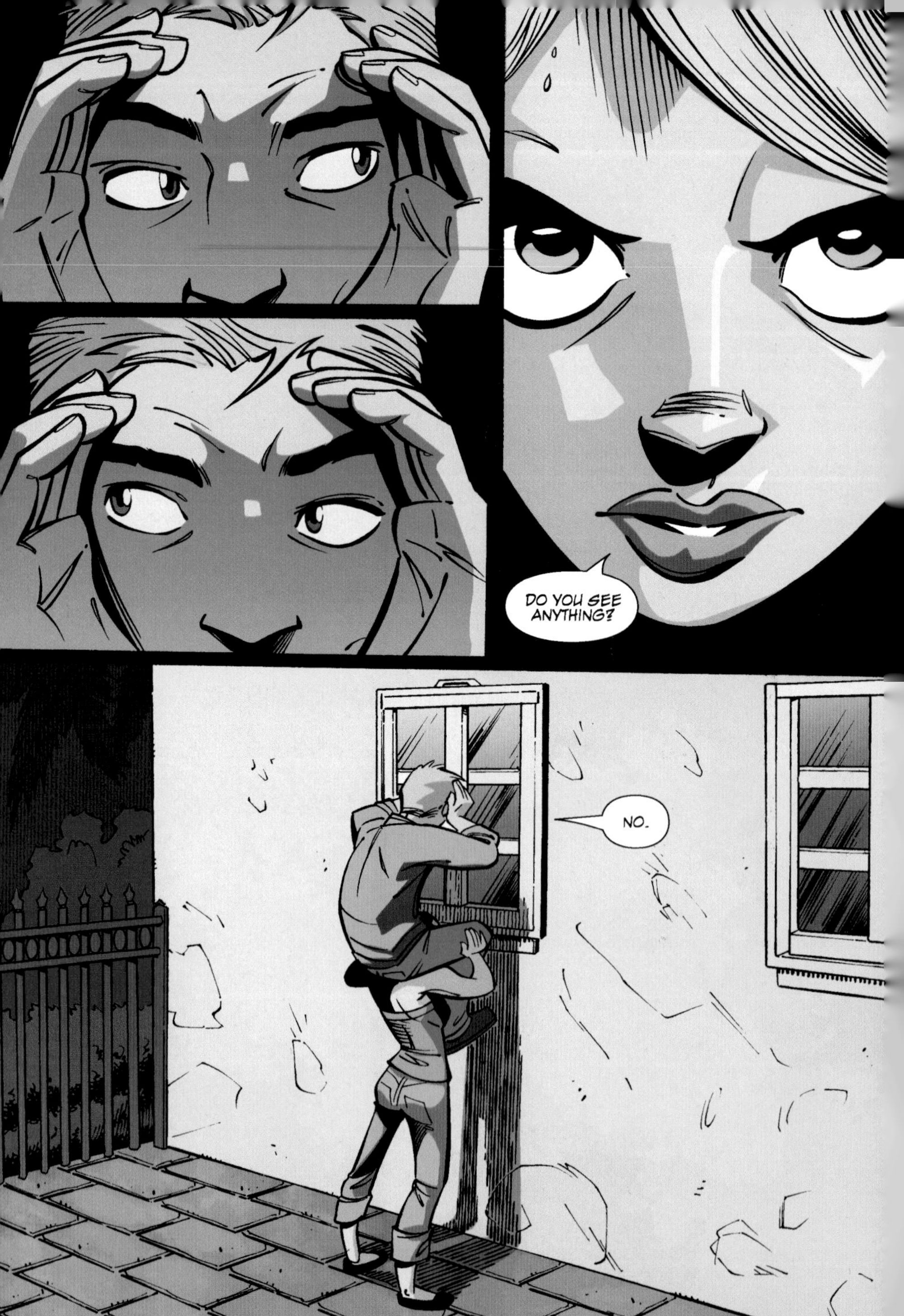
DO YOU SEE ANYTHING?
NO.

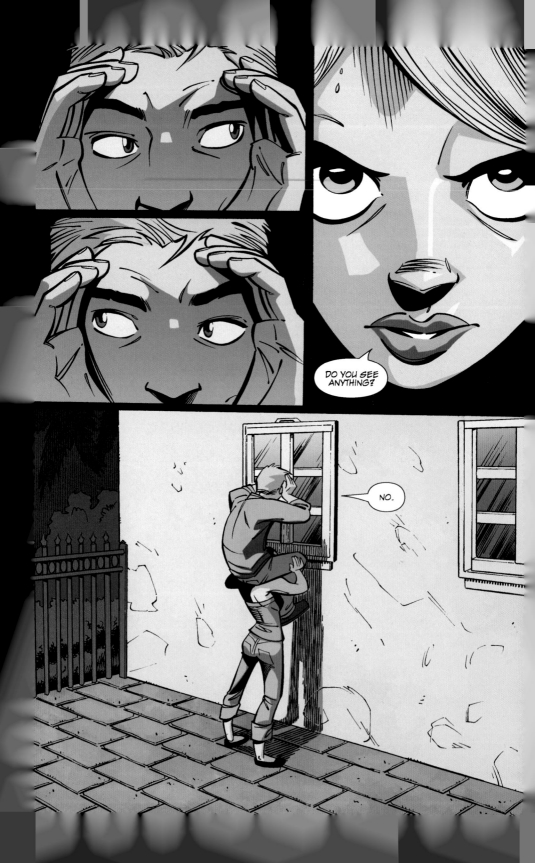

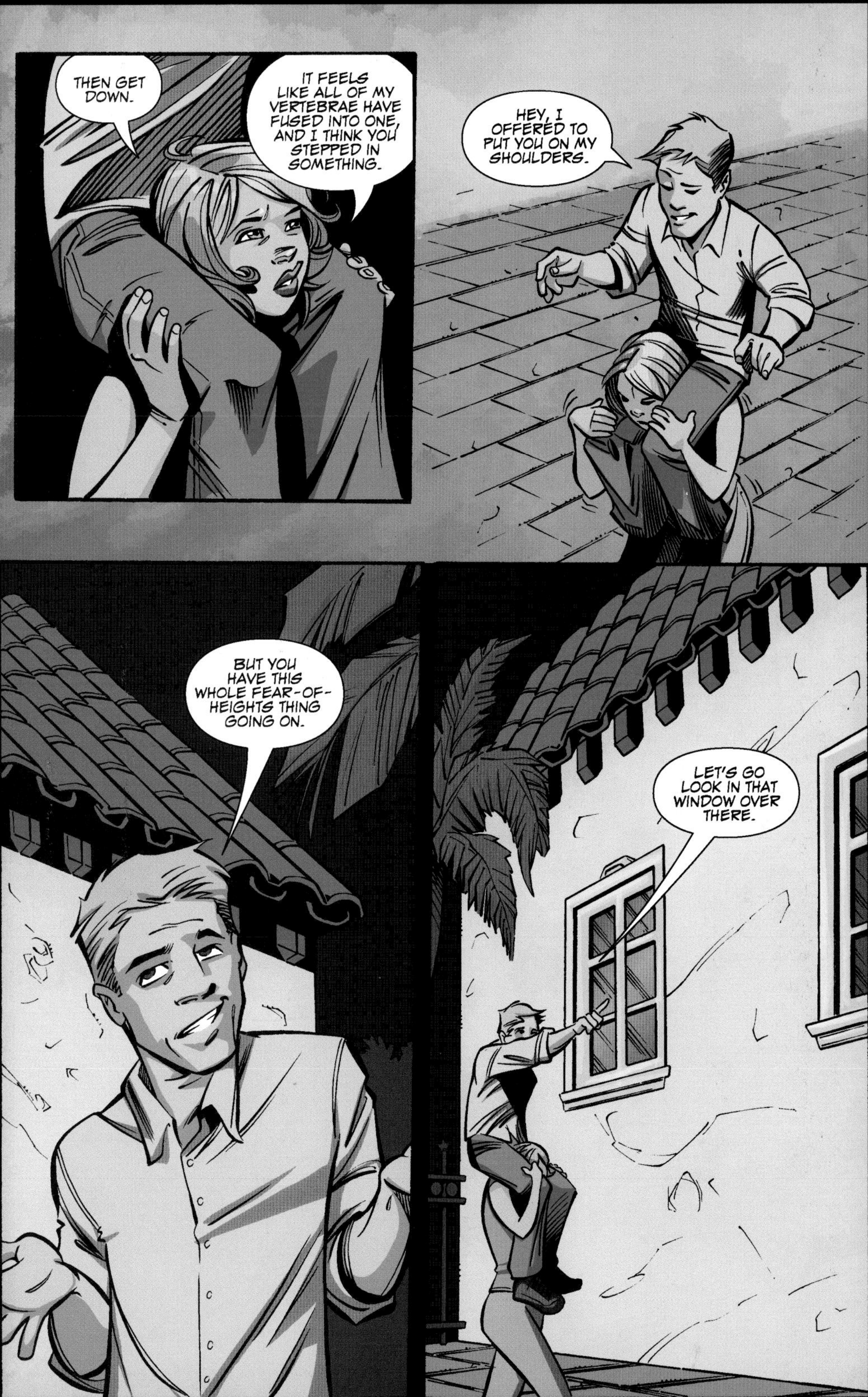

THEN GET DOWN.
IT FEELS LIKE ALL OF MY VERTEBRAE HAVE FUSED INTO ONE, AND I THINK YOU STEPPED IN SOMETHING.
HEY, I OFFERED TO PUT YOU ON MY SHOULDERS.
BUT YOU HAVE THIS WHOLE FEAR-OF-HEIGHTS THING GOING ON.
LET'S GO LOOK IN THAT WINDOW OVER THERE.

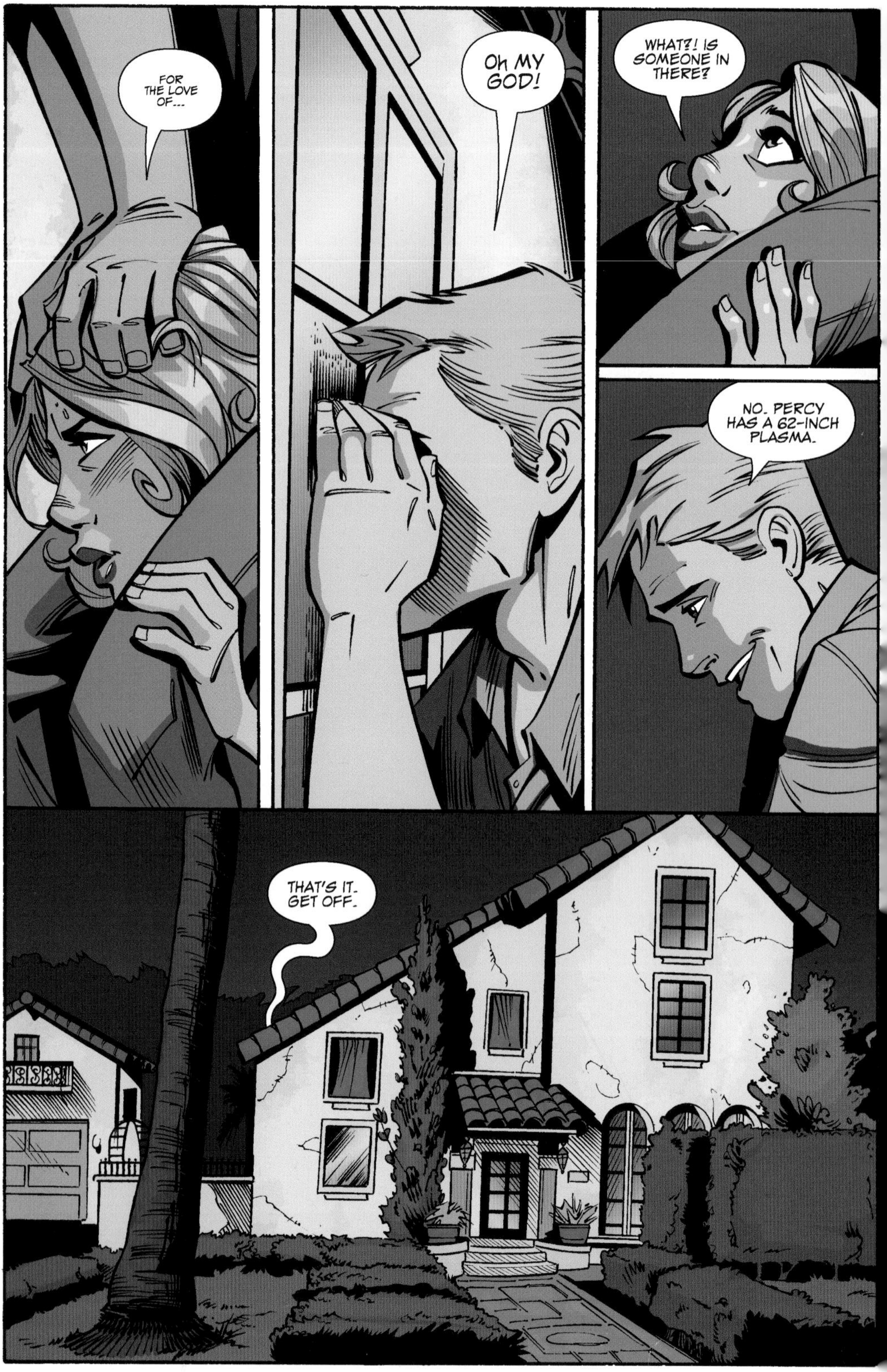
FOR THE LOVE OF...
Oh MY GOD!
WHAT?! IS SOMEONE IN THERE?
NO. PERCY HAS A 62-INCH PLASMA.
THAT'S IT. GET OFF.

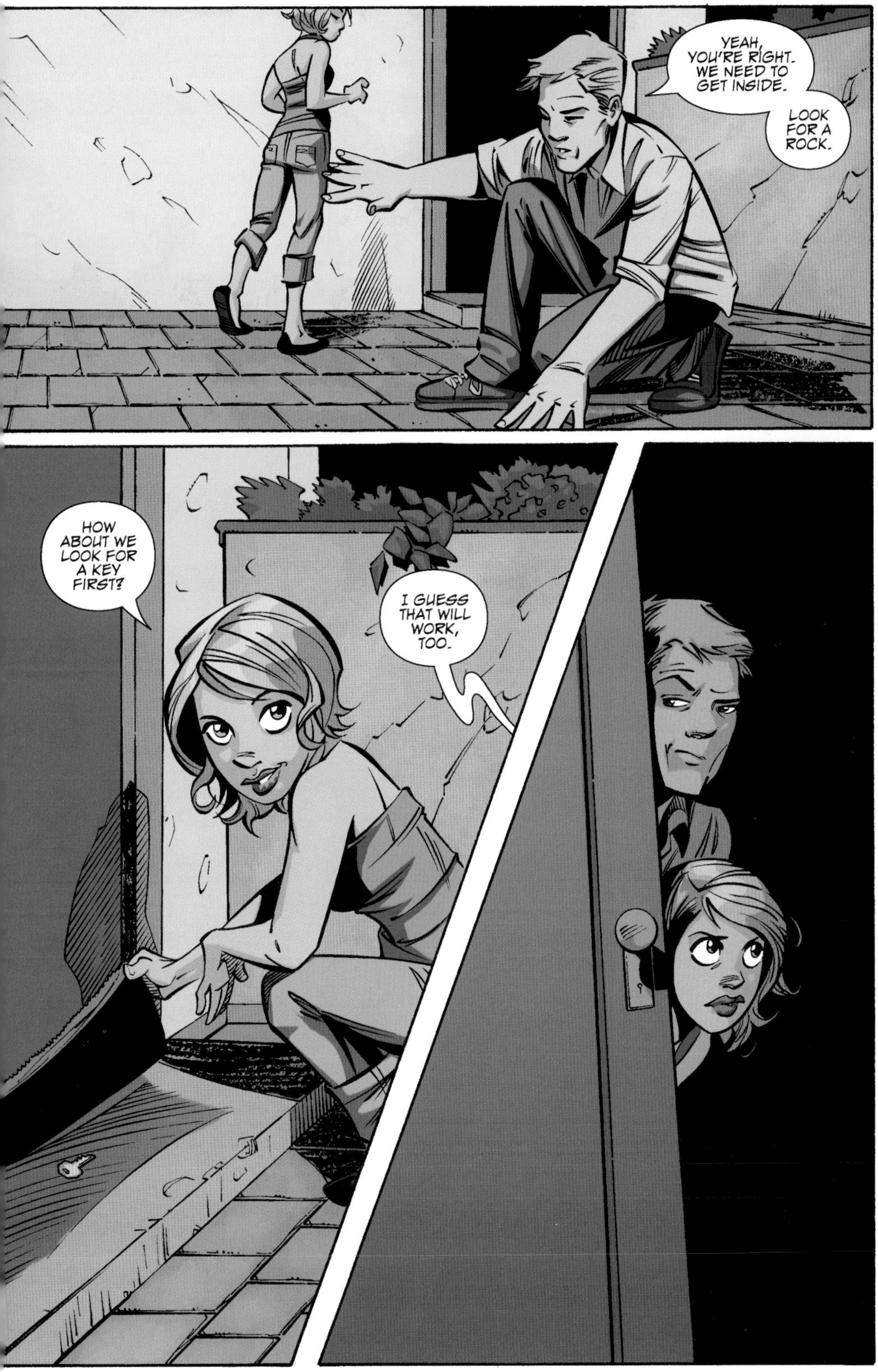
YEAH, YOU'RE RIGHT. WE NEED TO GET INSIDE.
LOOK FOR A ROCK.
HOW ABOUT WE LOOK FOR A KEY FIRST?
I GUESS THAT WILL WORK, TOO.

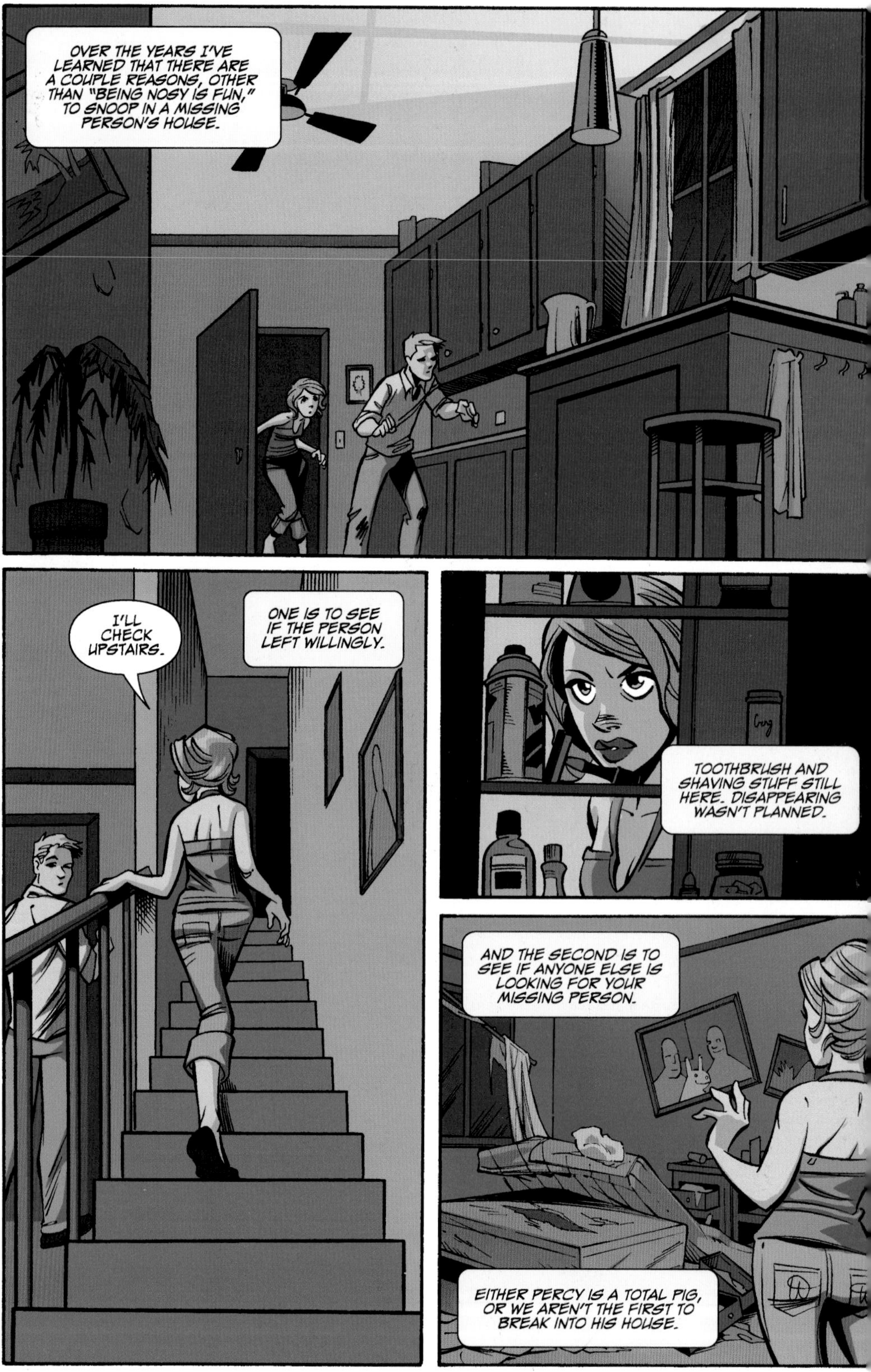
OVER THE YEARS I'VE LEARNED THAT THERE ARE A COUPLE REASONS, OTHER THAN "BEING NOSY IS FUN," TO SNOOP IN A MISSING PERSON'S HOUSE.
I'LL CHECK UPSTAIRS.
ONE IS TO SEE IF THE PERSON LEFT WILLINGLY.
TOOTHBRUSH AND SHAVING STUFF STILL HERE. DISAPPEARING WASN'T PLANNED.
AND THE SECOND IS TO SEE IF ANYONE ELSE IS LOOKING FOR YOUR MISSING PERSON.
EITHER PERCY IS A TOTAL PIG, OR WE AREN'T THE FIRST TO BREAK INTO HIS HOUSE.

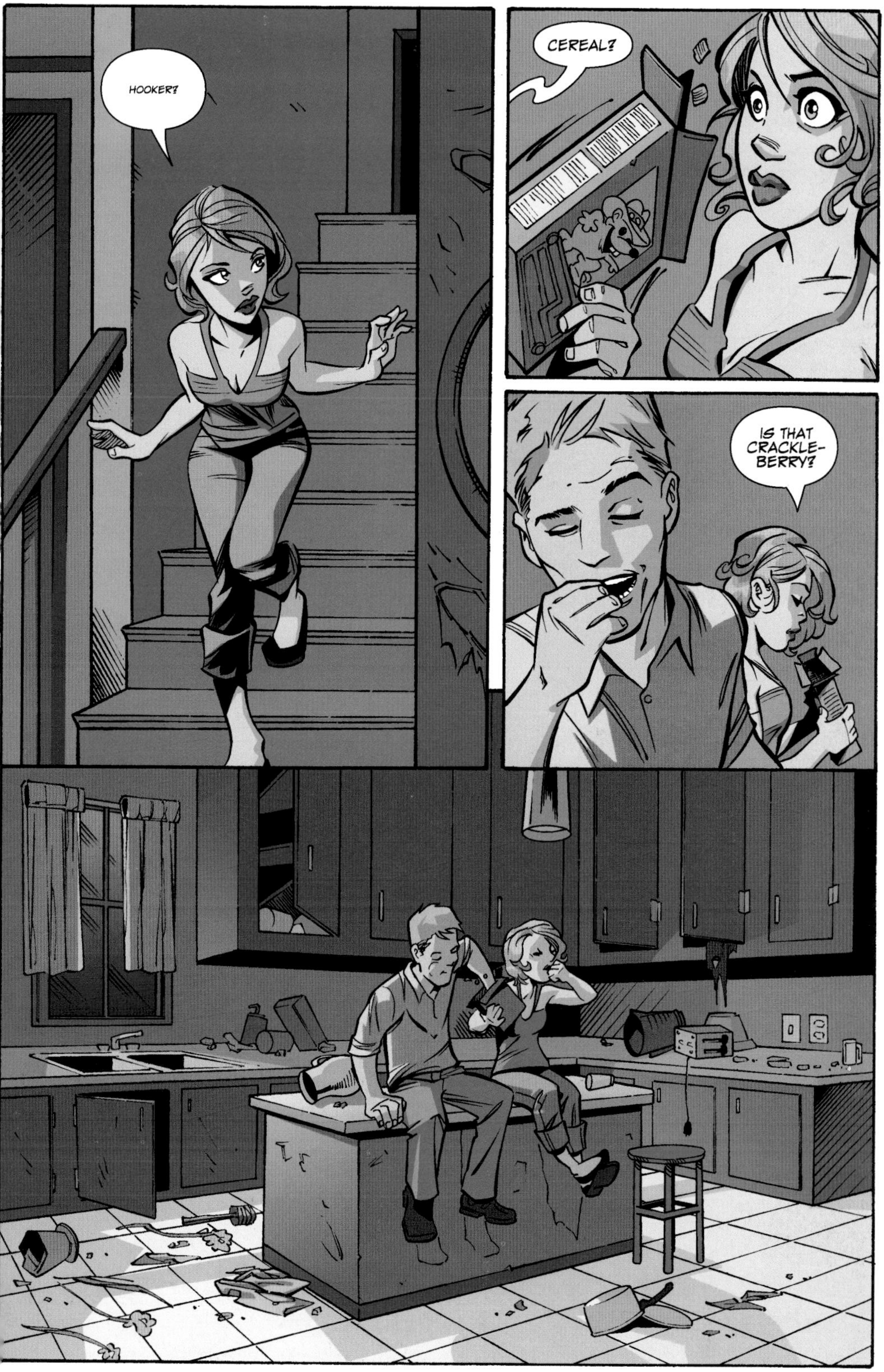
HOOKER?
CEREAL?
IS THAT CRACKLE-BERRY?

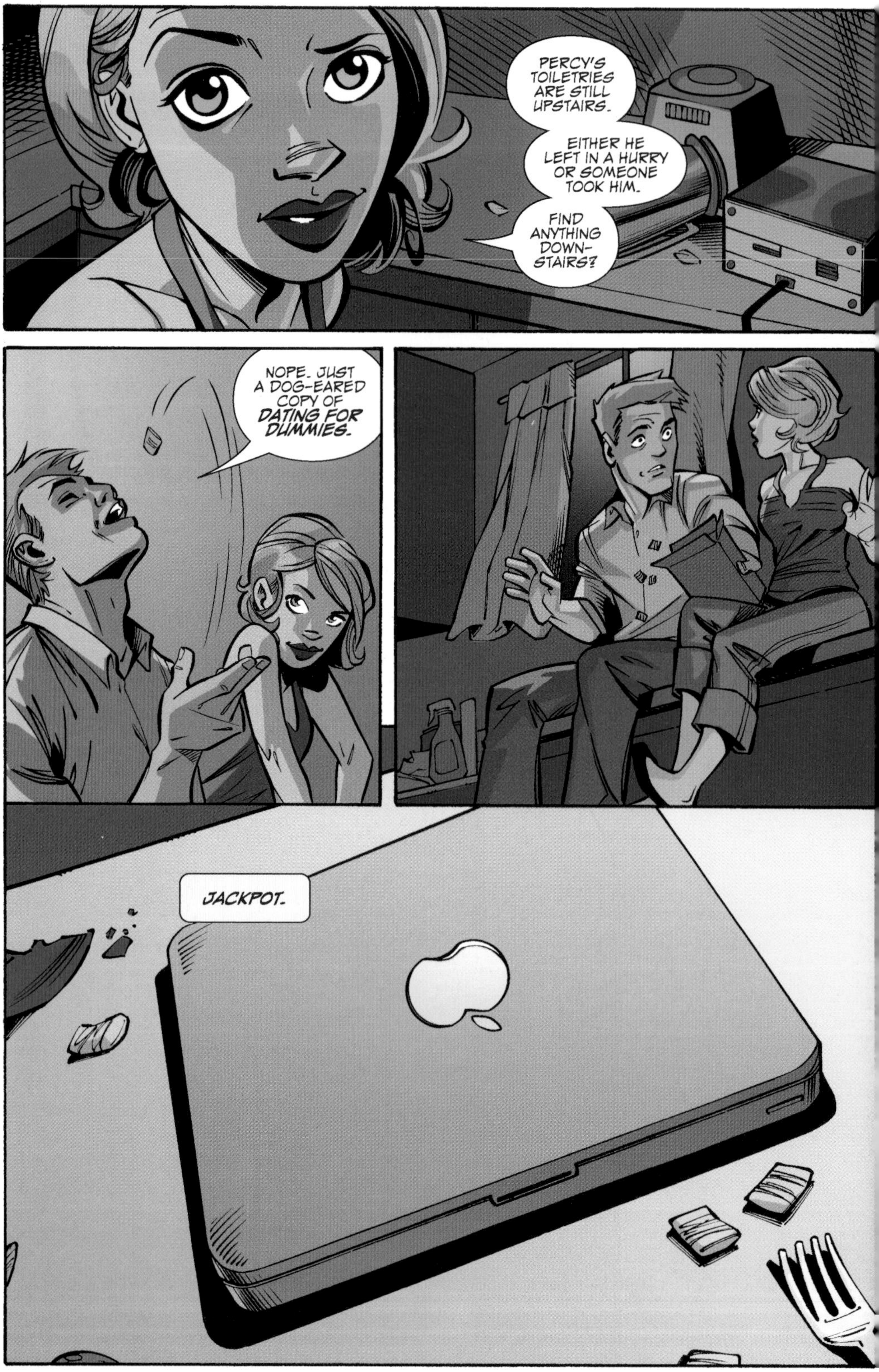

PERCY'S TOILETRIES ARE STILL UPSTAIRS.
EITHER HE LEFT IN A HURRY OR SOMEONE TOOK HIM.
FIND ANYTHING DOWN-STAIRS?
NOPE. JUST A DOG-EARED COPY OF *DATING FOR DUMMIES.*
JACKPOT.

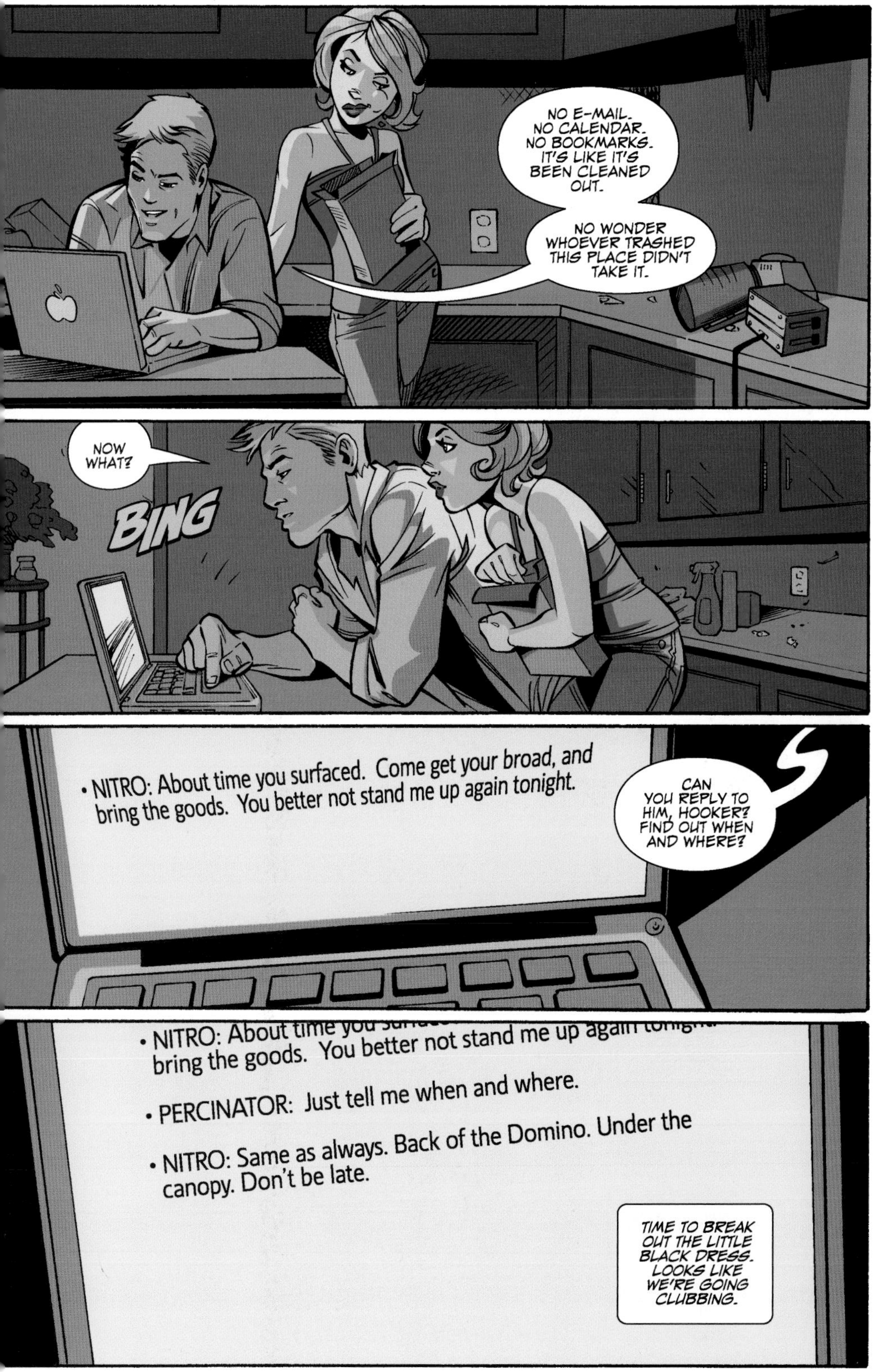
NO E-MAIL. NO CALENDAR. NO BOOKMARKS. IT'S LIKE IT'S BEEN CLEANED OUT.
NO WONDER WHOEVER TRASHED THIS PLACE DIDN'T TAKE IT.
NOW WHAT?
BING
• NITRO: About time you surfaced. Come get your broad, and bring the goods. You better not stand me up again tonight.
CAN YOU REPLY TO HIM, HOOKER? FIND OUT WHEN AND WHERE?
• NITRO: About time you surfaced. Come get your broad, and bring the goods. You better not stand me up again tonight.
• PERCINATOR: Just tell me when and where.
• NITRO: Same as always. Back of the Domino. Under the canopy. Don't be late.
TIME TO BREAK OUT THE LITTLE BLACK DRESS. LOOKS LIKE WE'RE GOING CLUBBING.

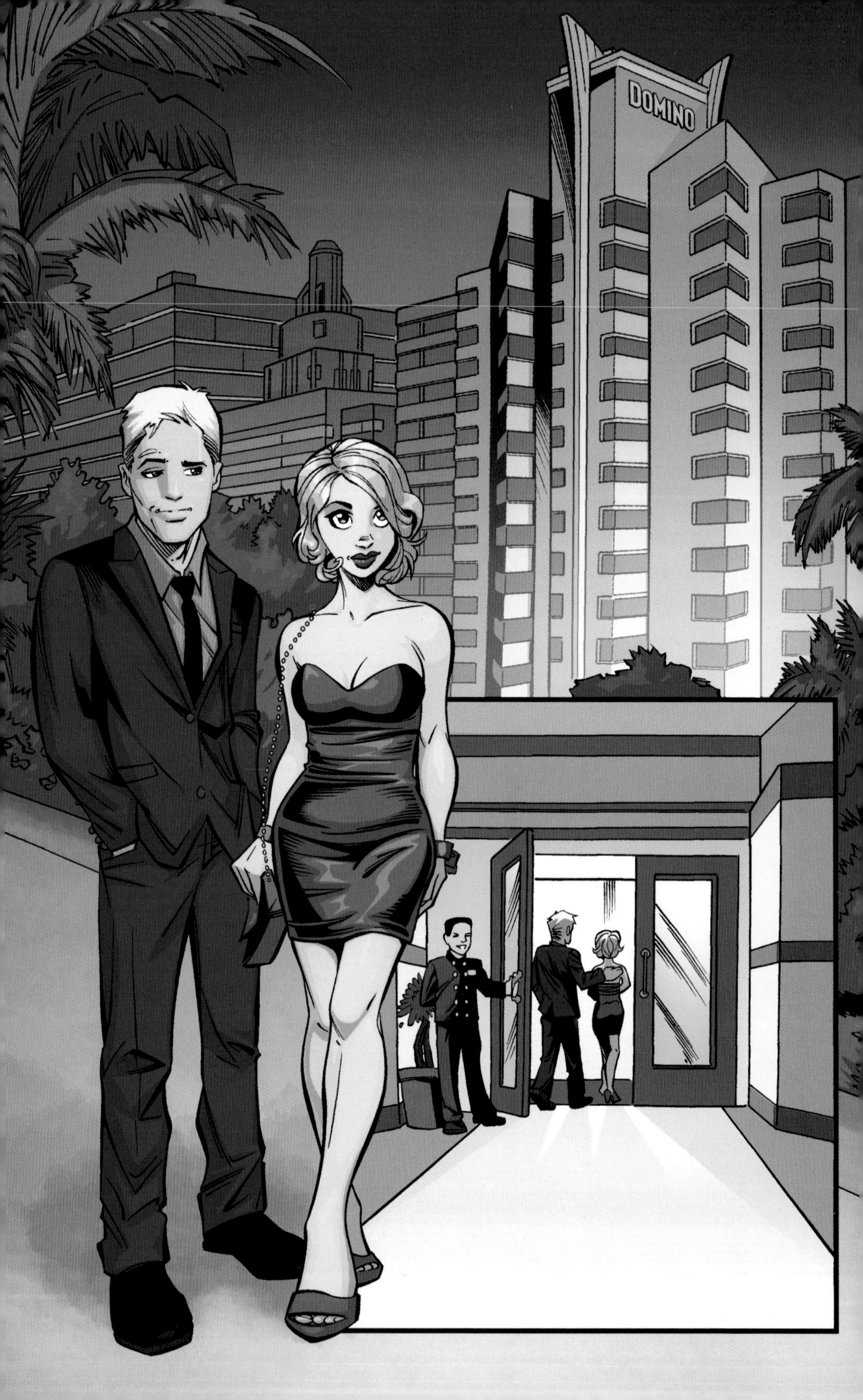
DOMINO

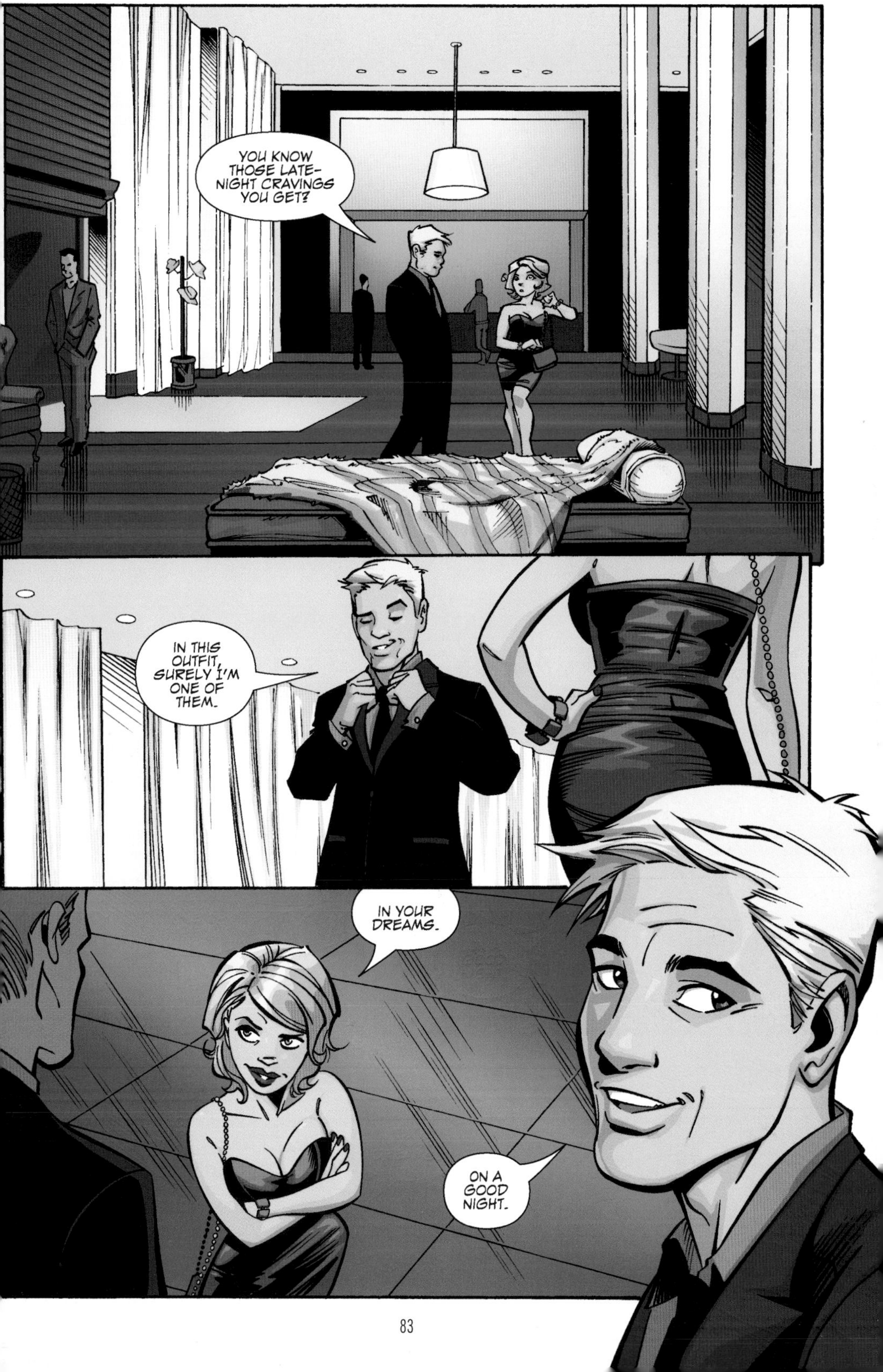
YOU KNOW THOSE LATE-NIGHT CRAVINGS YOU GET?
IN THIS OUTFIT, SURELY I'M ONE OF THEM.
IN YOUR DREAMS.
ON A GOOD NIGHT.

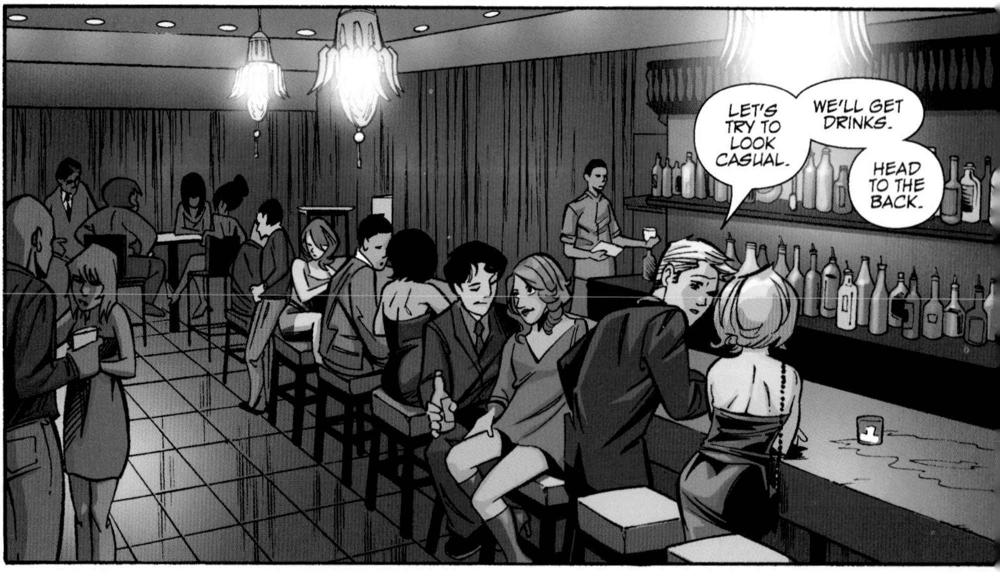
LET'S TRY TO LOOK CASUAL.
WE'LL GET DRINKS.
HEAD TO THE BACK.

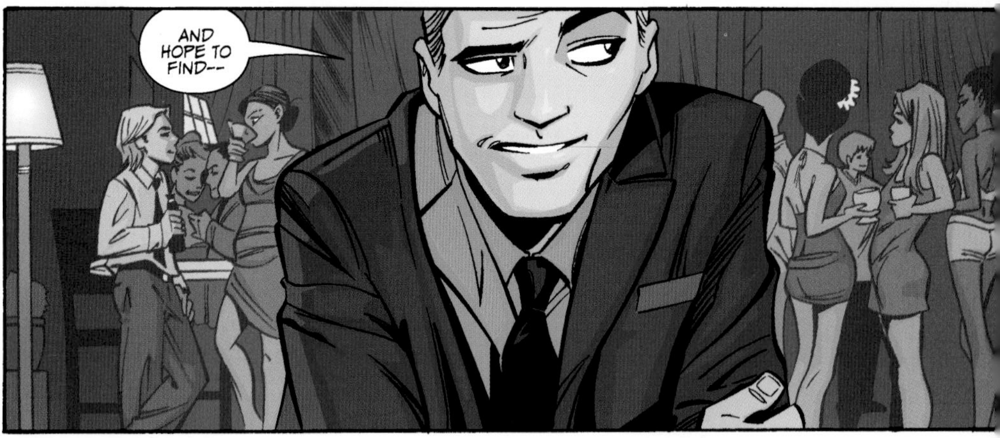
AND HOPE TO FIND--

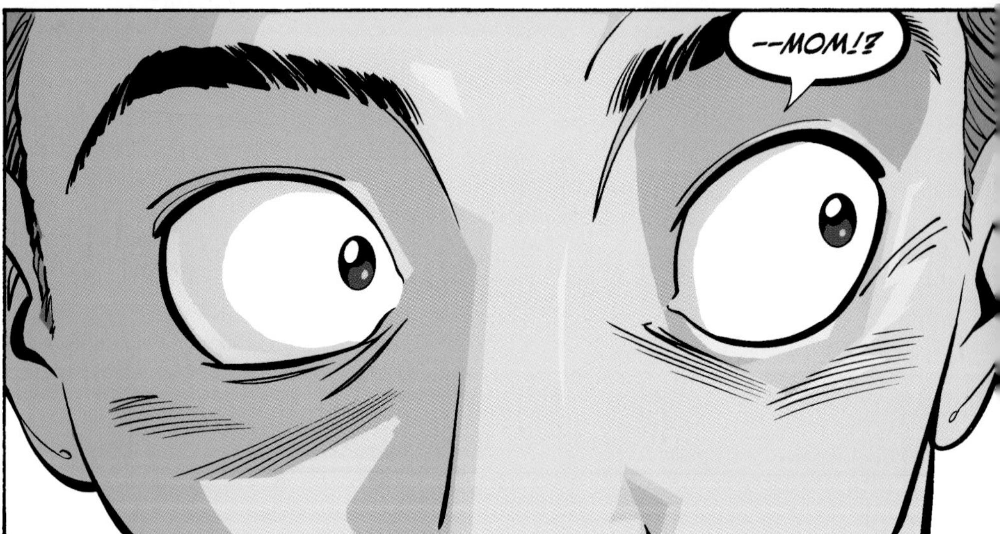
--MOM!?

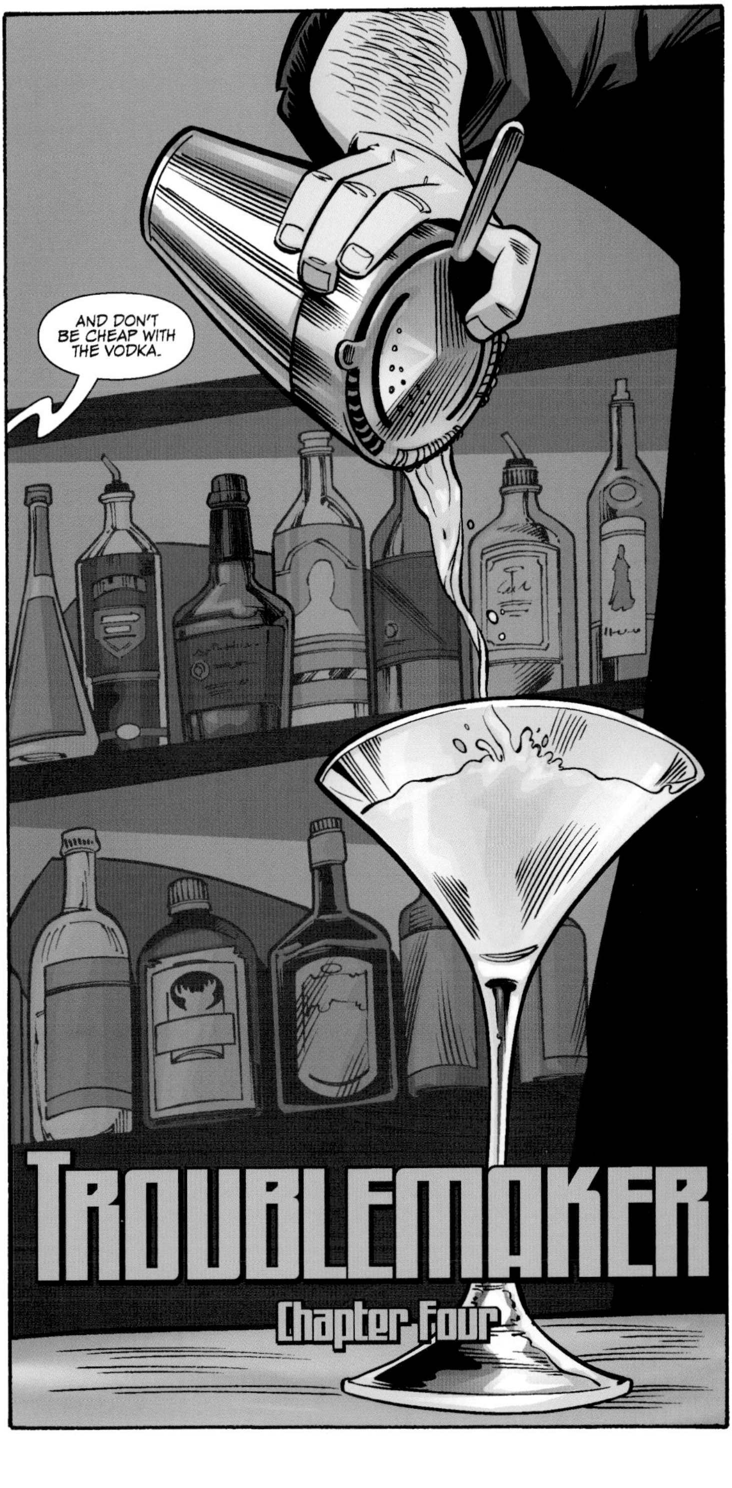
AND DON'T BE CHEAP WITH THE VODKA.
TROUBLEMAKER
Chapter Four

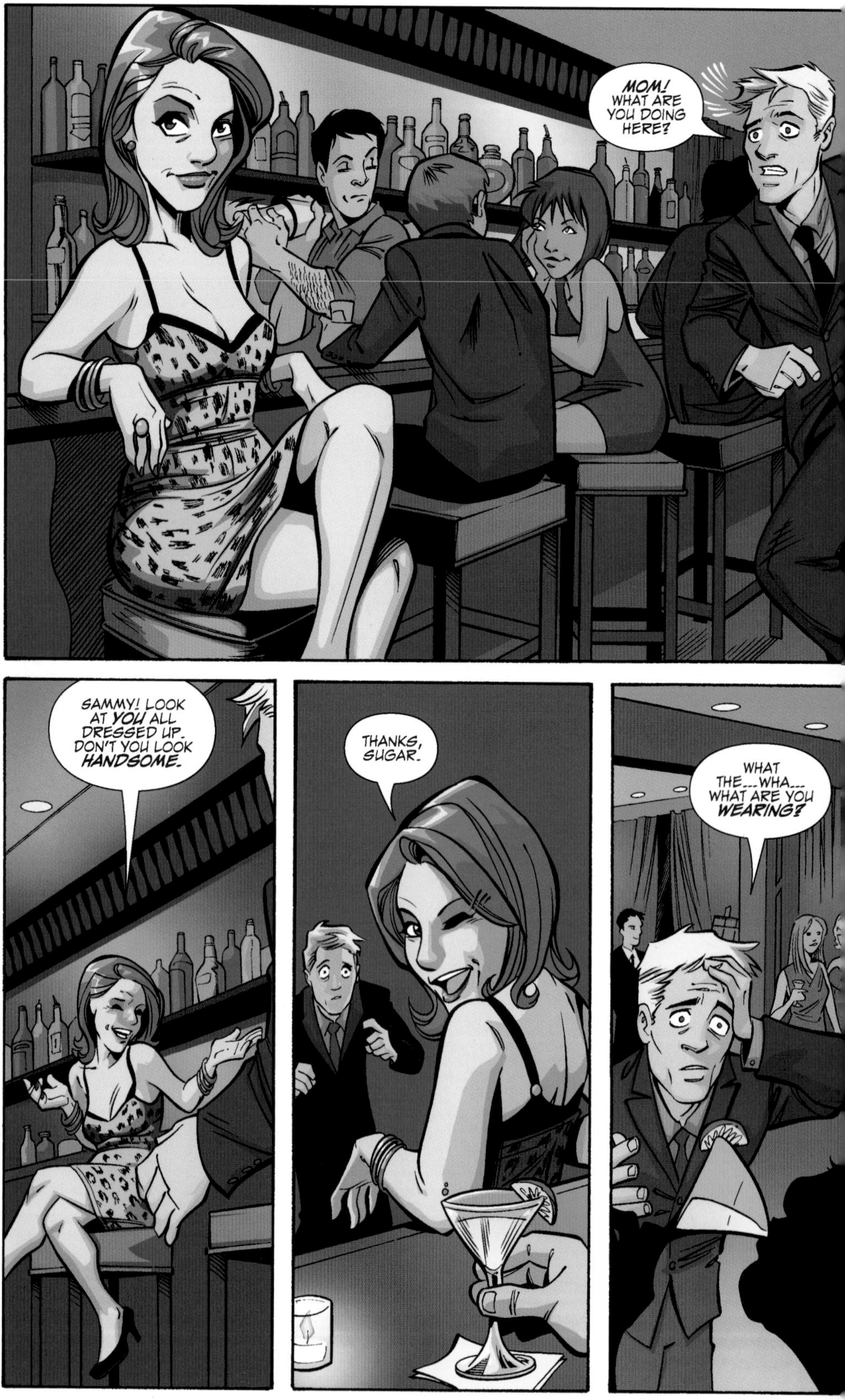
MOM! WHAT ARE YOU DOING HERE?
SAMMY! LOOK AT YOU ALL DRESSED UP. DON'T YOU LOOK HANDSOME.
THANKS, SUGAR.
WHAT THE...WHA... WHAT ARE YOU WEARING?

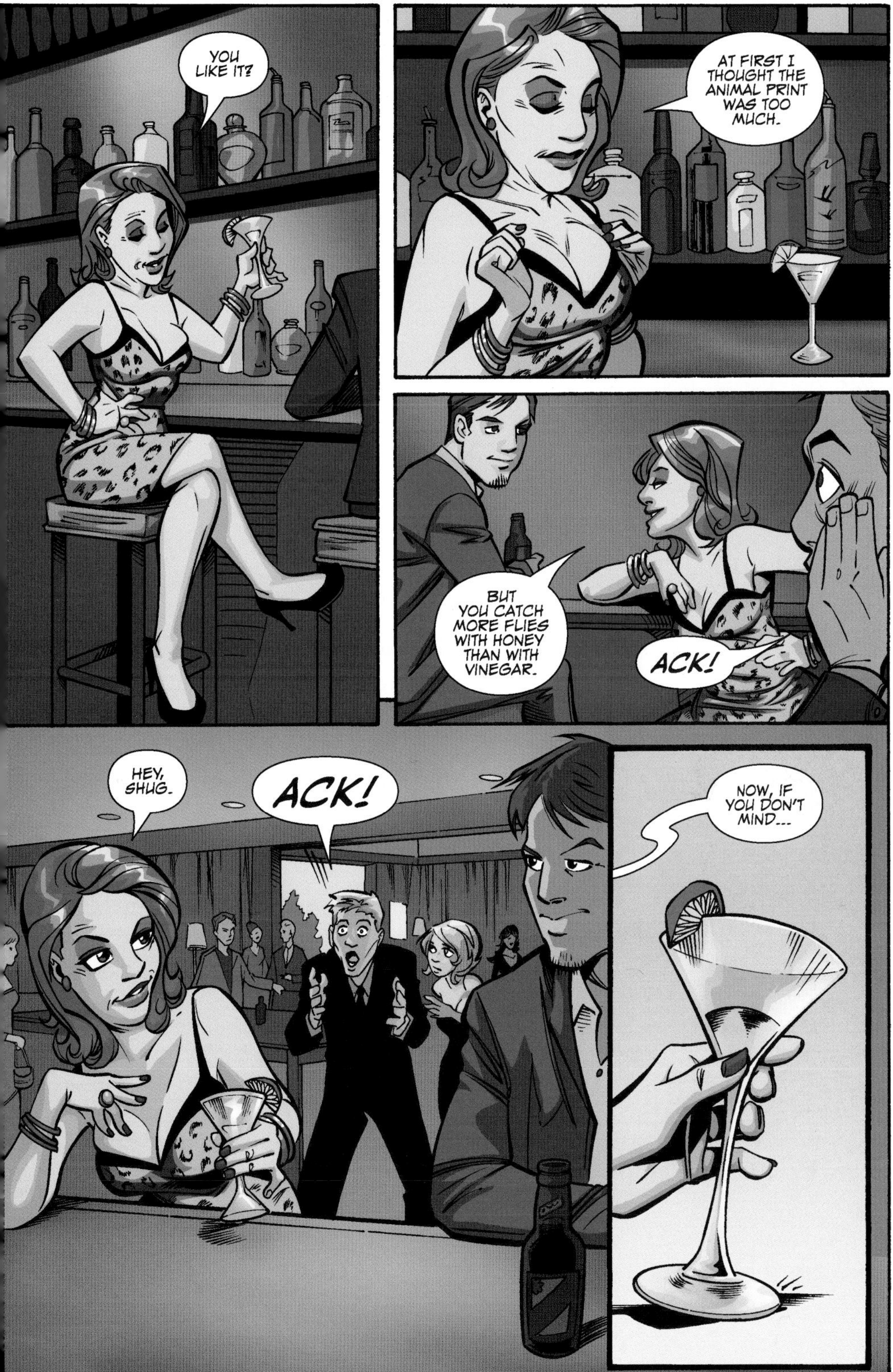
YOU LIKE IT?
AT FIRST I THOUGHT THE ANIMAL PRINT WAS TOO MUCH.
BUT YOU CATCH MORE FLIES WITH HONEY THAN WITH VINEGAR.
ACK!
HEY, SHUG.
ACK!
NOW, IF YOU DON'T MIND...

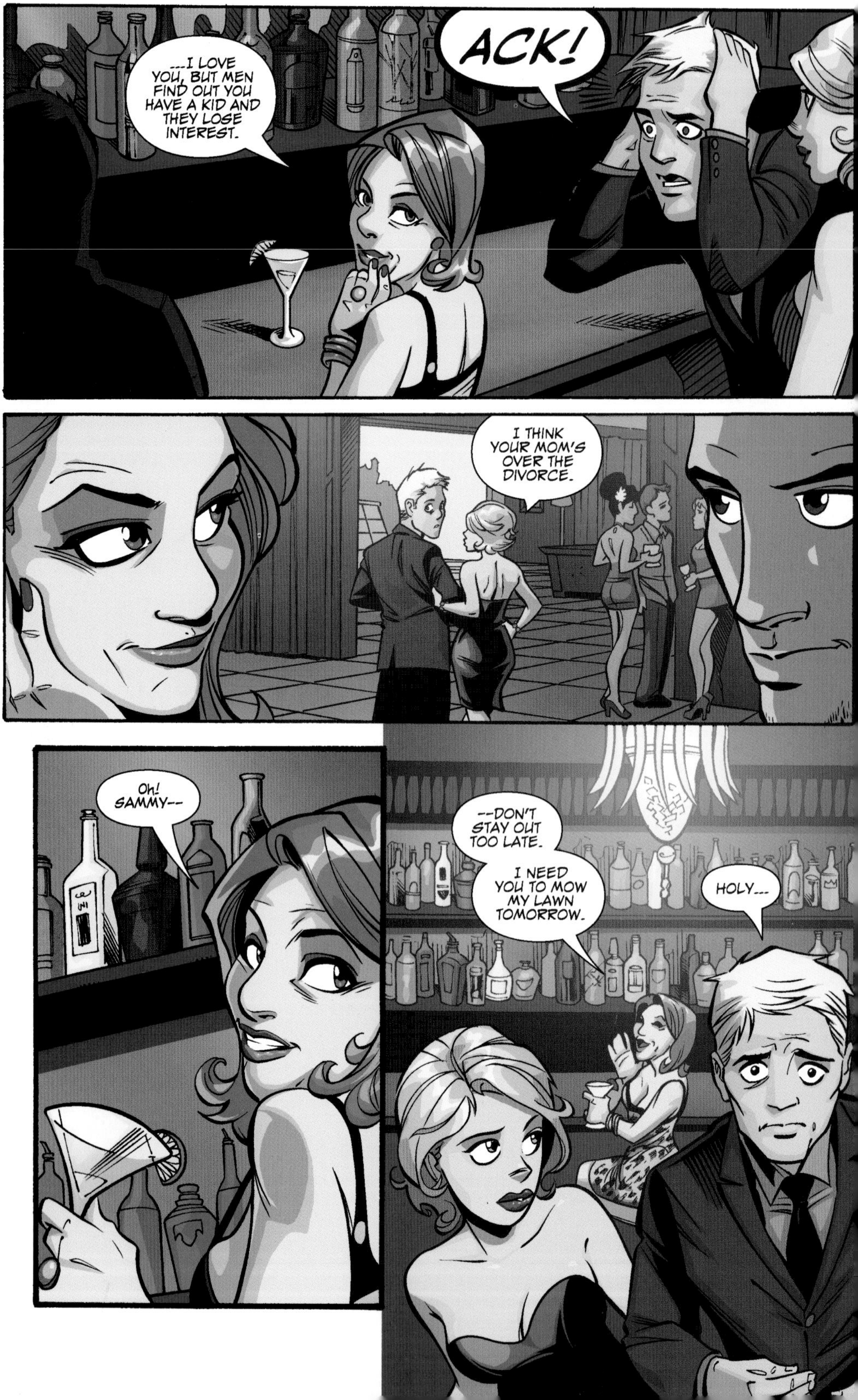
---I LOVE YOU, BUT MEN FIND OUT YOU HAVE A KID AND THEY LOSE INTEREST.
ACK!
I THINK YOUR MOM'S OVER THE DIVORCE.
Oh! SAMMY--
--DON'T STAY OUT TOO LATE.
I NEED YOU TO MOW MY LAWN TOMORROW.
HOLY...

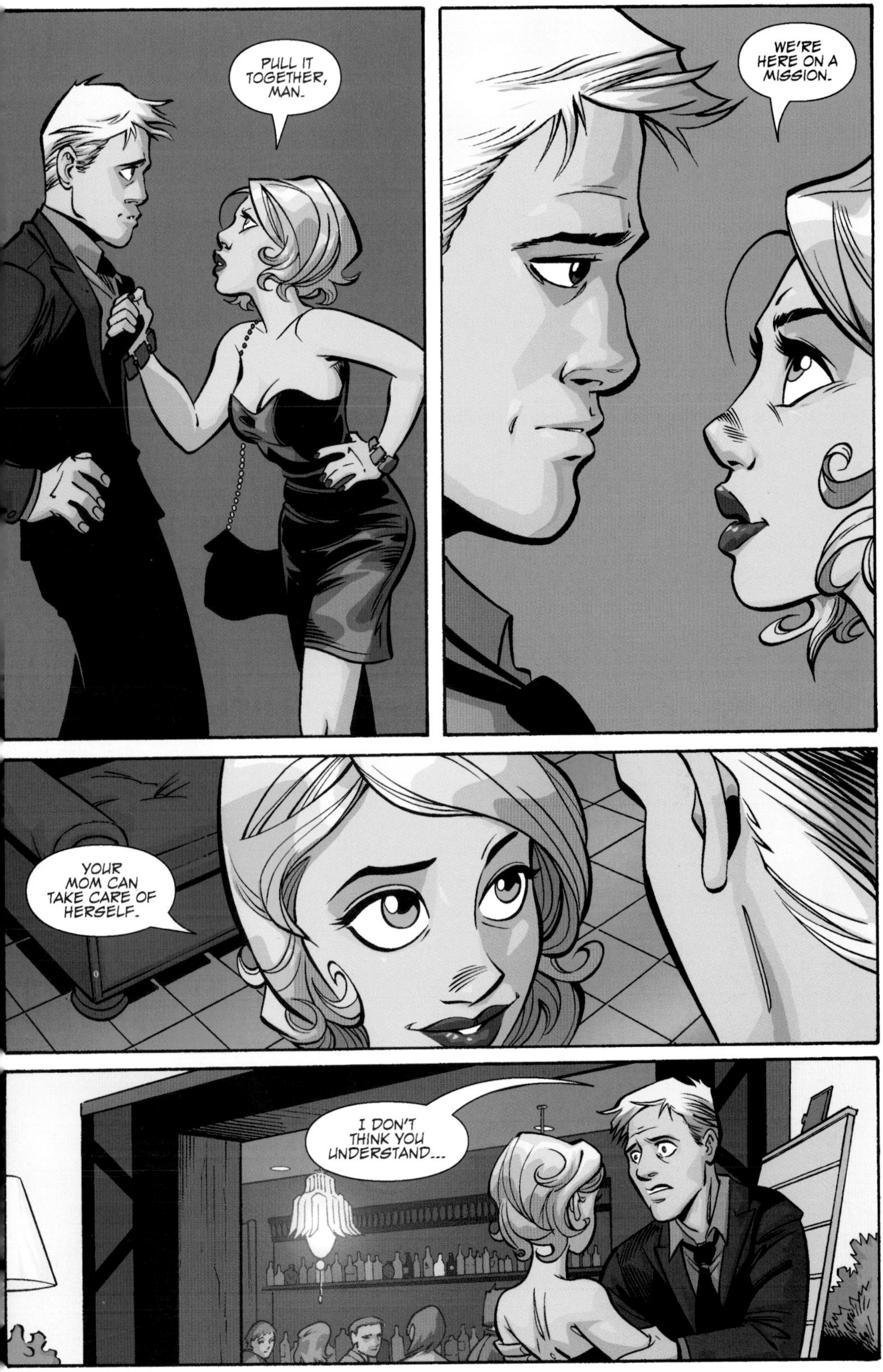
PULL IT TOGETHER, MAN.
WE'RE HERE ON A MISSION.
YOUR MOM CAN TAKE CARE OF HERSELF.
I DON'T THINK YOU UNDERSTAND...

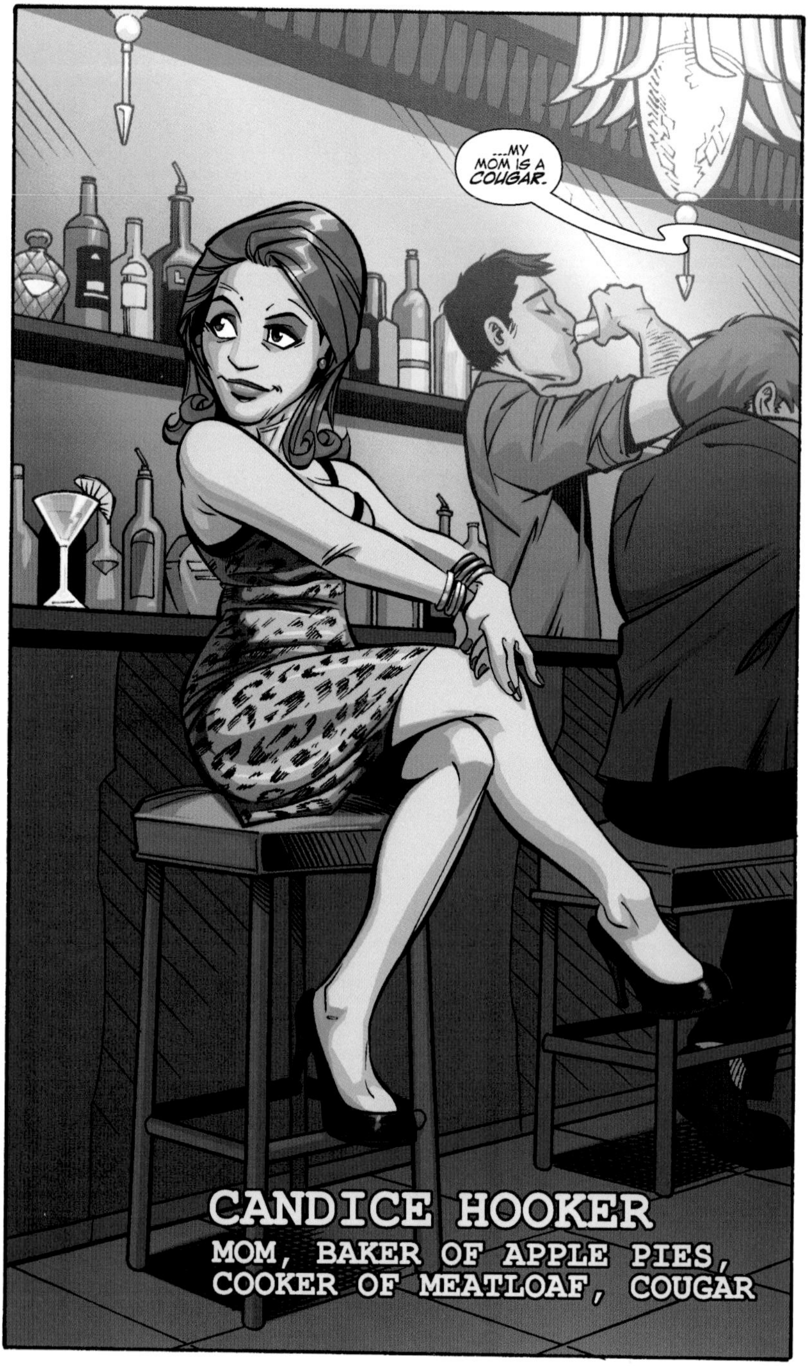
...MY MOM IS A COUGAR.
CANDICE HOOKER
MOM, BAKER OF APPLE PIES, COOKER OF MEATLOAF, COUGAR

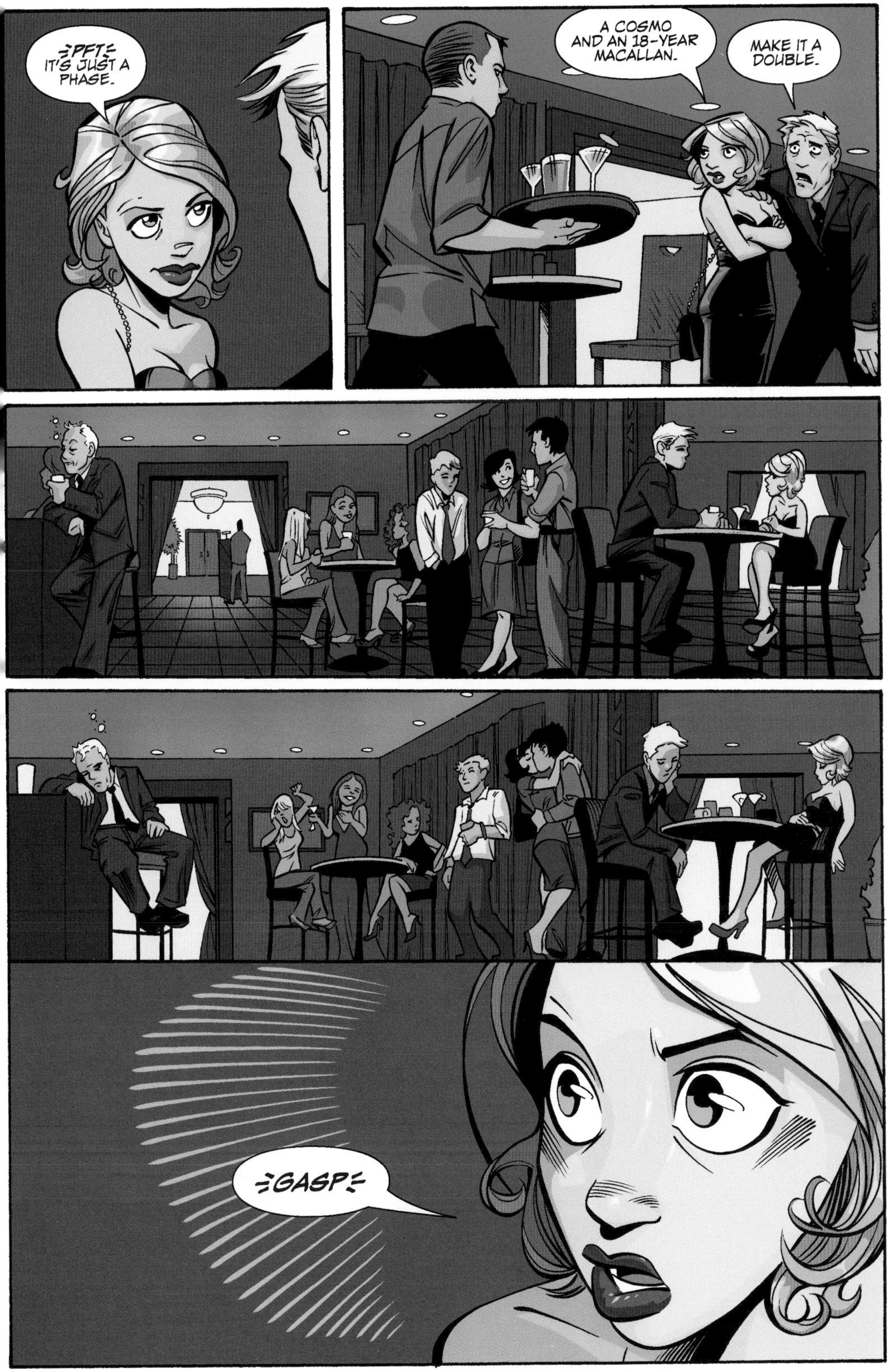

PFT
IT'S JUST A PHASE.
A COSMO AND AN 18-YEAR MACALLAN.
MAKE IT A DOUBLE.
GASP

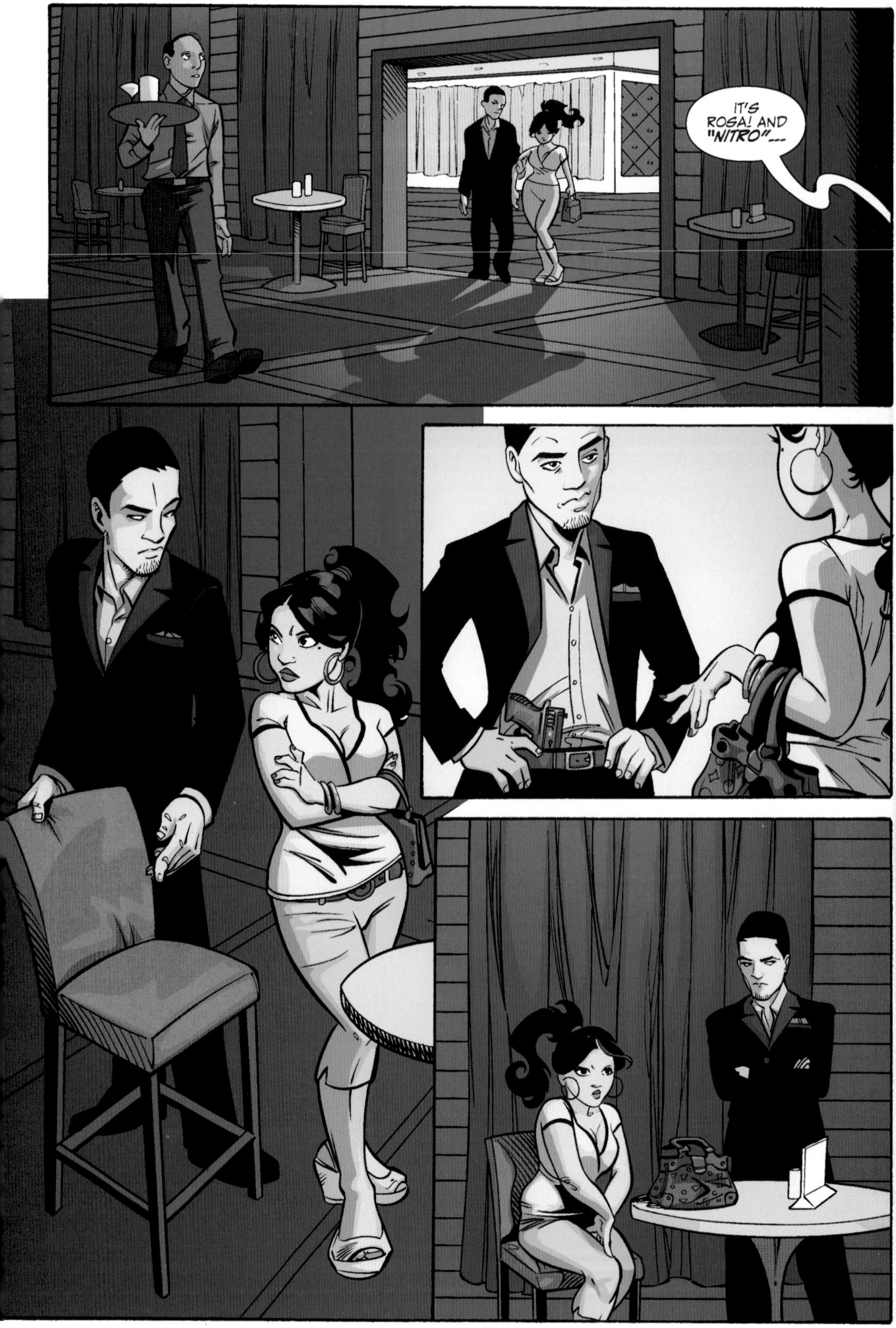
IT'S ROSA! AND "NITRO"...

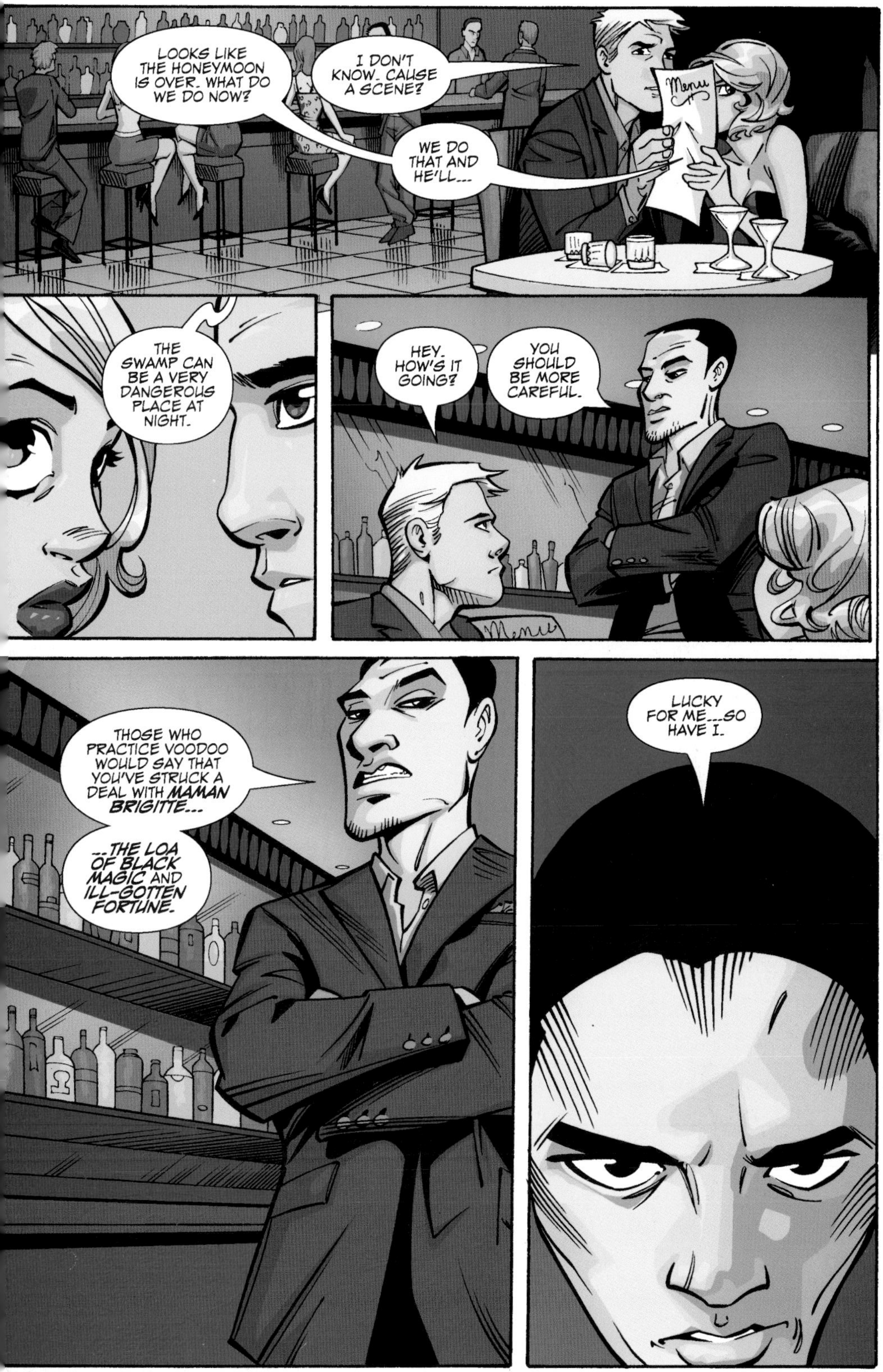
LOOKS LIKE THE HONEYMOON IS OVER. WHAT DO WE DO NOW?
I DON'T KNOW. CAUSE A SCENE?
WE DO THAT AND HE'LL...
THE SWAMP CAN BE A VERY DANGEROUS PLACE AT NIGHT.
HEY. HOW'S IT GOING?
YOU SHOULD BE MORE CAREFUL.
THOSE WHO PRACTICE VOODOO WOULD SAY THAT YOU'VE STRUCK A DEAL WITH MAMAN BRIGITTE...
...THE LOA OF BLACK MAGIC AND ILL-GOTTEN FORTUNE.
LUCKY FOR ME...SO HAVE I.

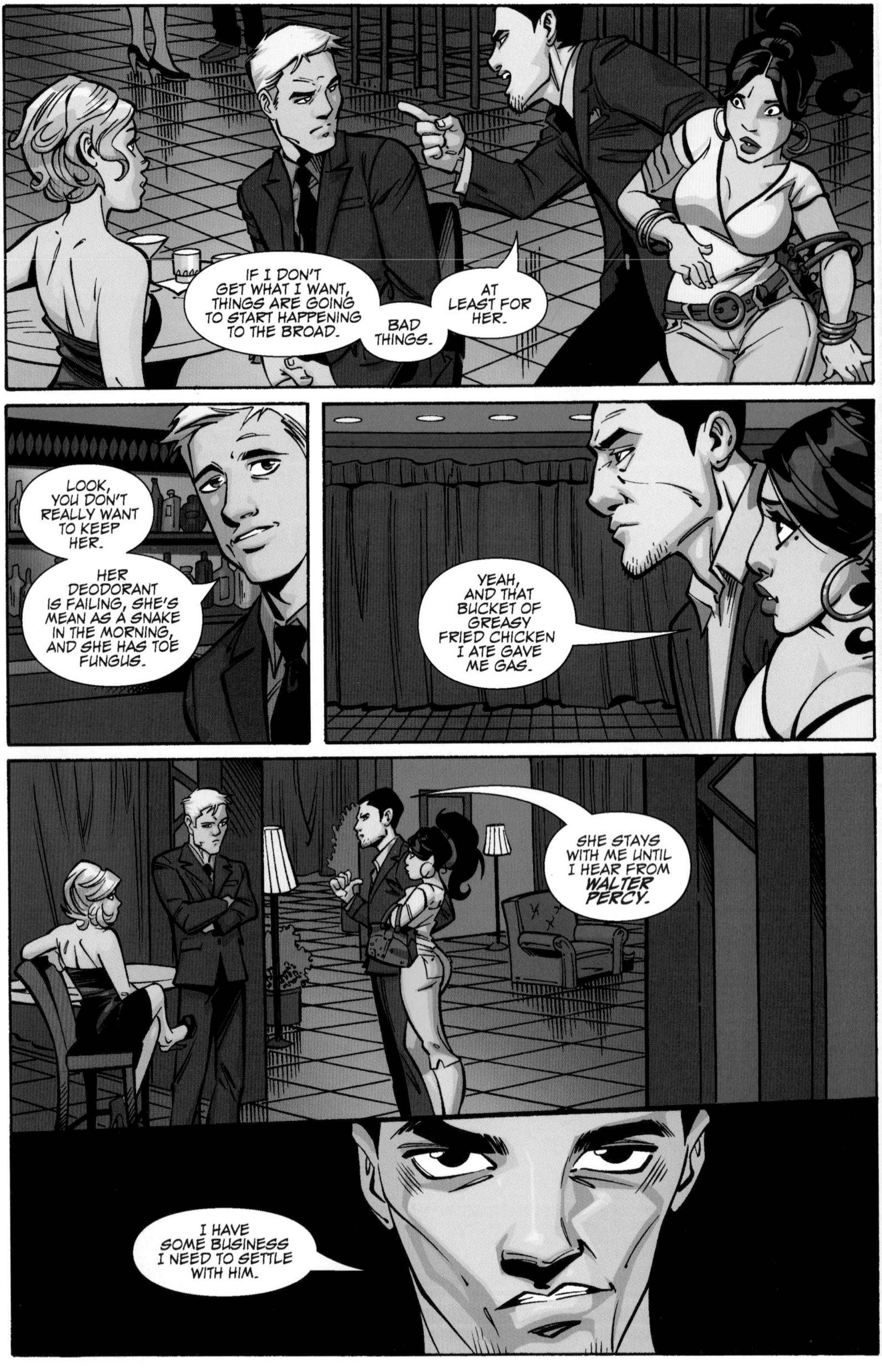
IF I DON'T GET WHAT I WANT, THINGS ARE GOING TO START HAPPENING TO THE BROAD.
BAD THINGS.
AT LEAST FOR HER.
LOOK, YOU DON'T REALLY WANT TO KEEP HER.
HER DEODORANT IS FAILING, SHE'S MEAN AS A SNAKE IN THE MORNING, AND SHE HAS TOE FUNGUS.
YEAH, AND THAT BUCKET OF GREASY FRIED CHICKEN I ATE GAVE ME GAS.
SHE STAYS WITH ME UNTIL I HEAR FROM WALTER PERCY.
I HAVE SOME BUSINESS I NEED TO SETTLE WITH HIM.

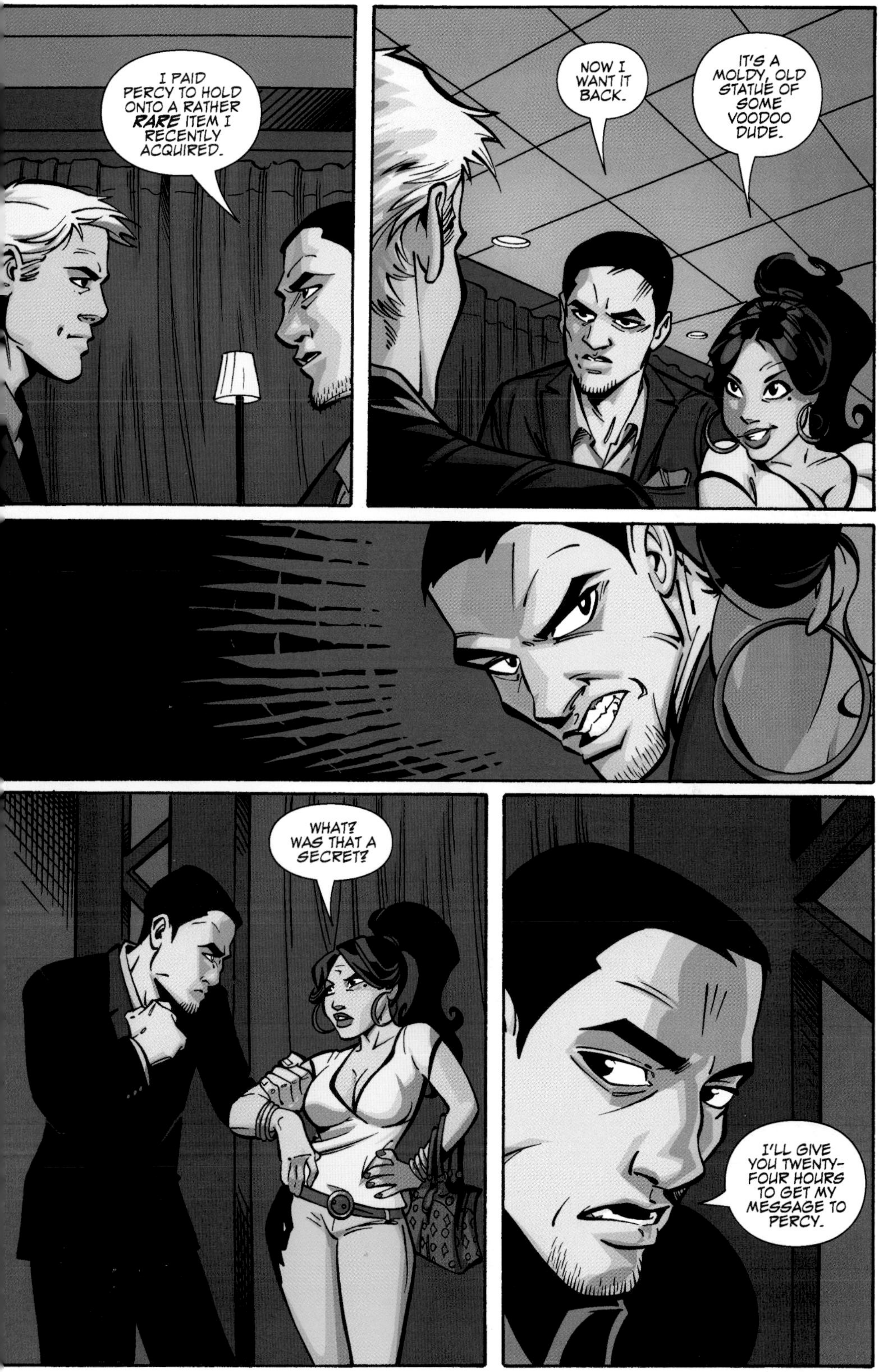
I PAID PERCY TO HOLD ONTO A RATHER RARE ITEM I RECENTLY ACQUIRED.
NOW I WANT IT BACK.
IT'S A MOLDY, OLD STATUE OF SOME VOODOO DUDE.
WHAT? WAS THAT A SECRET?
I'LL GIVE YOU TWENTY-FOUR HOURS TO GET MY MESSAGE TO PERCY.

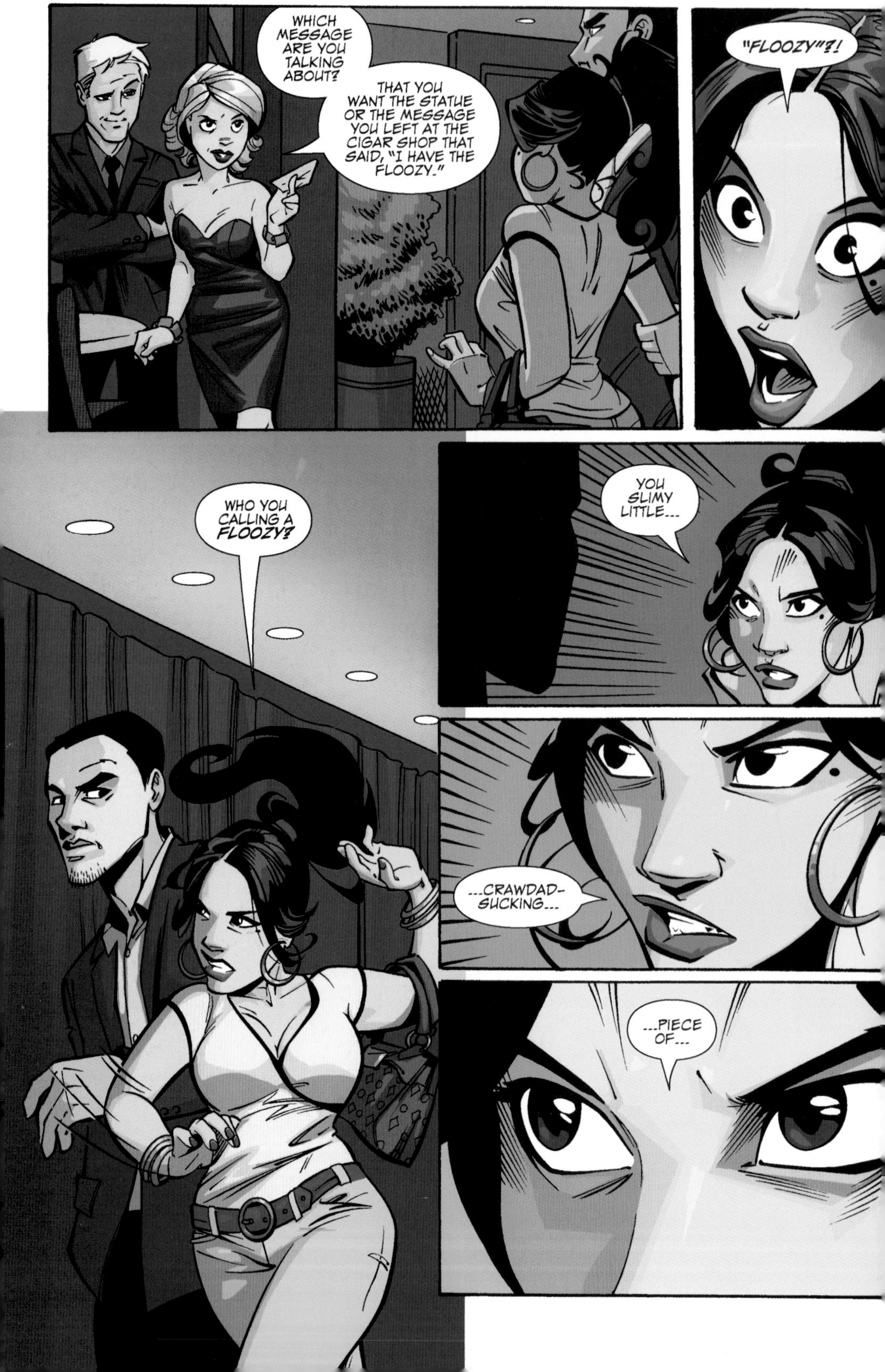
WHICH MESSAGE ARE YOU TALKING ABOUT?
THAT YOU WANT THE STATUE OR THE MESSAGE YOU LEFT AT THE CIGAR SHOP THAT SAID, "I HAVE THE FLOOZY."
"FLOOZY"?!
WHO YOU CALLING A FLOOZY?
YOU SLIMY LITTLE...
...CRAWDAD-SUCKING...
...PIECE OF...

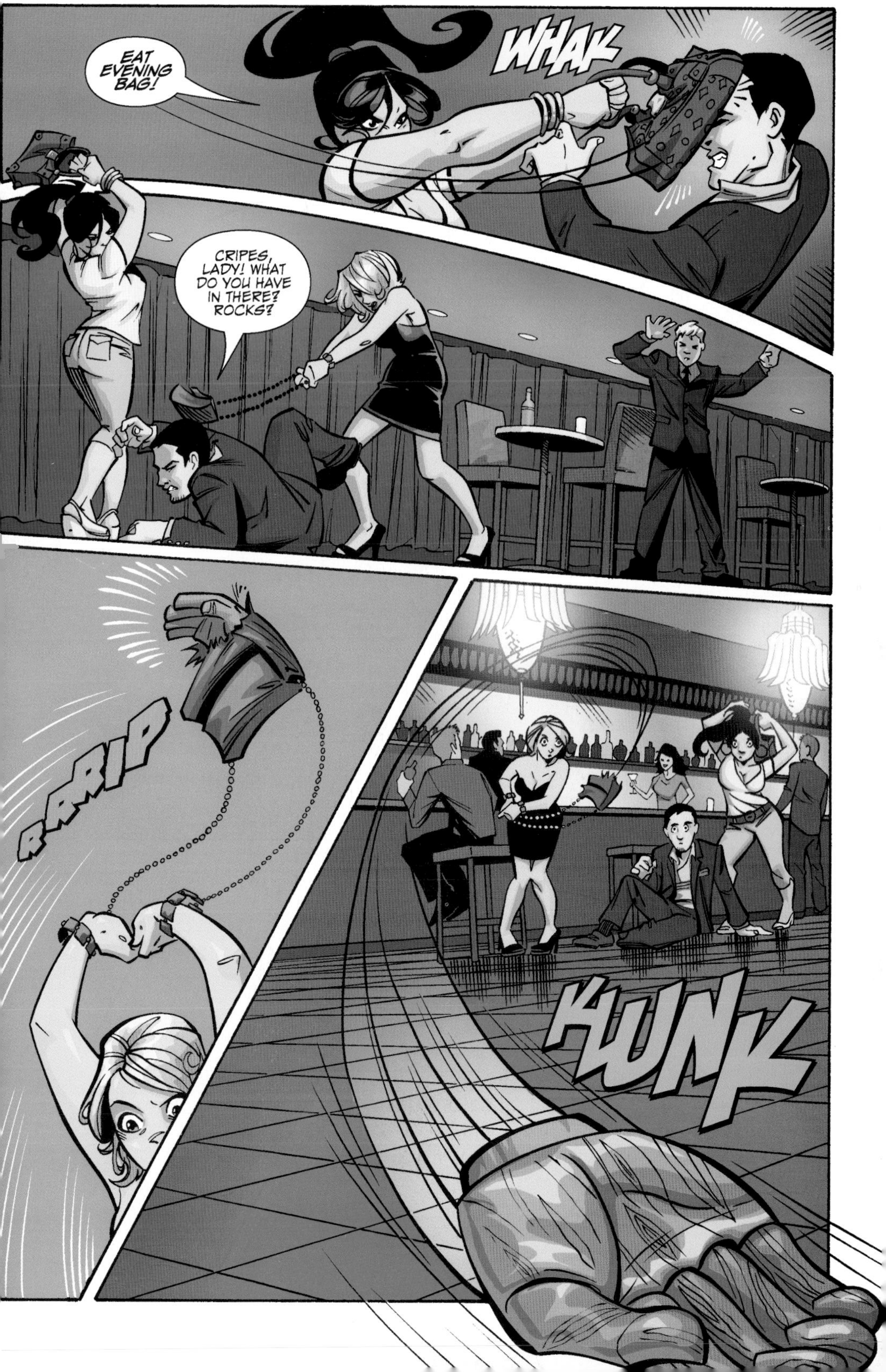
EAT EVENING BAG!
WHAK
CRIPES, LADY! WHAT DO YOU HAVE IN THERE? ROCKS?
RRRIP
KLUNK

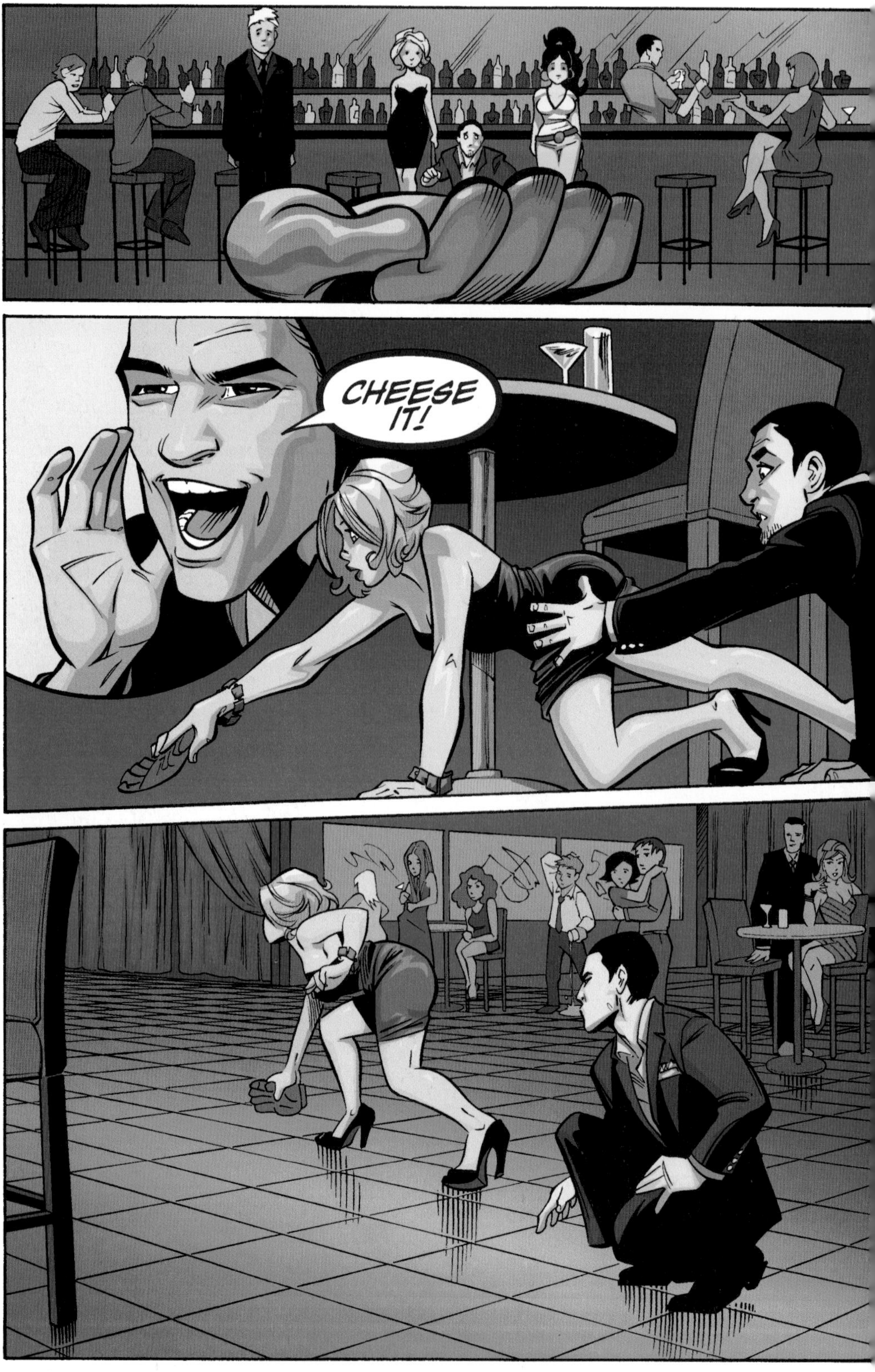
CHEESE IT!

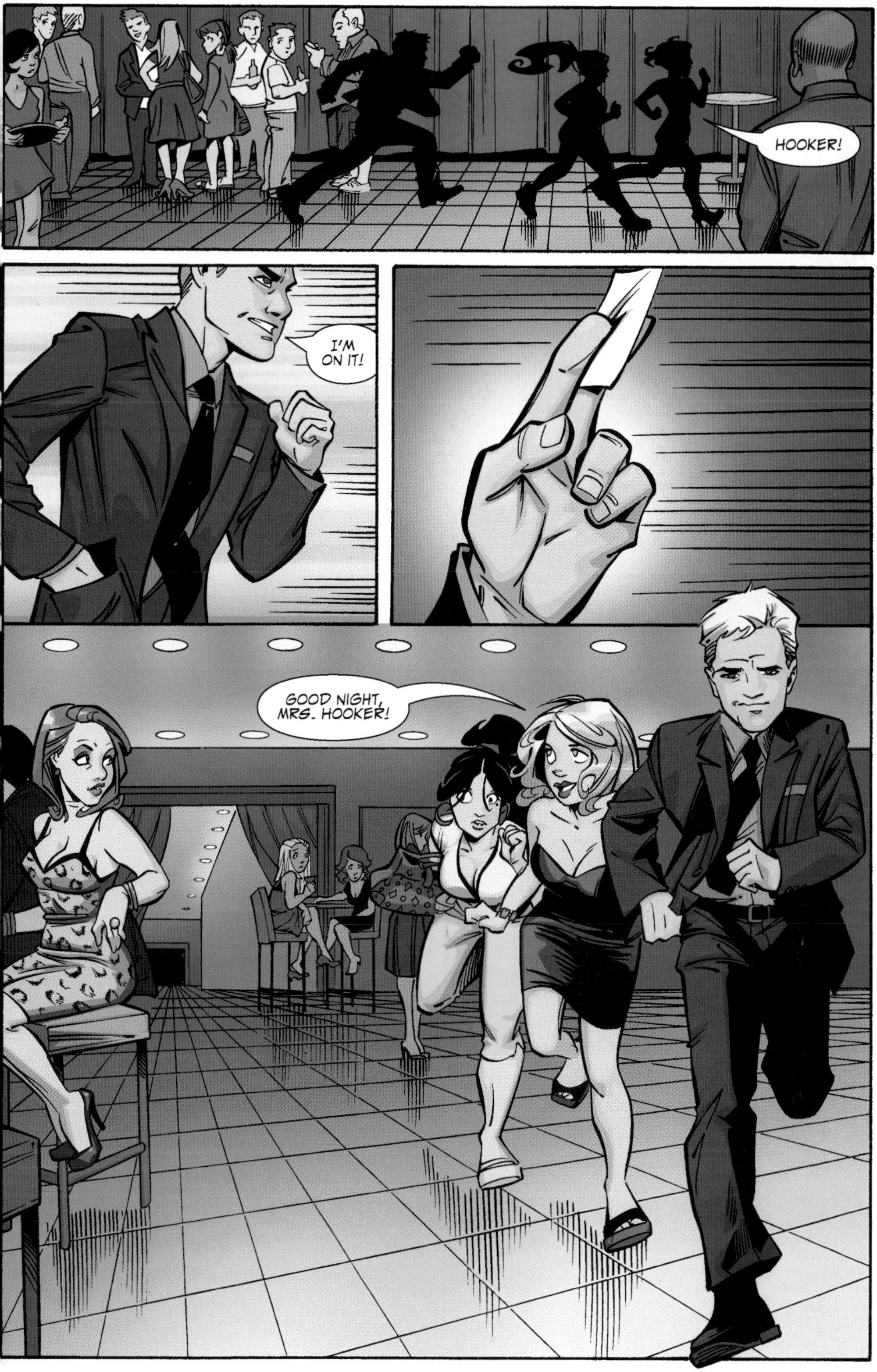
HOOKER!
I'M ON IT!
GOOD NIGHT, MRS. HOOKER!

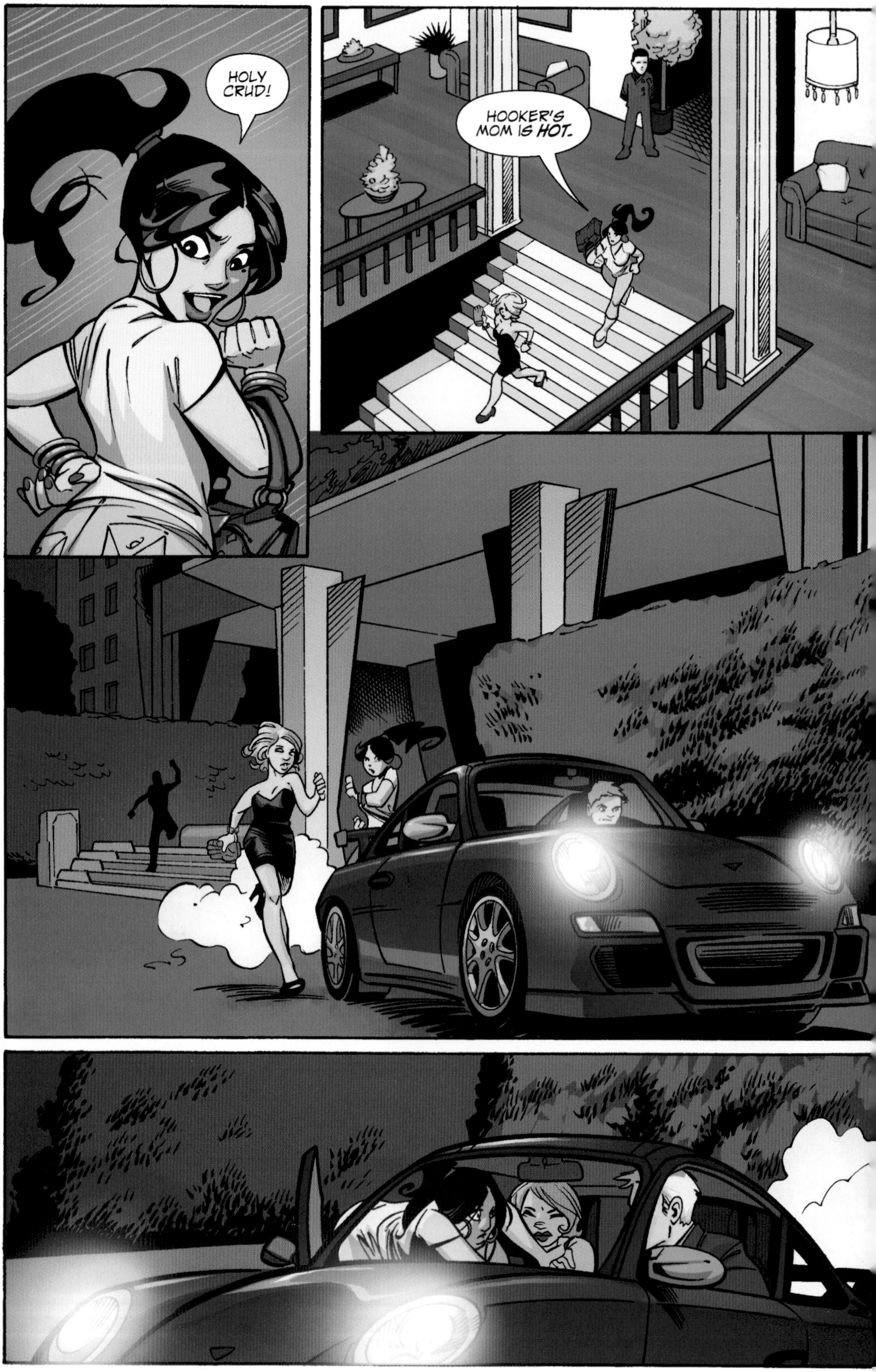
HOLY CRUD!
HOOKER'S MOM IS HOT.

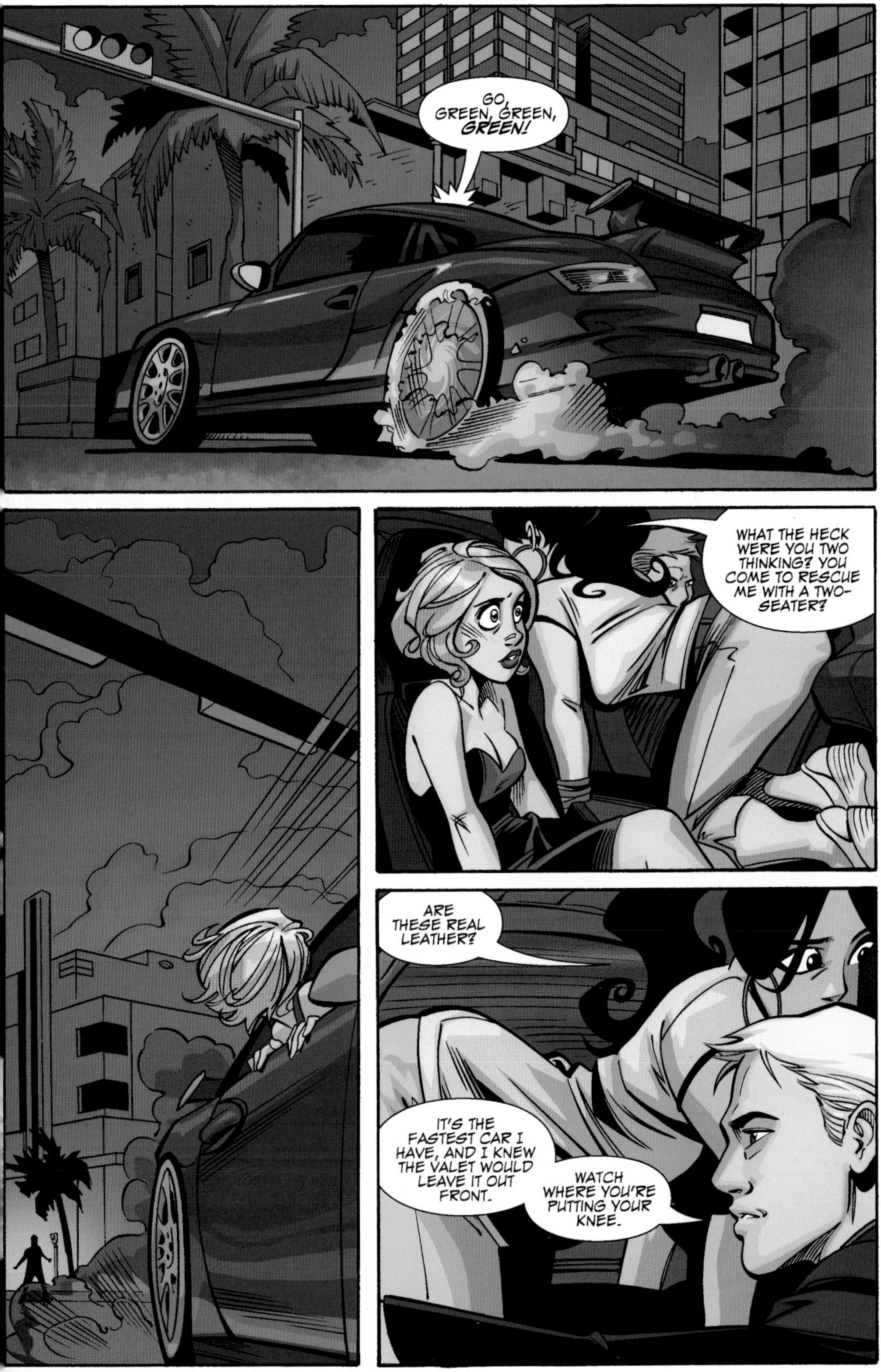
GO, GREEN, GREEN, GREEN!
WHAT THE HECK WERE YOU TWO THINKING? YOU COME TO RESCUE ME WITH A TWO-SEATER?
ARE THESE REAL LEATHER?
IT'S THE FASTEST CAR I HAVE, AND I KNEW THE VALET WOULD LEAVE IT OUT FRONT.
WATCH WHERE YOU'RE PUTTING YOUR KNEE.

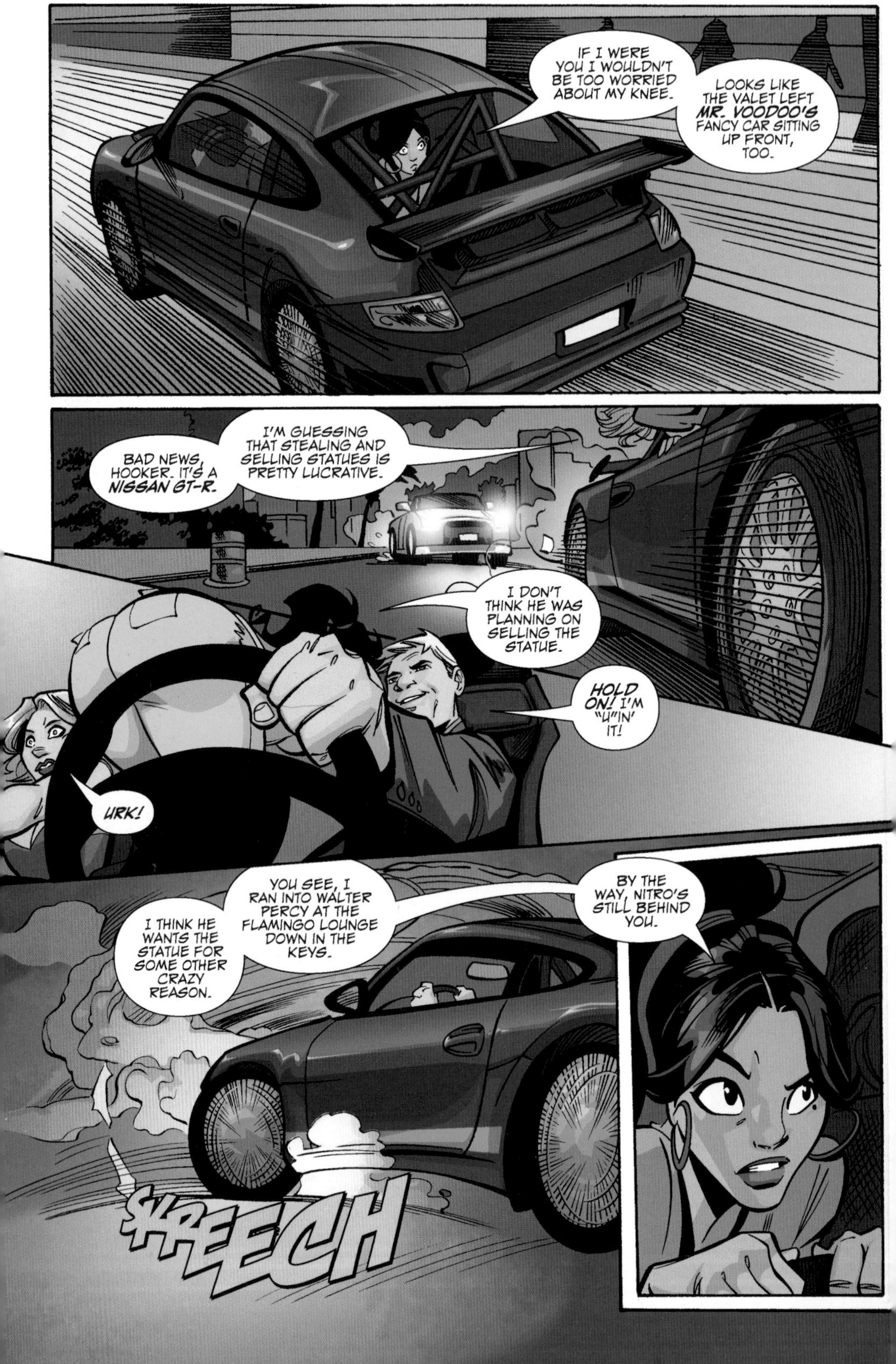

IF I WERE YOU I WOULDN'T BE TOO WORRIED ABOUT MY KNEE.
LOOKS LIKE THE VALET LEFT **MR. VOODOO'S** FANCY CAR SITTING UP FRONT, TOO.
BAD NEWS, HOOKER. IT'S A **NISSAN GT-R.**
I'M GUESSING THAT STEALING AND SELLING STATUES IS PRETTY LUCRATIVE.
I DON'T THINK HE WAS PLANNING ON SELLING THE STATUE.
HOLD ON! I'M "U"IN' IT!
URK!
I THINK HE WANTS THE STATUE FOR SOME OTHER CRAZY REASON.
YOU SEE, I RAN INTO WALTER PERCY AT THE FLAMINGO LOUNGE DOWN IN THE KEYS.
BY THE WAY, NITRO'S STILL BEHIND YOU.
SKREECH

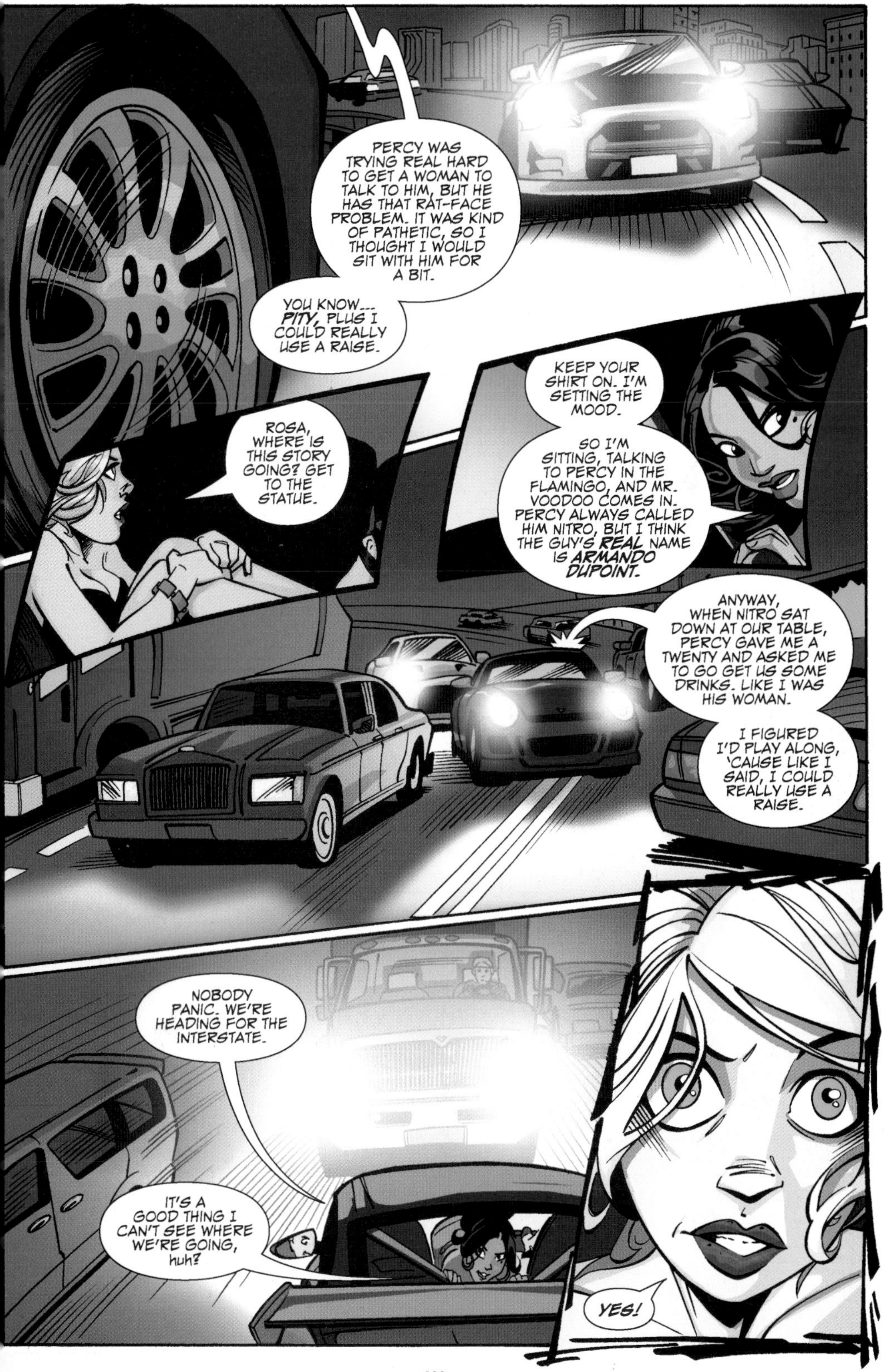
PERCY WAS TRYING REAL HARD TO GET A WOMAN TO TALK TO HIM, BUT HE HAS THAT RAT-FACE PROBLEM. IT WAS KIND OF PATHETIC, SO I THOUGHT I WOULD SIT WITH HIM FOR A BIT.
YOU KNOW... PITY, PLUS I COULD REALLY USE A RAISE.
ROSA, WHERE IS THIS STORY GOING? GET TO THE STATUE.
KEEP YOUR SHIRT ON. I'M SETTING THE MOOD.
SO I'M SITTING, TALKING TO PERCY IN THE FLAMINGO, AND MR. VOODOO COMES IN. PERCY ALWAYS CALLED HIM NITRO, BUT I THINK THE GUY'S REAL NAME IS ARMANDO DUPOINT.
ANYWAY, WHEN NITRO SAT DOWN AT OUR TABLE, PERCY GAVE ME A TWENTY AND ASKED ME TO GO GET US SOME DRINKS. LIKE I WAS HIS WOMAN.
I FIGURED I'D PLAY ALONG, 'CAUSE LIKE I SAID, I COULD REALLY USE A RAISE.
NOBODY PANIC. WE'RE HEADING FOR THE INTERSTATE.
IT'S A GOOD THING I CAN'T SEE WHERE WE'RE GOING, huh?
YES!

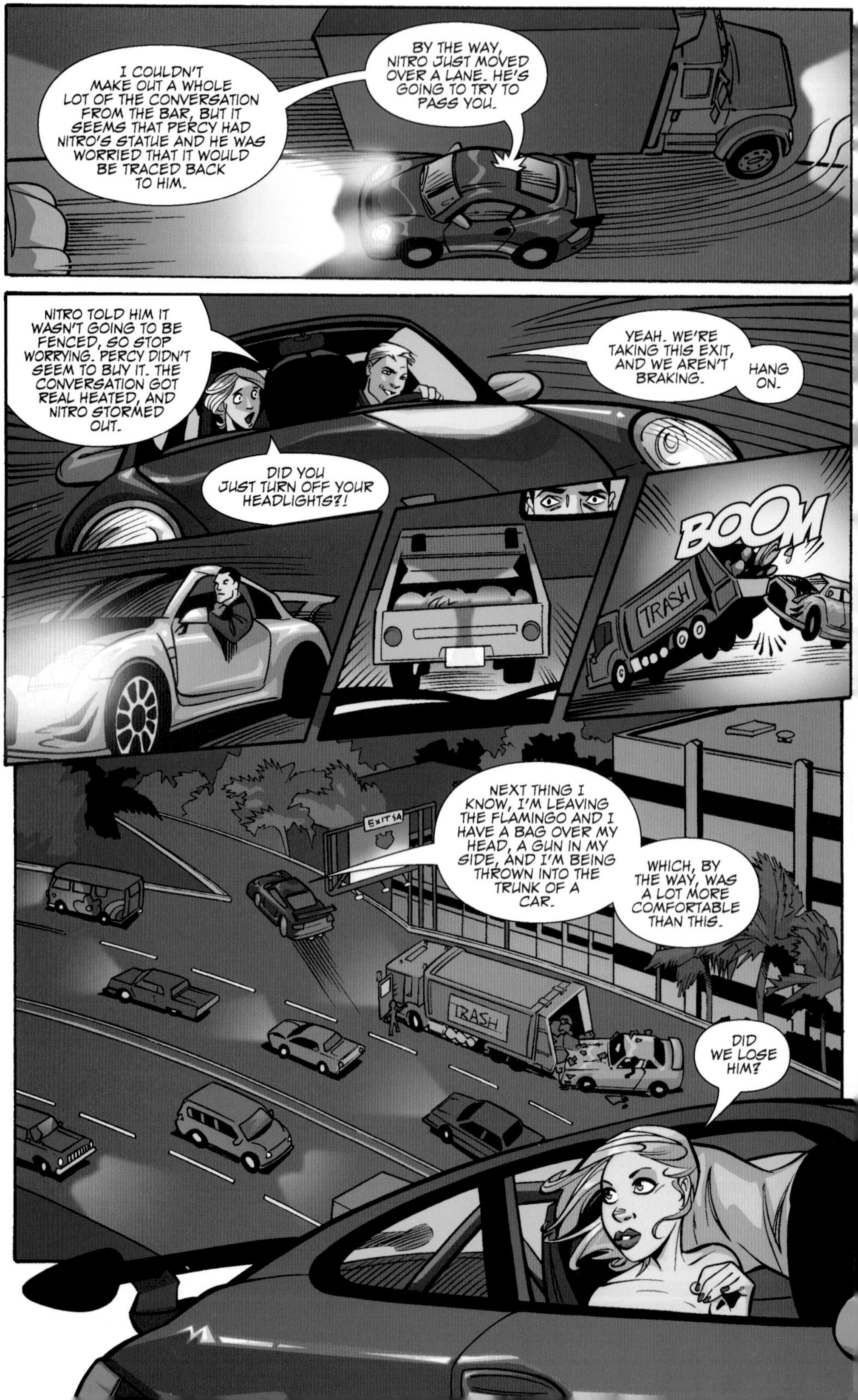
I COULDN'T MAKE OUT A WHOLE LOT OF THE CONVERSATION FROM THE BAR, BUT IT SEEMS THAT PERCY HAD NITRO'S STATUE AND HE WAS WORRIED THAT IT WOULD BE TRACED BACK TO HIM.
BY THE WAY, NITRO JUST MOVED OVER A LANE. HE'S GOING TO TRY TO PASS YOU.
NITRO TOLD HIM IT WASN'T GOING TO BE FENCED, SO STOP WORRYING. PERCY DIDN'T SEEM TO BUY IT. THE CONVERSATION GOT REAL HEATED, AND NITRO STORMED OUT.
YEAH. WE'RE TAKING THIS EXIT, AND WE AREN'T BRAKING.
HANG ON.
DID YOU JUST TURN OFF YOUR HEADLIGHTS?!
BOOM
TRASH
EXIT 5A
NEXT THING I KNOW, I'M LEAVING THE FLAMINGO AND I HAVE A BAG OVER MY HEAD, A GUN IN MY SIDE, AND I'M BEING THROWN INTO THE TRUNK OF A CAR.
WHICH, BY THE WAY, WAS A LOT MORE COMFORTABLE THAN THIS.
TRASH
DID WE LOSE HIM?

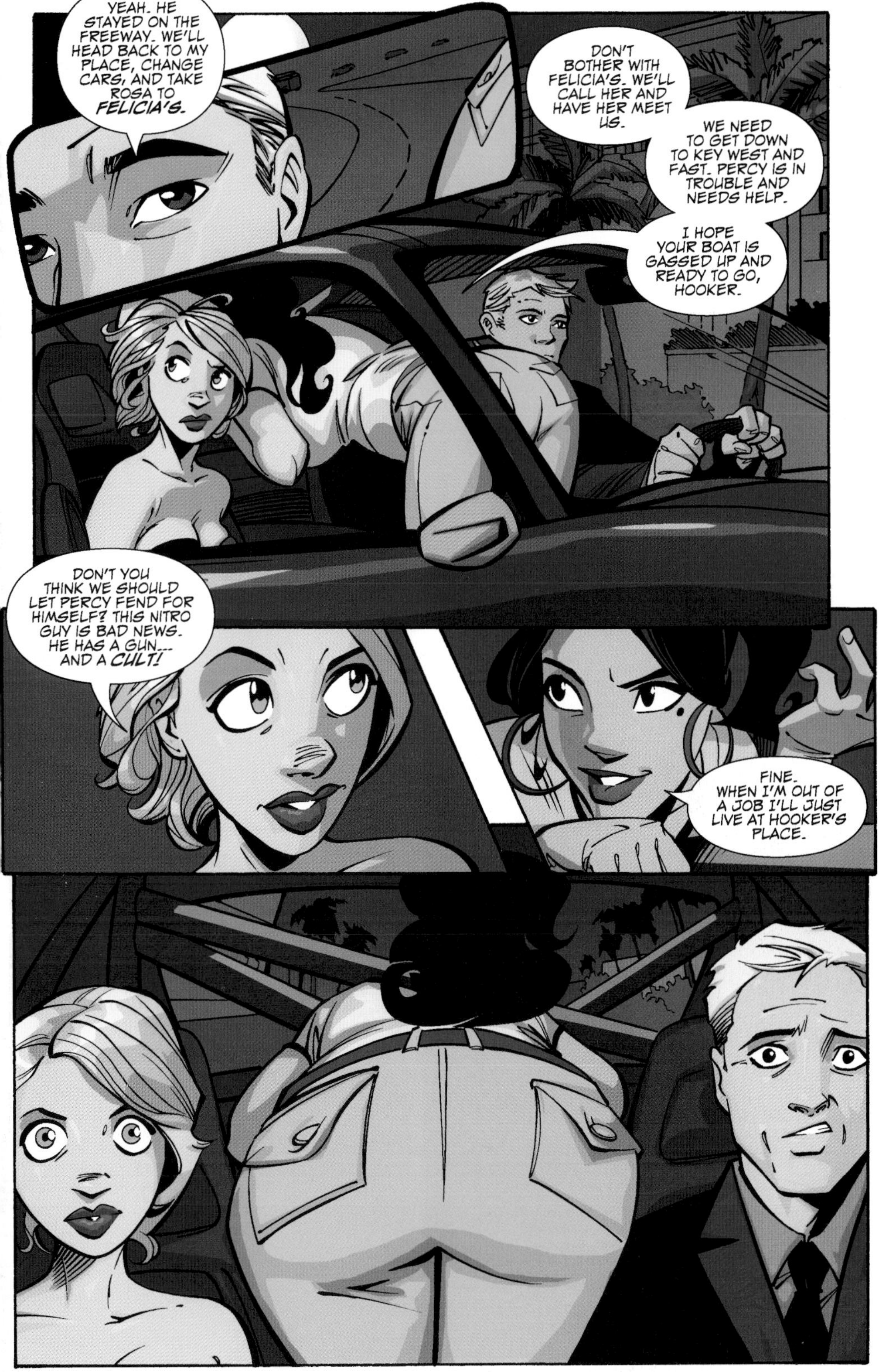
YEAH. HE STAYED ON THE FREEWAY. WE'LL HEAD BACK TO MY PLACE, CHANGE CARS, AND TAKE ROSA TO FELICIA'S.
DON'T BOTHER WITH FELICIA'S. WE'LL CALL HER AND HAVE HER MEET US.
WE NEED TO GET DOWN TO KEY WEST AND FAST. PERCY IS IN TROUBLE AND NEEDS HELP.
I HOPE YOUR BOAT IS GASSED UP AND READY TO GO, HOOKER.
DON'T YOU THINK WE SHOULD LET PERCY FEND FOR HIMSELF? THIS NITRO GUY IS BAD NEWS. HE HAS A GUN... AND A CULT!
FINE. WHEN I'M OUT OF A JOB I'LL JUST LIVE AT HOOKER'S PLACE.

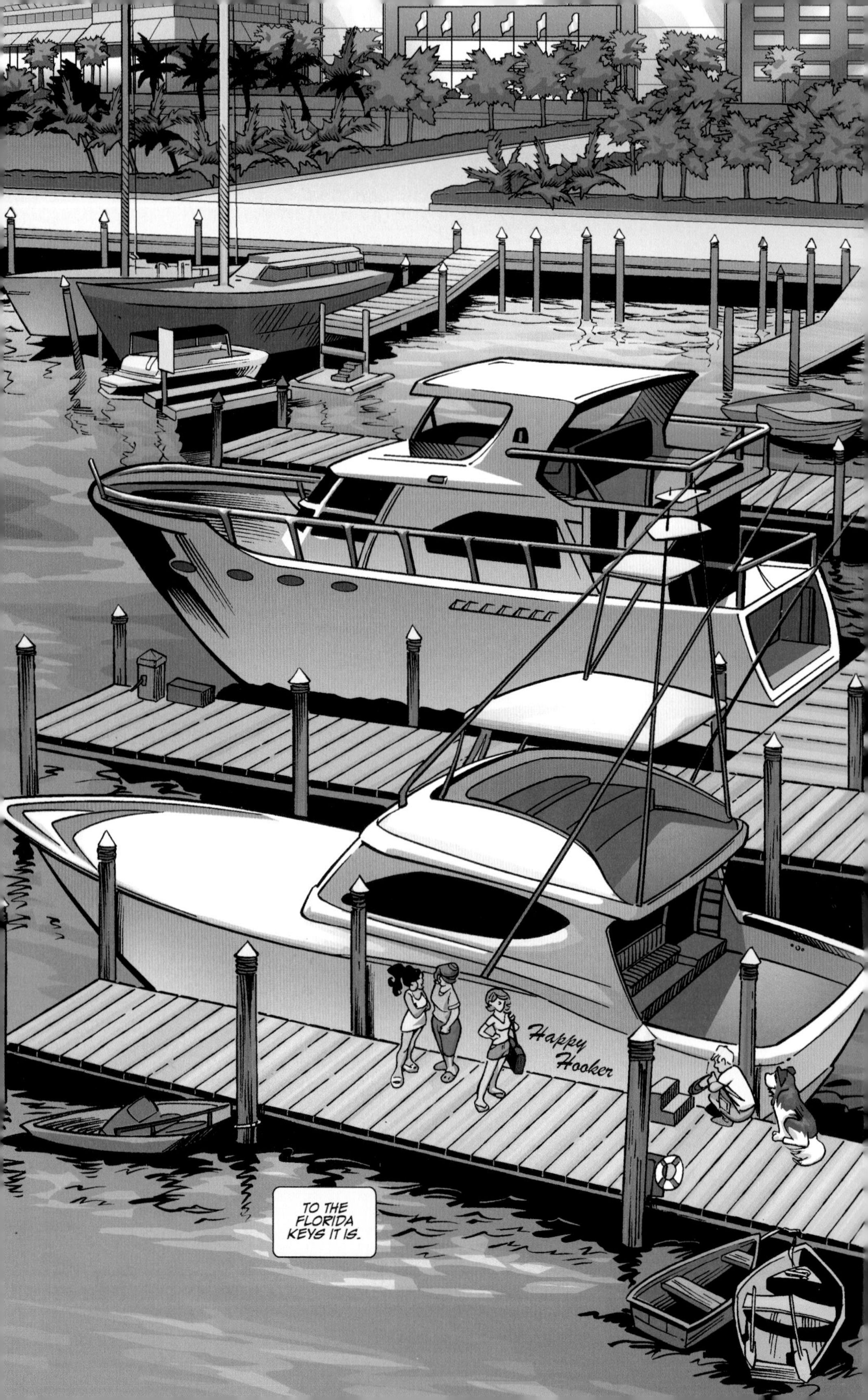
Happy Hooker
TO THE FLORIDA KEYS IT IS.

THE ADVENTURE CONTINUES!

TROUBLE MAKER

BOOK TWO

#1 *NEW YORK TIMES* BEST-SELLING AUTHOR
JANET EVANOVICH
BRINGS YOU THE NEXT CHAPTER IN THE LIVES OF CRACK AUTO MECHANIC ALEX BARNABY
AND NASCAR RACER SAM HOOKER IN
NOVEMBER 2010!

There's no smooth sailing for Barnaby and Hooker when they find themselves caught up in an adventure involving voodoo, thinly veiled threats, and the hunt for a missing relic. Together again with friends Rosa and Felicia, Barney, Hooker, and their St. Bernard, Beans, begin a search for Walter Percy—the man at the heart of this ongoing mystery.

Written by Janet and Alex Evanovich, and illustrated by Joëlle Jones, *Troublemaker* Volume 2 brings you double the trouble in the heart of Miami and on the shores of the Keys!

www.evanovich.com

ISBN 978-1-59582-573-5
$17.99 U.S.

www.joellejones.com

AVAILABLE AT YOUR LOCAL COMICS SHOP OR BOOKSTORE
To find a comics shop in your area, call 1-888-266-4226.
For more information or to order direct visit darkhorse.com or call 1-800-862-0052 • Mon.–Fri. 9 AM to 5 PM Pacific Time.
*Prices and availability subject to change without notice.

CREATOR BIOGRAPHIES

Photo © Roland Scarpa

Janet and her granddog, Barnaby.

JANET EVANOVICH is the number-one *New York Times* best-selling author of the Stephanie Plum series, as well as the Alex Barnaby and Sam Hooker novels *Metro Girl* and *Motor Mouth*. Janet lives in Florida with her husband and her Havanese, Ollie. This is her first foray into writing comics.

ALEX EVANOVICH is the daughter of Janet Evanovich. She's been working with Janet for over fourteen years doing Internet work, newsletters, and editing, and is one of the coauthors of *How I Write*. She lives in Florida with her husband and her St. Bernard, Barnaby.

JOËLLE JONES debuted in comics in 2006, contributing a short story to the Dark Horse anthology *Sexy Chix*. She followed this a year later with the full graphic novel *12 Reasons Why I Love Her*, her first collaboration with author Jamie S. Rich. She went on to illustrate the crime graphic novel *You Have Killed Me* and most recently the teen-witch comedy *Spell Checkers*. Joëlle has also drawn the young-adult book *Token* with Alisa Kwitney, worked with Zack Whedon on a comic-book spinoff of the popular *Dr. Horrible's Sing-Along Blog* web series, and drawn two issues of the Eisner-nominated series *Madame Xanadu*, written by Matt Wagner. She is currently working on a long-form comic for DC/Vertigo called *The Starving Artist*. You can visit her online at www.joellejones.com.

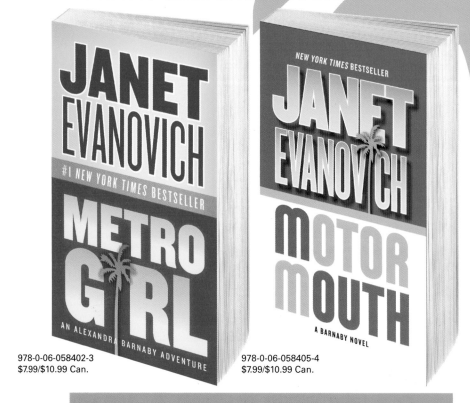

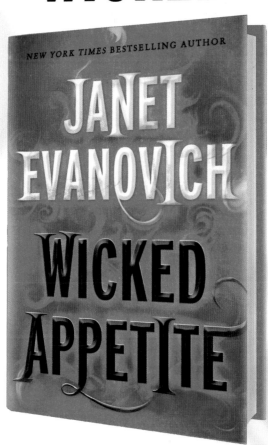

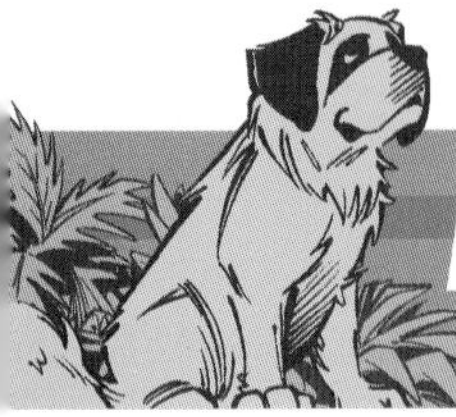

RECOMMENDED
DARK HORSE READING . . .

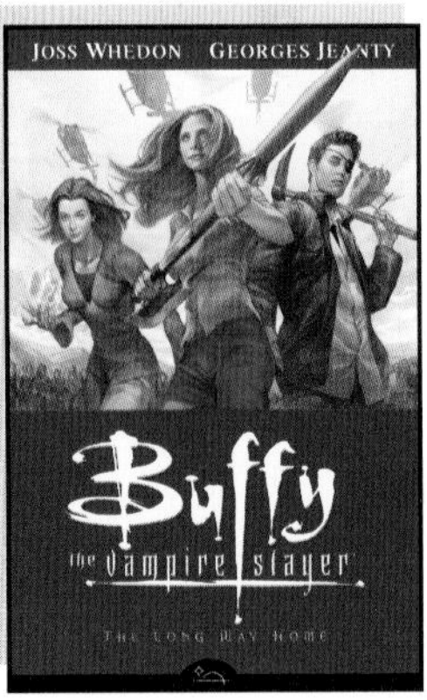
JOSS WHEDON GEORGES JEANTY
Buffy the vampire slayer
THE LONG WAY HOME

BUFFY THE VAMPIRE SLAYER SEASON EIGHT VOLUME 1: THE LONG WAY HOME

JOSS WHEDON, GEORGES JEANTY

Since the destruction of the Hellmouth, the Slayers—newly legion—have gotten organized and are kicking some serious undead butt. But not everything's fun and firearms, as an old enemy reappears and Dawn experiences some serious growing pains. Meanwhile, one of the "Buffy" decoy slayers is going through major pain of her own.

Buffy creator Joss Whedon brings Buffy back to Dark Horse in this direct follow-up to season seven of the smash-hit TV series.

$15.99
ISBN 978-1-59307-822-5

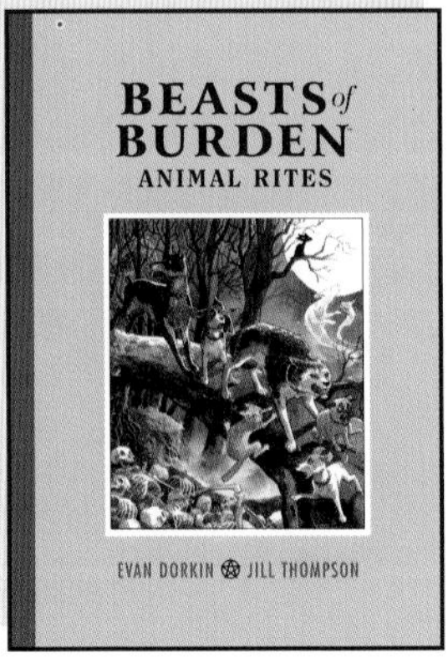
BEASTS of BURDEN
ANIMAL RITES
EVAN DORKIN JILL THOMPSON

BEASTS OF BURDEN VOLUME 1: ANIMAL RITES

EVAN DORKIN, JILL THOMPSON

Welcome to Burden Hill—a picturesque little town adorned with white picket fences and green, green grass, home to a unique team of paranormal investigators. Beneath this shiny exterior, Burden Hill harbors dark and sinister secrets, and it's up to a heroic gang of dogs—and one cat—to protect the town from the evil forces at work. Can our heroes overcome these supernatural menaces? Can evil be bested by a paranormal team that doesn't have hands? And even more importantly, will Pugs ever shut the hell up?

$19.99
ISBN 978-1-59582-513-1

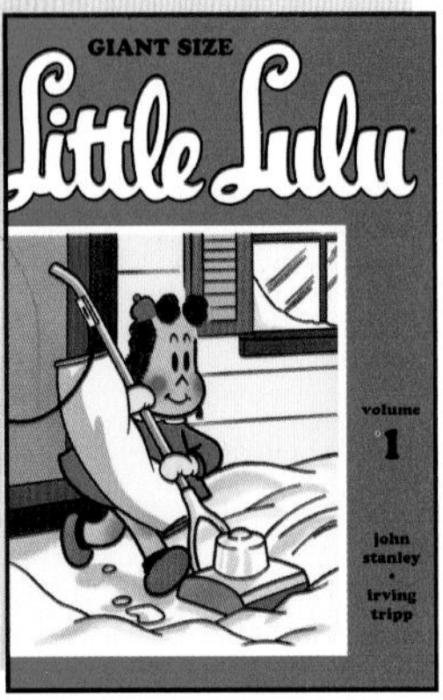
GIANT SIZE
Little Lulu
volume 1
john stanley • irving tripp

GIANT SIZE LITTLE LULU VOLUME 1

JOHN STANLEY, IRVING TRIPP

John Stanley and Irving Tripp's long run on *Little Lulu* is a milestone in American comics, as hilarious to grownups as it is to their children. With Stanley's popularity at an all-time high, Dark Horse is proud to take you back to the beginning of this legendary run. Collecting some of the earliest out-of-print volumes of Dark Horse's acclaimed reprint series, this massive 664-page omnibus contains the first fourteen issues where Little Lulu appeared.

$24.99
ISBN 978-1-59582-502-5

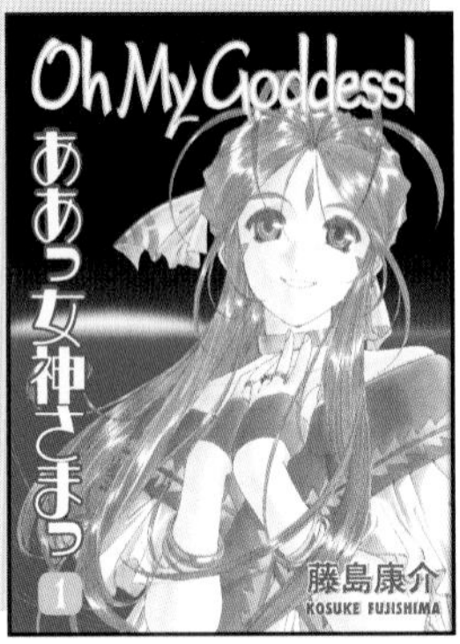
Oh My Goddess!
ああっ女神さまっ
1
藤島康介
KOSUKE FUJISHIMA

OH MY GODDESS! VOLUME 1

KOSUKE FUJISHIMA

Alone in his dorm, Nekomi Tech's Keiichi Morisato dials a wrong number that will change his life forever—reaching the Goddess Technical Help Line. Granted one wish by the charming young goddess Belldandy, Keiichi wishes she would stay with him always! Complications are bound to ensue from this; the immediate first being the new couple getting tossed out of the dorm—it's males only! How is his new "exchange student" companion going to be received on the NIT campus? A little too well for normal life to ever return . . .

$10.99
ISBN 978-1-59307-387-9

DARK HORSE BOOKS

AVAILABLE AT YOUR LOCAL COMICS SHOP OR BOOKSTORE
To find a comics shop in your area, call 1-888-266-4226.

For more information or to order direct visit darkhorse.com or call 1-800-862-0052 • Mon.–Fri. 9 AM to 5 PM Pacific Time.
*Prices and availability subject to change without notice.